From Film Practice to Data Process

In loving memory of
David Arnold
1951–2016

From Film Practice to Data Process

Production Aesthetics and Representational Practices of a Film Industry in Transition

Sarah Atkinson

EDINBURGH
University Press

Edinburgh University Press is one of the leading university presses in the UK. We publish academic books and journals in our selected subject areas across the humanities and social sciences, combining cutting-edge scholarship with high editorial and production values to produce academic works of lasting importance. For more information visit our website: edinburghuniversitypress.com

© Sarah Atkinson, 2018

Edinburgh University Press Ltd
The Tun – Holyrood Road
12 (2f) Jackson's Entry
Edinburgh EH8 8PJ

Typeset in 11/13 Ehrhardt by
IDSUK (DataConnection) Ltd

A CIP record for this book is available from the British Library

ISBN 978 0 7486 9358 0 (hardback)
ISBN 978 0 7486 9359 7 (webready PDF)
ISBN 978 1 4744 2647 3 (epub)

The right of Sarah Atkinson to be identified as author of this work has been asserted in accordance with the Copyright, Designs and Patents Act 1988 and the Copyright and Related Rights Regulations 2003 (SI No. 2498).

Contents

Acknowledgements

I would like to extend my sincere thanks and gratitude to the following people and organisations who, collectively, have made all the different elements of the research for this book possible:

Staff from the Open University (OU) Support Centre for Open Resources in Education (SCORE), in particular Jonathan Darby and Tim Seal.

Clare Holden, Sally Potter, Christopher Sheppard, Mike Manzi, Stella Corradi, Kurban Kassam at *Adventure Pictures*. All of the interviewees from the crew of *Ginger & Rosa*.

Nordisk Film: Shortcut, Copenhagen.

Mainstream, Copenhagen.

All of the digital imaging technicians from the UK, USA and Canada.

The Higher Education Academy & Joint Information Services Committee (JISC) Pedagogical development from Open Educational Resources Project.

Lucy Bolton, Charles Drazin and Ros Attwood from Queen Mary, University of London.

David Arnold, Roger Evans, Anne Galliot, Tony Inglis, Helen W. Kennedy, Gillian Youngs, Karen Norquay from the University of Brighton.

Professor Andrew Prescott and The Arts & Humanities Research Council (AHRC).

My fellow Deep Film Access Project (DFAP) Team: Roger Evans and Jos Lehmann.

University of Brighton in Hastings students Adam Johnson and Chalice Bartholomew.

Catherine Grant, Film Studies for Free.

Steve Mallinder, Debbie Flint and Jennifer Embleton at the Art Design and Media Higher Education Academy (ADM-HEA) Subject Centre.

Chris Follows & Process Arts, John Casey & Arts Learning and Teaching Online (ALTO–UK) project.

British Film Institute (BFI): Paul Gerhardt, Gabriele Popp, Wendy Russell, MariJose de Esteban, Peter Todd and Richard Paterson.

National Media Museum (NMM), Michael Terwey, Jen Skinner, Toni Booth and Simon Braithwaite. Tom Vincent of the Bradford International Film Festival 2013, Mark Goddall at the University of Bradford and Rhona Murray.

BBC Archive Development – Bill Thompson, Oliver Bartlett and Alex Tucker.

Screen Archive South East (SASE): Frank Gray, Ine van Dooren, Elaine Sheppard and Nick Clark.

University of Southern California, School of Cinematic Arts, Vicki Callahan, Virginia Kuhn and the VAT project (formerly the large-scale video analytics project).

Franck Trebillac for the design of the DFAP promotional material.

Artificial Eye: Ben Luxford and Marcel Karst.

The Duke of York's Picture House and Jimmy, the projectionist.

Filmmaker at Large: Alex Frois and Adam El Sharawy.

Bullet Creative: Kathy Barber and Gorm Ashurst.

University of Surrey, Janco Ćalic.

To all those who have hosted and kindly invited me to various forums and events that have enabled me to share the research of this book with wider audiences, including:

University of Essex and AHRC/CHASE 'Going Digital' workshop: Sanja Bahun and Heidi Wilkins.

Cinecity: Tim Brown.

COSMAT Conference: Martin Sohn-Rethel and Varndean School.

Archives 2.0: Saving the Past, Anticipating the Future conference, National Media Museum, Bradford, 2014: Michael Terwey.

Archaeologies of Media and Film 2014 Conference: University of Bradford.

Digital Echoes symposium: Digital Archives and Open Archival Practices, jointly hosted by Coventry University and the University of Brighton (2014) & Digital Echoes Symposium: The Digital Economy, Coventry University, 2013: Professor Sarah Whatley and Lilly Hayward-Smith.

Convergence: The International Journal of Research into New Media Technologies: Julia Knight and Alexis Weedon.

Screen Seminars at Glasgow University, 2015: David Archibald.

Digital Archives and Humanities: From Memory Curation to Innovation Seminar, Estonian Institute of Humanities, Tallinn University, 2015: Indrek Ibrus.

Digital Cultures and Film Studies, Institute for Collaborative Research in Humanities, Queen's University Belfast, 2015: Stefano Baschiera.

Big Humanities Data Workshop, 2014 IEEE International Conference on Big Data, Bethesda, Maryland, USA, 2015.

The Semantic Web: ESWC 2015 Satellite Events, Portorož, Slovenia, 2015.

European Network for Cinema and Media Studies Conference, Archives of/for the future, 2015. Wendy Russell, Karl Magee, Phil Wickham and Philip Drake.

Open Education Week: Opening minds, sharing resources and developing collective practice, HEA sponsored workshop, Sussex University, 2014.

The Higher Education Academy Annual Conference 2014, Aston University.

'Expertise?' workshop, 2012 CCN+ Digital transformations, communities and culture project: Caroline Bassett, Aristea Fotopoulou and Katie Howland.

Eric Faden at Bucknell University.

Besides the Screen conference, Goldsmiths College, London, December, 2012.

Living British Cinema Conference, Queen Mary University of London, 2012.

My amazing peer reviewers, Helen W. Kennedy, Jane Arthurs, Paula Hearsum, Virginia Crisp and Aylish Wood.

And finally, for keeping me sane, loved and alive throughout the process – my wonderful partner Helen, my parents, my daughters Maisie and Martha, Robbie, Ella, Helen Senior, my brothers, sisters, nieces and nephews, and my trusty dog Jess.

Preface

This book represents a departure from my previous monograph, *Beyond the Screen* (Atkinson, 2014) in which I interrogated the new and emergent spaces of cinematic engagement and film consumption from audience perspectives. Whilst *Beyond the Screen* offered considerations of the overlapping spaces where film audiences and producers inhabited the same (online) spaces, it was predominantly focused on new modes of cinema exhibition and film *consumption*. In contrast, *Film Practice to Data Process* explores the processes, people, spaces and representations of film and cinema *production* within a prolonged period of film-to-digital transition.

Research for this book began in 2011 when I was awarded an Open University (OU) SCORE fellowship – to explore the potential and realisation of Open Educational Resources with Film and Media education. It was at that point that I first made contact with Sally Potter's film company *Adventure Pictures*, since I was excited to discover that they had released a vast majority of the production materials from Potter's 1992 film *Orlando* in the framework of an online archive – SP-ARK.

Using a WordPress interface and Creative Commons licensing, SP-ARK had been made openly available to members of the public to explore and engage with. SP-ARK incorporated an online blogging tool which enabled users to trace 'pathways' through the archive and to allow others to follow in their archival footsteps.

I joined the SP-ARK team as part of my OU fellowship work and undertook a case study of the archive and its use with a number of Higher Education Institutions (Reported in Atkinson, 2012).

I experienced a moment of serendipity at the time of this work, since Sally Potter's then forthcoming film (*BOMB*, to eventually be titled *Ginger & Rosa*, and released in autumn 2012) went into Pre-Production. Situated in the Production Office, I was able to engage in observational activities around the film's making with a view to the further development and evolution of SP-ARK. These activities involved the collation of all of the materials of production and the interviewing of every crew member working on the film from the runners right up to the Director herself –

and taking in the entire process – from development and financing right through to distribution, exhibition and reception.

This resulted in a number of outputs and outcomes, such as the inclusion of some of the audiovisual materials about the research on the UK Blu-ray release of the film, in an interactive featurette entitled *Anatomy of a Film* which I conceived, co-produced and designed. The interface enabled viewers to scroll through excerpts from the interviews that had been undertaken with selected crew members, whilst simultaneously viewing archival materials and behind-the-scenes footage from that particular crew member in the adjacent windows.

A holistic picture of all aspects of industrial feature filmmaking was therefore achieved through my direct experience as a participant observer, embedded as I was in the processes of production – working and liaising directly with the Director, Producer, postproducers and distributors in the conception, design and production of this featurette. During the cinema distribution and exhibition phase, I convened and hosted a preview screening of *Ginger & Rosa* in October 2012 at the Duke of York's Picture House for university students in Brighton. I also hosted a further educational screening with Q&A for A-level students at CineCity Film Festival in Brighton, December 2012.

These activities led to the successful award of an AHRC Big Data grant in the autumn of 2013 for the Deep Film Access Project (DFAP) to develop an archival ontology using the *Ginger & Rosa* dataset. Further interviews were undertaken with filmmaking practitioners during this project who were at the heart of technological changes affecting the workflow of filmmaking (in particular with Digital Imaging Technicians or 'DIT's) who are critical agents in managing and marshalling the emergent and complex digital film production workflow.

Within these projects, there were many moments when I was required to articulate and explain the production workflow to non-expert audiences – to the visual designers who worked on the graphical representations included within this book and on the front cover, to the computer scientists working to design a knowledge bank of the processes and people involved in filmmaking. The notion of *translation* is a core and recurring theme of this book, from translations of the film-to-digital process, to translations of the communication of working practices to broader audiences, and a translation through decoding various industry and archival explanations of filmmaking practice.

These activities all underpinned and facilitated the research work of this book which enabled the generation of in-depth and unique insights from my incredibly fortunate perspective, able to observe the entirety of the filmmaking process in a period of transition.

Understanding the impacts of this transitionary moment is key to understanding film production for contemporary students, who do not intuitively recognise the analogue referents that are embedded in the terminology, practices and operational interfaces in filmmaking hardware and software tools. Their understanding requires a historical perspective which takes in the art, craft and practice of filmmaking.

There are also limited opportunities to engage directly with the materials and people of film production, given their professional ability to represent themselves through their own tools and mediums of their making (predominantly through commercialised 'making-of' materials which have a tendency to celebrate the novel and the spectacular – through the professions and processes they repeatedly represent – Visual Effects (VFX) work – at the expense of the mundane and the daily) invoking a skewed perception of the realities of filmmaking. Critical approaches to these materials by film scholars and students are therefore imperative.

It is a moment worthy of capture in terms of the challenges and opportunities that it presents to both practitioners and scholars of film production, contributing to emergent fields of production studies and digital film production studies.

The research for this book also builds on my own fascination as a film fan which has evolved since I was a child, sneaking into my brother's bedroom to read his *Fangoria* magazines to satisfy my inquisitiveness about how on-screen effects were achieved in horror films like *Hellraiser* and *A Nightmare on Elm Street*; or persuading the production team to allow me access to part of the set of *Anna and the King* which I stumbled across in Penang whilst backpacking in South East Asia in 1999, or becoming an accidental extra on *24-hour Party People*, whilst it filmed on location in Manchester in 2001. I also worked as an on-set photographer for a short time in Manchester on a number of independent film shoots.

I have always wanted to know how films are made and who is involved in their making, which I believe, to varying extents, is a universally shared curiosity of film audiences – shared by film students, cinephiles, cineastes and aficionados of film.

This book takes this curiosity to deeper levels – setting its frame around the labour conditions, the working practices, workflows and production processes and, crucially, the people, networks and materials of production in the film industry in 2012.

Tables and Figures

Tables

Figures

CHAPTER 1

Digital Film Production Studies

Book overview

From Film Practice to Data Process explicitly interrogates what is happening at the frontiers of contemporary 'digital film' production at a key transitional moment in 2012, when both the film industry and film-production practices were situated between the two distinct medium polarities of film and digital.

Evidence of this transition can be found across a swathe of institutional sites. Industry discourse at this particular moment was rife with representations and images of the impacts of digital technologies upon film production. Chris Kenneally's documentary *Side by Side,* which examined Hollywood's response to the digital transition of cinematographic practice, captures the coexistence of film and data in both the title and the content. In a similar vein, Tacita Dean's *FILM* installation in Tate Modern's Turbine Hall, which ran from October 2011 to March 2012, simultaneously expressed the threat to film in that current moment whilst also celebrating its unique aesthetic qualities. The emergence and visibility of the new labour conditions of the digital film economy were evident in a crisis in the special effects (VFX) industry as it adjusted to exponential international growth and global competition. Significant changes to the UK's film funding regime were signalled by the closure of the UK Film Council (UKFC) and the transfer of its responsibilities to the British Film Institute (BFI). Publications proliferated during this time as the academic community and the film industry responded to this period of intense change. The transitional moment is exemplified in Andrew Utterson's *From IBM to MGM* (2011), while the threat to industry stability is captured in the title of the USA Science and Technology Council's second 'Digital Dilemma' report (2012). The Hollywood Costume exhibition at London's V&A Museum in 2012 manifested what I will analyse as a temporally-specific and distinctive hybridised-aesthetic. In this case, the juxtaposition of material and digital is made manifest through augmenting the physical display of the costume by means of projected images of the performers' heads on screens which were mounted on the shoulders of the mannequins. To frame the work of the book, I have deliberately chosen to give emphasis to the terms – 'film' and 'data' – as opposed to *analogue* and *digital* although I do still use these when referring to a 'signal' transmission process and medium specificity. The fundamental questions underpinning and driving the research for this book are, what are the continuities and discontinuities of the *film*-to-*data* transitional moment?

What are the transformational characteristics which frame this transitional epoch where there is this shift between film practice and data process? As we shall see, these tensions are not unique to the intervention of the digital, indeed there has always been a constant friction between 'practice' (as it relates to creativity) and 'process' (as it relates to the logistical aspects of film production) since the birth of cinema. In some of the discussions that follow, we see that these tensions are first made most explicit during the period of industrialisation, Fordism and what were referred to as the 'factory-like conditions of film-making . . .' (Perkins 1972:158).

Through a close examination of 2012, this pivotal year for an industry where 'films have become files' (Bordwell 2012: 8), the book reveals the impacts and effects of this transition on the practices of film production, and the implications for practitioners working within the British film industry, and examines the various causative forces behind their adoptions and resistances. Importantly, in showing how this transmogrification was made manifest in film-production materials, processes and practices, it explains why film in its material form continued to persist in the digital.

I critically examine the entire film production process and its attendant representations through the case study of a single film made in this significant year. This approach allows me to explore industrial film production practice[1] in terms of the day-to-day experiences of its practitioners – how they work, how they communicate with one another, how they negotiate networks of operations and how they employ representational practices in order to communicate their work to wider audiences.

First, I lay bare the various 'aesthetics of production' – a phrase which I use to refer to a set of practices, behaviours and their attendant manifestations (in spoken nomenclature, written documentation, software, hardware, etc.). The identification of these in turn leads to the establishment of a specific 'Production Aesthetic' which is used to characterise a *specific* film production. In the example under examination here (*Ginger & Rosa*, Dir. Sally Potter, 2012), the resultant Production Aesthetic is specific to an independent location-based film – these would clearly be different to the Production Aesthetic for a different type of film or mode of production such as a Computer Generated Imagery (CGI) film or a studio-based film.

The emphasis on and elaboration of a 'Production Aesthetic' makes legible and accessible the ways in which a film production is made visible and visualised through its own tools, processes and ritualistic practices. Through an understanding of these, we can begin to gain full insights into what 'film practice' and 'data process' and all that is in between, looks, sounds and feels like.

Second, by extension, the book examines 'representational practices' – when the film's Production Aesthetic is mobilised and translated for wider audiences. Representational practices are the modes by which the film industry and its constituent practitioners present what they do, by drawing on this recognisable and iconographic visual palette of the codes and conventions of film production, and how these are then subject to further interpretation, extension, remediation and commodification by other (third-party) individuals, organisations and media.

Work such as this, which examines any temporally-specific transitional moment becomes increasingly important, as we might advance towards an era of total transformation, before the chance is lost to capture its aesthetics and impacts. As Slavoj Žižek cautions:

> One should adopt towards cyberspace a 'conservative' attitude, like that of Chaplin *vis-a-vis* sound in cinema: Chaplin was far more than usually aware of the traumatic impact of the voice as a foreign intruder on our perception of cinema. In the same way, today's process of transition allows us to perceive what we are losing and what we are gaining – this perception will become impossible the moment we fully embrace, and feel fully at home in, the new technologies. In short, we have the privilege of occupying the place of 'vanishing mediators.' (1997: 130–1)

A study focused on this 'digital film' moment is particularly significant, where understandings of the history of film production and key moments in its evolution can *only* be tracked and understood in the vestiges of celluloid material practice which, in 2012 continued to resonate and reside in the emergent digital terminology, iconography, practice and process. It is therefore essential for students and scholars of film to become attuned to this increasingly embedded and occluded system of signification in order to ensure and sustain their film production literacy.

Towards a Digital Film Production Study

A 'Digital Film Production Study' theoretical and conceptual framework is proposed through the unique synthesis of Production Studies, Film Studies and Digital Humanities, in order to be able to grapple with this complex industry at a critical moment of transition. I deploy this range of methodologies across the different Chapters as appropriate; in Chapter 2 (Digital Film Production People) and Chapter 3 (Digital Film Production Time) I use an augmented production studies approach, described below. In its proposition of collaborative auteurship, Chapter 2 also continues a film studies approach. In Chapter 4, I extend this use of a Film Studies approach, adopting textual analysis, digital film studies, new media and software studies, and visual media analysis to examine Digital Film Production Space. In its consideration of representation, and my use of in-depth textual analysis, Chapter 5 builds on Film Studies' work in an examination of the complexities of self-representational practices within and about the film industry. Chapter 6 – in its focus on digital archives, draws on and extends existing work within the wider Digital Humanities field.

Much has been written about the impact of the digital upon all other aspects of the film industry including: the aesthetics of mainstream and commercial film (McClean, 2008; Manovich, 2011; Christian 2011; and Purse 2013); digital performance practices (North 2008 and Desjardins, 2016); the (economic) impact of the digital upon film industry structures, operations, markets, changing distribution models (Wasser 2009, Knight, 2007; Hagener et al., 2016); alternate distribution and exhibition models (Lohmann, 2007; Lobato, 2009; Reiss, 2010; Bordwell, 2012; Tryon, 2013, Perren, 2013; Crisp, 2015); audience cultures (Rose, 2011; Atkinson, 2014); the new 'spaces' of digital cinema (Shaw and Weibel, 2003; Taylor and Hsu, 2003; Snickars and Vonderau, 2009; Atkinson, 2014); and new digital funding models (Sorensen, 2012); however, little attention has been afforded to the impact of the digital upon industrial film production practice, and the day-to-day experiences of the practitioners, how they work, how they communicate with one another, their networks of communication and crucially their representational practices.

I undertake this study through an examination of the people and processes involved in the entire lifecycle of one film – released under the title of *Ginger & Rosa* in October 2012. Through access to the people, the agglomeration of materials of production throughout the pre-production, production, post-production, distribution and reception of the film, I was able to make set visits, conduct interviews, attend test screenings, and undertake post-production observation in Denmark. I was also directly involved in the production process through the creation of a featurette for the Blu-ray release of the film, and through the design and delivery of a public-facing workshop as part of a Sally Potter Retrospective at Bradford International Film Festival 2013 (see Prescott, 2015). I then went on to develop an archival strategy and ontology through the AHRC-funded Deep Film Access Project (DFAP)[2]. Drawing on the methodological traditions of embedded ethnographic approaches and thick description (Geertz, 1973), I was particularly fortunate to truly 'get amongst' my field of study and through this could draw on the insights of the cultural anthropological tradition underpinning Geertz's approach to vivid detailed, and ultimately analytically significant, description. This method was further augmented by the use of virtual and textual ethnographic approaches (Hine, 2015).

Ginger & Rosa is emblematic of the transitional film-to-data period in many ways. It was one release in the context of the many independent films of 2012, many directed by British directors, and filmed in the UK, which included – *The Angels Share* (Dir. Ken Loach), *Sightseers* (Dir. Ben Wheatley), *Papadopoulos & Sons* (Dir. Marcus Markou), *Byzantium* (Dir. Neil Jordan), *Everyday* (Dir. Michael Winterbottom), *Broken* (Dir. Rufus Norris), *I, Anna* (Dir. Barnaby Southcombe), *Suspension of Disbelief* (Dir. Mike Figgis), *Berberian Sound Studio* (Dir. Peter Strickland), *My Brother the Devil* (Dir. Sally El Hosaini), *Good Vibrations* (Dir. Lisa Barros D'Sa and Glenn Leyburn) and *Holy Motors* (Dir. Leos Carax). All were in the context of a seemingly burgeoning UK film industry which was responsible for 'directly generating 43,900 full-time equivalent (FTE) jobs and contributing £1.6 billion to national GDP' (Oxford Economics, 2012: 6).

Ginger & Rosa exemplifies all aspects of the film production process which are applicable within the traditional and conventional film industries transnationally.

The case study of *Ginger & Rosa* reveals the complex social, cultural, financial, political and ethical influences which are at play, and how they can affect the creative and artistic decisions that are made. *Ginger & Rosa* was one of the first films shot in the UK to use the digital *Arri Alexa* camera. As a location-based feature film, set and filmed in London, it is (almost) entirely digital in all aspects of its production and output. It simultaneously embraced and eschewed digital technologies.

It embraced digital post-production in its removal of digital traces in the post-production process (cables, wires and satellite dishes were meticulously removed in order to sustain an authentic 1950s' verisimilitude of post-war Britain), and in its addition of very minor digital visual effects. The Director also embraced social media as a form of casting. It eschewed these digital technologies in the Director of Photography's use of rear netting across the cameras lens in order to restrain the camera's digital high definition. Furthermore, as an international co-production with Denmark, it was one of the last films to be processed through the soon-to-be-closed *Short Cut* Copenhagen film laboratory.

Ginger & Rosa involved the work of a diversity of film practitioners including many renowned and experienced film-production practitioners in the UK and International film industry, whose experience spans several decades, not least of which is Director Sally Potter herself. Potter's work is a common feature of the curriculum and syllabi of university courses both in the UK and abroad within the film, media and literature subject areas (see Sophie Mayer, 2008 and 2009; Fowler, 2009; Giuliana, 2008; McKim, 2006 and Fischer, 2004). Potter has been notable for her engagement with digital developments including her 2009 film *Rage*, the first feature film to be launched and distributed on mobile phones, and her SP-ARK archival website, which hosts 3,000 assets of *Orlando* (1992) (and will be discussed in more detail in Chapter 6). But whilst Potter is considered to be an auteur in her creative style and output, her working practices are notably highly collaborative and inclusive, the extent to which I will give fuller considerations within Chapter 2. *Ginger & Rosa* involved some new collaborations such as Robbie Ryan (Director of Photography, who has worked with Andrea Arnold, Ken Loach and Stephen Frears), and Anders Refn (Editor, and long time collaborator of Lars von Trier) whilst also extending a number of enduring partnerships including with Irene Lamb (Casting Director, who has worked extensively with Terry Gilliam). These latter partnerships have since extended further – at the time of writing both Lamb and Refn were working on Potter's new film (*The Party*, 2017). Interviews with these key collaborators and others, provided further insights into the broader context of the international film industry. A full illustrative filmography of each of the people interviewed is included as an appendix.

Although the creative and technical production team of this single film – *Ginger & Rosa* – provided the locus of my research, I approached the interviewees from the perspective that these were practitioners working within a wider professional field and able to draw from a diversity of affiliations and a heterogeneous range of experiences. The professionals and practitioners that I interviewed are a representative slice taken from a cross-section of their own 'project network.' The interviewees spoke about their own particular material practices on a micro-level, with regard to their immediate surroundings within this particular production, and also with reference to the macro context of their place within the film industry ecosystem. The interviews took place while they worked on the production of *Ginger & Rosa*, since it would be almost impossible to gain access to them once they had moved on to their next jobs. This set of interviews was augmented by interviews with other film practitioners from different films (mainly Digital Imaging Technicians) as they are at the forefront of implementing the changes of the film-to-digital transition.

Ginger & Rosa was an international co-production between the UK and Denmark and therefore allowed for the examination of distinctive processes such as an international cast and crew, and funding by multiple partners. The interviews were supplemented by the content and discourse analysis of the materials and tools of the production process which I undertook retrospectively after the production was completed. I worked with the collection of materials generated by *Ginger & Rosa* which include the film itself, rushes, stills photographs, director's notes, scripts, contracts, call sheets, production designs, sketches and schedules.

Digital film definition

I need to define what I mean when I use the term 'digital film', by tracing its etymology since many agree with Thomas Elsaesser on the 'oxymoronic nature of 'digital cinema' ' (2014a :32). Others who have discredited the use of 'digital film' as doublespeak, usually do so upon the basis of a specific hermeneutic assumption – that the term 'film' exclusively pertains to the material form of the medium. These protestations are located in discourses of imperilment, and are propounded by those seeking to protect film's medium specificity, purity and integrity.

Rather than 'film' implying the material condition, I use film in the phrase 'digital film' to refer to it as a cultural object in the way that the many terms across different cultures have referred to it: i.e. Motion Pictures, Movies, 'The' Pictures, Cinema. I would agree with David Bordwell and Kristin Thompson's observation, that 'The term "digital film" may seem contradictory, but almost immediately everyone understood it. Just as audio books and e-books were still called books, digital films counted as films, even though they never involved light hitting celluloid' (2013: 13), and would support Thomas Elsaesser's assertion that ('digital cinema') 'suggests a smooth transition between the traditional film experience and its digitally reworked successor' (2014a: 25).

However, even if one disputes this position and we return to the original 'material' definition of film – I would still maintain that 'digital film' is an exceptionally useful phrase since it is endemic in the hybridity of the transitional moment in which the film industry was caught in 2012, and which I also capture through the book's title – 'From Film Practice to Data Process'. It is a provocative juxtaposition of terms that appear to be in continual dialogue and tension. So I would argue that the 'digital film' locution, on the one hand, is most useful since it provides an accurate description of the current cultural object, a film made digitally, and on the other, it is a transitional term which communicates the instability of the 2012 film production moment.

I would not frame this as an intermedial moment – which would imply a clear transitional shift from one medium to the other – rather it is characterised by the coterminous existence of film and data, and the persistent aesthetic presence of celluloid.

This instability and the tension felt by people in the film industry in 2012 was profound and is communicated most clearly in this claim made by film director Christopher Nolan: 'A transition starts with people offering a new choice, but it finishes with taking the old choice away, and I don't think technically we're ready to do that yet' (2012 in *Side by Side*, Dir. Chris Kenneally). 'This transitional situation is manifest in the text of Christopher Nolan's 2010 film *Inception*, where the physical mechanical effects (of the infamous rotating corridor scene) coexist alongside the ground-breaking kaleidoscopic VFX of folding and morphing cityscapes.

Beyond my assertion that the term 'digital film' is itself both very clear and critically coherent, the implications for the 'digital film' form of production and its conditions of production are not so clearly understood. They are highly complex and subject to much debate. As Erin Hill has stated: 'Texts are created through an interlocking series of soft systems, developed over a century of massive technological and social change, and are held together by multiple, contradictory industrial mythologies, resulting in *production processes that are often as messy, disconnected, and chaotic* as their most successful products are clean, harmonious, and balanced.' (Hill, 2014: 142, emphasis added).

It is the messy, disconnected and chaotic production processes of 'digital film', that are the focus of this book. I have explored these in detail through the consideration and analysis of the entire production process of one 'digital film'. *Ginger & Rosa*[3] is a digital film in both senses of the phrase as I have defined it. Firstly, it is a film (as cultural object) that has been shot on a digital camera. Secondly, it is a film that is characteristic of the transitional moment within the 2012 temporal framing of this study, as we shall see, in its reliance upon film-based technologies, processes, practitioners, principles and politics.

This case study enabled a unique interrogation of the conditions film production in the present moment. It contributes to the growing attention given to the working practices and procedural aspects of all members of the crew and their respective input and impact on the film production *process* and the resultant film.

Before continuing with the main work of the book, it would be useful to contextualise the contribution that it is making to the wider academic fields of study.

Drawing together production studies, film studies, digital humanities and elements of computer science into a unified 'Digital Film Production Study', my research process also included moments of collaboration and co-research with film production professionals and film archivists. During these encounters, I inhabited a complex and amorphous researcher subjectivity in which I became both exegete and expositor in the navigation and translation between these diverse spheres of professional practice in film production and film archiving, translating the sometimes arcane and very often oblique terms to practitioners within both these two domains.

Production Studies

Production Studies, which frames and consolidates these various strands of enquiry and sharpens the research agenda, is considered to be 'a subfield of Media Industry Studies (MIS)' (McDonald, 2013: 149). Studies of the media industries normally tend to adopt a macro, political economy approach, examining the overall shape, dynamics and trends within the industry and often the industry organisation on a global scale (Miller et al., 2005; Miller 2011 and Jin 2012). But as Havens et al. propose, these studies provide an '. . . incomplete explanation of the role of human agents' (Havens et al., 2009: 236). Instead they propose a 'Critical Media Industry Studies' approach defined by Havens as 'midlevel fieldwork' (2009: 234) and an emphasis on more 'microlevel industrial practices' (2009: 235). Then there are those who look below the line – looking at exploitative factors, or technical roles, for example (Banks, 2009; Mayer, 2011).

Haven and Lotz contend that: 'By analysing how media industries operate, we can better appreciate how and why the texts we interact with come to be created' (Havens and Lotz, 2012: 2). I would propose that the production studies approach that I have adopted reverses this claim – *by analysing how and why texts interact and come to be created, we can better appreciate how media industries operate.*

'Production Studies'[4] is a multi and inter-disciplinary area. Studies of production have been undertaken by scholars within sociology, management studies, business studies, organisational studies, economics, cultural policy and arts management studies, and cultural studies, but it has only very recently been acknowledged as a significant, legitimate and growing field of enquiry in film and media studies, and its attendant methods have been validated. John Caldwell has stated that: 'I have always imagined that "production studies" or "production culture research" might become useful and productive institutional "contact zones" – not necessarily "fields" or "disciplines" in the traditional sense of intellectual activities that have clear and discrete borderlines' (Caldwell quoted in Vonderau, 2013: 22).

Whilst a production studies approach did not explicitly contribute to the original shaping of my thinking and my research design, it has certainly proved useful in being able to retrospectively frame my methodological approaches and theoretical positions. I place my work, and my Digital Film Production Study on a production studies continuum, despite the fact that the production studies field was not so established when I was undertaking field work in 2012.

There is clearly a need for studies into film production method, as noted by Jean-Pierre Geuens: 'Renewed attention therefore should be brought on the nub of film production *for the methods used to make films are far from neutral.* The "invisible hand" of the market in fact guides the entire production process' (Geuens, 2007: 411, emphasis added).

Methods in Production Studies

The business of conventional feature-film production assembles a huge company of people from multiple-disciplines on a temporary basis to engage in the collaborative endeavour of producing a unique, one-off output. The study of this phenomena is replete with significant methodological challenges. As Caldwell has suggested:

> We need to augment the traditional tools used in textual analysis and archival research with ethnographic and cultural-economic frameworks that allow us to see and account for the institutional logic [. . .] if we are to fully understand today's complex systems of film and television. (Caldwell, 2013: 163)

Through direct access to the film and all of its collaborators, in-depth filmed interviews with every person involved have been undertaken, from the runners right up to the producer: the crew involved with camera, lighting, sound, stunts, production coordination, editing, art, costume and make-up, as well as the financiers, lawyers, publicists and distributors. This testimony has been augmented in my own study through the close analysis of the by-products of production, as well as the equipment, hardware and software of production and is founded in empiricism (semi-structured interviews with practitioners) which is combined with a textual analysis approach and addresses the lacunae identified in the studies above.

Production Studies validates a number of methodological approaches traditionally employed in social science disciplines. Take, for example, early studies such as *Hollywood: The Movie Colony* (Rosten, 1941) and *Hollywood: The Dream Factory* (Powdermaker, 1951) which both used interviews as their main evidence base. Butler (1971) shapes his study of the making of feature films around the first-person testimonies of key workers (these are mostly above-the-line creative workers, but he does also include considerations of 'the continuity girl,' the distributor, the censor and the cinema). Many more recent studies are built solely upon practitioner interviews and industry testimony (Petrie, 1996b; Singer, 1998; Duchovnay, 2004; Perkins and Stollery, 2004). McKinlay and Smith propose a 'labour process perspective' (McKinlay and Smith, 2009: 5) which examines the processes and procedures of production. This, they argue, 'looks inside the experience or actuality of production processes and reveals how inputs of human labour, machinery and 'raw materials' are transformed into finished products' (McKinlay and Smith, 2009: 5).

Meehan and Wasko argue that '. . . research must address not only media corporations and markets but also the people whose collective labour creates media artifacts, the artifacts themselves, and the people who engage with or are exposed to those artifacts' (2013: 153). I will be doing so through an analysis of the objects, ephemera and tools of film production, the impacts of the digital and the imbrication of the digital as it manifests in craft-based location film production[5], the last bastion for the digital to fully penetrate in the film production industry overall.

A holistic consideration of the entire digital film production process in the context of the independent British film industry is an inherently inter-disciplinary endeavour. In order to gain insights of all elements of the production process – the people, networks and materials of production, different frameworks of analysis and subfields of academic studies were required.

In its investigations of the people and their working conditions, the book works within a production studies framework or a critical media industries framework (as defined by Havens et al., 2009) deploying textual, content and discourse analyses of the various texts and aesthetics of production throughout the creation, processing, release, exhibition and reception of the film. As such, it could be considered an 'integrated cultural-industrial study' as defined by John Caldwell through its use of 'ethnographic, sociological, critical, and industrial methodologies' (Caldwell, 2009b: 200).

Whereas Curtin and Sanson would suggest that: 'production studies [. . .] tend to stop short of linking their analysis to a global political economy, preferring instead to offer specific claims about the internal dynamics of media industries and workplaces' (2016: 9), the study of *Ginger & Rosa*

builds on the widely held belief that all film productions have been acknowledged to follow the same pattern of work:

> The business or the art (or both) of producing, distributing and exhibiting films
> follows a pattern largely similar, in warp and woof, around the civilised world.
> Because of the established and irrefutable superiority of the American product,
> and the business technique created around that product, it is understandable how
> and why the Hollywood impress has made itself felt wherever the motion picture
> finds an outlet. (Kann, 1938: 185)

This has always been considered to be the case but now with such a global
workforce and, as many of the interviewees of my study attest, international distinctions between film production practices at a local, departmental level are very limited. Just as an established (yet contested) notion
of 'Film Language' (Metz, 1974) and 'Film Grammar' (Spottiswoode,
1950; Nichols, 1975; Thompson 2002; Thompson and Bowen, 2009)
exists in relation to narrative film, so, too, a universal language of film
production process has emerged. As one of the Producers of *Ginger &
Rosa* stated, upon reflecting on the impacts of the film's status as an international co-production, and the potential challenges of spoken-language
issues: 'The good thing about film is there's a film language which *is* film,
which is different to English, French, Danish.'[6]

The film industry has been examined through many different thematic
and critical lenses. Looking back through the annals of film production
studies and the studies of production contexts and conditions, the different traditions fall into at least seven thematic approaches – coinciding
with key paradigm shifts in the film industry. These are: Film Industry
studies; Studio as space/location studies; Studio as organisation studies;
Labour studies; Filmmaking (production) studies; Specific (professional)
disciplinary studies and Individual film/author studies.

Broad **Film Industry Studies** were first initiated in the US in the
1930s and 1940s (Hampton, 1931; Lewis, 1933 and Huettig, 1944), and re-
emerged as a focus in the 1960s (Jobes, 1966) with studies which focused
on specific aspects of the film industry including legal analyses (Conant,
1960) and an entire study dedicated to the Hollywood system (Powdermaker, 1963). The British film industry received critical attention, from
an early study in 1921 (Boughey, 1921) to the British film industry in the
sixties (Walker, 1974), with more contemporary studies including British
cinema as a canon (Fitzgerald, 2010) and British Cinema (Murphy, 2010).
Additionally, Hollywood filmmaking (Kapsis, 1986) and the Hollywood
film industry (McDonald and Wasko, 2008; Schatz 2009a and 2009b)
have continued to be the source of ongoing academic enquiry. The film

industry has been approached from a number of different dimensions: as industry (Barrow, 2011); as its status as a business (Lees and Berkowitz, 1981; Baillieu and Goodchild 2002); and through the examination of women's involvement and representation (Cook and Dodd, 1993; Bell and Williams, 2010). The film industry has also been interrogated through economic perspectives including studies focused on specific national film economies including Switzerland (Cucco, 2010), Austria (Sperlich, 2011) and Spain (Kogen, 2005), through to interrogations of co-productions (Hoskins, McFayden, Finn and Jackel, 1995; Neumann and Appelgren, 2007) and comparative film production regimes (Mathieu and Strandvad, 2008).

The **spaces of film production**, their geographic locations and local film ecologies have historically received much attention (Johns, 2010). In the UK, studies of British film studios include: Shepperton (1932– present) (Sweet, 2005 and Threadgall, 1994); J. Arthur Rank (established Pinewood Studios) (Macnab, 1993); Goldcrest Films 1977–86 (Eberts and Ilott, 1990), Forever Ealing (1902– present) (Perry, 1981), Studies of Ealing Studios (Barr, 1998), Mitchell and Kenyon (Toulmin et al., 2004). Such studies are relatively straightforward to undertake, since all of the resources are contained under one roof. The dispersal of production across networks, which characterises contemporary film productions, creates an additional challenge for researchers seeking to capture and study them. A focus on particular movie **studios in the organisational sense** have included Warner Brothers (Gomery, 1985), Columbia Pictures Organisation (Buscombe, 1985) and Nordisk Film (Larsen and Nissen, 2006).

Labour Studies emerged in the 1970s, when the studio model in the US and UK became less influential and new organisational structures emerged. Michael Chanan's 'Labour Power in the British Film Industry' criticised the trend 'towards cumbersome intellectual systems of analysis, purporting to reveal the ideological superstructure of the cinema, as if this were possible without first understanding the basic *conditions of production*' (Chanan 1976: italic emphasis added). As Siân Reynolds similarly has observed 'what might be called the "labour history" of the cinema is on the whole a less-prospected territory' (1998: 66).

There were further labour organisation studies undertaken in the US film industry including Lois Gray and Ronald Seeber's 1996 historical study into the labour union movement, whilst studies into industry work continued in the UK (Langham, 1996). More than a decade on, the focus is seen to shift to freelance careers in Hollywood (Randle and Culkin, 2009) and Production careers in Europe (Mathieu, 2013). More general labour-based accounts can be found which take broader overviews of the digital media industries (Ursell, 2006; Deuze, 2007; Ashton, 2015 and Curtin and Sanson, 2016), and the impact of the digital and convergence upon working cultures and practices (Jenkins, 2006a; Deuze, 2009).

Filmmaking (production) studies were initiated by an early analysis of movie-making – (Gans, 1963). Modes of production and production practices became the focus of later studies, including the Hollywood mode of production (Staiger, 1981), expanded and advanced in Bordwell et al. (1985).

In the project-based mode of film production which relies on a constellation of practitioner networks, studies have started to proliferate which focus on **particular groups of professionals** within film (and cultural) productions. The focus upon groups of practitioners includes: British and Irish Film Directors (Allon, Cullen and Patterson, 2001), Cinematographers (Cowan, 2012a); Costume Designers (Banks, 2009); Screenwriters (Conor, 2014); Casting Directors (Hill, 2014); Editors (Perkins and Stollery, 2004); and Costume in British Cinema (Cook, 1996).

Women have also been studied as a specific group of professionals through gendered studies of film production, such as Sue Harper's examination of female Producers, Writers, Directors, Costume Designers, Art Directors and Editors (Harper, 2000); Female film editors (Hatch, 2013); Freelance Hollywood Women (Carman, 2016) and Continuity Girls (Williams, 2013: 603). Melanie Williams' study marks a departure from the usual studies of 'above-the-line' professionals, to below-the-line workers and technical staff. As Paul and Kleingartner state, the 'line' has been 'found in [motion picture, television, and other cultural industry] project budgets. Creative work is accounted for above the line; below-the-line expenses include craft and technical labor, materials and supplies, and so on' (1996: 161).

In addition to Williams' work, other studies which have focused on below-the-line professions include Sound (Hilmes, 2013); VFX workers (Curtin & Vanderhoef, 2014; Atkinson, 2015a); the VFX industry (Venkatasawmy, 2013); VFX 'services industry' (Mukherjee et al., 2013) and Runners (Szczepanik, 2014).

Above-the-line contributions have been celebrated within literature that draw out the artistic, 'exciting' aspects of production, often fetishising production work and certain roles – such as the Directors, Editors and Production Designers, as focused upon by the *FilmCraft* book series (some of the first were Chang, 2011; Halligan, 2012; Goodridge, 2012, and there have subsequently been more published) reaffirms the hierarchies of production and the creative leads – those that already feature in the paratextual surround of a film. These tend to be aestheticised with glossy colour images – interviews taking place with practitioners after, and not during, the process – and are retrospective romanticised accounts.

Individual Film/Author Studies

Given that a film '. . . manifests thousands of parameters, from acting and body language to lighting, cutting and cinematography, and each of these parameters exists in, and is developed in connection with, artistic traditions that for each parameter may have its own relative autonomous history' (Grodal et al., 2004: 9), there has been a historic lack of attention given to the collaborative and collective film production process within film studies scholarship. This lack, and the subsequent invisibility of agents in the film production process has been compounded by the dominant critical paradigm of auteur theory within film studies. As Dai Vaughan has noted in his study of film editors:

> The auteurists have created a criticism in which no one but the director may be discussed; and this, while not even satisfying the desiderata of critical purity, sets the seal of academic approval upon the exclusion of 'technicians' from all other discourses: and film, the most collaborative of the arts, is stuck with a literature which cannot at any level handle the idea of collaboration. (1983: 13)

In comparison to the innumerable studies that focus upon individual directors, there is a notable dearth of studies which focus on non-directorial, although highly influential industry figures. There is the autobiography of Michael Balcon, the Ealing Film Producer (Balcon, 1969) and, more recently, a study into Michael Klinger, the British film producer (Spicer and McKenna. 2013). Similarly, there have been limited academic studies that focus upon the production of singular films (Robert Carringer's study of *Citizen Kane* in 1985 being a notable exception).

Compared to the attention bestowed upon finished films and macro-level industry study in its assessment of the impacts of the digital – limited consideration has been afforded to the actual impacts this has upon day-to-day working practices, as McKinlay and Smith note '. . . how work is structured and what people do when they make creative products remains relatively under-researched' (2009: 5).

There are a number of notable exceptions where process and people are the locus of the research in film studies – although limited to Hollywood models of production – (Lovell and Sergi, 2005; Caldwell, 2008a; Corrigan and White, 2012). There is even less consideration given in terms of what effect these working practices have upon production aesthetics and the end product. There have been some studies that examine the intersection and influence between industrial factors and film *style* (as summarised by Holt and Perren, 2009, including Bordwell et al., 1985 and Wyatt, 1994), and more recently there have been studies focused upon the impacts of Computer Generated Imagery (CGI) and stereoscopic *style* (including Wood, 2013 and Ross, 2015).

What is unique in my approach is that I have selected one film; a close analysis of this enables novel insights which touch all aspects of those domains: Film Industry, Studio as space/location, Studio as organisation, Labour, Filmmaking (production), Specific (professional) disciplinary and Individual film/author studies. Implicated throughout my study are the insights now being enabled through the engagement with Digital Humanities approaches. The implicit influence of this field comes in to a more explicit relationship with the material under examination when I turn my attention to digital archives in Chapter 6. This situates this analysis of the archive within this wider Digital Humanities field and brings to bear these distinctive approaches (Berry 2012) where they can most usefully apply to film studies and the media industries (Acland and Hoyt, 2016). The recent intervention of digital methodologies in film studies is captured in a special issue of *The Frames Cinema Journal* – 'Re-Born Digital' (Grant 2012).

Data approaches towards film analytics include Barry Salt's 'Cinemetrics' project (Salt, 1985) in which he examines emergent patterns of editing and increased cutting rates and rhythms. Other digital film studies approaches such as Kuhn et al.'s (2012) large-scale video analytics study; the videographic approach to film criticism (Ferguson, 2015); the automated analysis of archive film material (Zeppelzauer et al., 2012), and the visualisation of data in Digital Cinema Studies (Verhoeven, 2016), are all informed by these Digital Humanities perspectives. These approaches have yet to be applied to a (digital) film production context which will be the major contribution of this volume.

Overview of Chapters

What follows in Chapter 2 is a critical examination of the wider context of the film industry taking *Ginger & Rosa* as a lens through which to examine the three main professional working frameworks that film industry professionals operate within. These are the network, the department and the project itself, the film. Drawing on the interviews with established film professionals who are both adept at and successful in the navigation and negotiation of temporary project-based working, I will examine these three distinctive, yet overlapping spheres, their intersections, their challenges and their moments of contradiction. I will extrapolate the organisational structure as specific to the *Ginger & Rosa* 'project' and examine in detail the structures and working relationships of a number of departments – Camera/Electrical, Assistant Director (AD), Production and Post-production. I pay particular attention to the challenges of cross-departmental communications within these structures and point to some of the conflicting tensions that emerge in the pervading discourses of 'flexibility.' I examine the complex interplay between, on the one side, a highly craft-based production, in which established film practitioners are engaged with the craft process of traditional classical narrative film production, and, on the other, the practices associated with the new digital technologies and how these may lead to lacunas in the training and development needs of the workforce and interstitial roles and work specific to the film-to-data moment. Through the mapping of a Personnel Structure and Working Relations model, as they pertained to *Ginger & Rosa*, I examine how Potter manages to nurture innovation and experimentalism within these seemingly inflexible structures through 'collaborative and transitional auteurism.'

In Chapter 3, I explore the notion of digital film production 'Time' and the various different temporalities of film production. Again, by drawing primarily upon the case-study materials of *Ginger & Rosa*, the Chapter maps the 2012 moment of transition from working with film to working with data, and the hybrid practices and protocols that manifested as a result. I examine how the introduction of new technologies and digital processes challenged the orthodoxies of long-established film industry production practice. I also explore how workflow patterns were effected with the advent of the digital in film production. These technologies have radically increased the speed and volume at which film data and metadata can be generated during the film production workflow. For instance, where once there were naturally appearing gaps in the photochemical process, to enable film reels to be changed between takes, and to give time for the processing to take place (overnight) which all enabled a space for contemplation and consideration by the Director and other key creative members of the crew. These have been compressed by the synchronous (through multiple monitors on set) and instantaneous (through playback) access to the material which is being shot that is enabled within the digital film production process. I propose a 'Creative Core' Structure of Production model with which to understand the determinants and impacts of on-set *workflow*. I propose the emergence of a specific aesthetic of production which I term 'workflow-warp' – which is temporally bending the traditional film structure and pace out of shape. I then conceptualise the interstitial and transitional practices noted in the previous Chapter as workflow-weft – the process of weaving together a complex blend of the film and the digital into an inextricable tapestry – which metaphorically meshes processes and their representation.

Chapter 4 picks up on this phenomenon, and addresses the challenge of disentangling deeply ingrained celluloid practices, from processes, practices and the tools of film production. In its close textual examination of Digital Film Production Space, this Chapter includes detailed considerations of the attendant 'production apparatus' of *Ginger & Rosa* (which is the same apparatus used by the film industry in a diversity of national contexts) and the manifestation of the film in digital and virtual representations. Through a process of abstraction, I expound how film/analogue motifs and nomenclature are inscribed and sustained in the digital film production process, in the professional practices and in the physical and digital manifestations of film production. Through the examination of embodied practices, onset processes and protocols, including the minutiae of hardware design, software and interface aesthetics, I trace the origins of the often perplexing film and celluloid skeuomorphs. The chapter goes on to consider the reasons for the persistence of these practices which conversely seek to simultaneously erase the analogue whilst at the same time mask the use of the digital medium. I consider the notion of 'Celluloid Pedagogies', and how the various practitioners on *Ginger & Rosa* learned their crafts, describing them through material practices and tactile experience. I examine the attendant politics of loss, erasure, absence and invisibility in the wider industry discourses of 2012. I conclude by identifying and defining the Production Aesthetic specific to *Ginger & Rosa*.

In Chapter 5, I proceed to expound how the industry appropriates and mobilises the Production Aesthetic, through an exploration of the various modes, tools and types of film industry representation, whereby film is the conduit through which we see film production, and is subject to its own representational modes, aesthetics and practices. I present a genealogy of different types of mediated films and their making, that have commercialised these aesthetics. As part of this more holistic overview, I detail how *Ginger & Rosa* communicated and embedded its Production Aesthetic in a number of different ways. I draw on the inherent paradox which is innate to these modes of representation where the film production attempts to make itself visible whilst simultaneously rendering itself invisible. This leads to a conflicting aesthetic of 'pseudo-visibility' and 'hyper-invisibility' – the simultaneous openness and foreclosure of film production practice obscuring people, histories and practices. Drawing on themes of invisible labour, invisible economies, politics of invisibility and aesthetics of erasure, I then turn to considerations where aesthetics of production are made manifest in modes of resistance – where the tools and aesthetics of production are subverted for moments of protest by film industry practitioners.

In Chapter 6, I examine how the history of digital cinema will be curated, compressed and encoded through an investigation into digital film production preservation and access in the moment of the 'Digital Dilemma' (2012). This Chapter focuses on the preservation, organisation and representation of digital film and the attendant challenges to the archiving of digital film which I summarise as Reliability, Vulnerability, Volume and Data Complexity. I consider different archival paradigms including film, born digital and *hybrid*, and the resultant archival aesthetics which emerge, drawing from various branches of enquiry within archival studies. I consider how archival structures support and replicate auteurism leading to omissions and occlusions. The Chapter includes considerations of Sally Potter's own online, interactive archive SP-ARK – whereby all film/analogue was digitised – and the archival structure developed by the Deep Film Access Project (DFAP) – designed to accommodate both film, data and hybrid assets, for a transitional moment. I provide evidence that the way in which an archive is conceived, shaped and organised captures the various 'aesthetics of production' and 'Production Aesthetics' of a moment in time, as well as its concomitant 'production legacy aesthetics', 'archival legacy aesthetics' and embedded paradoxes of representation.

The epilogue closes the book with a look back at 2012 through the contemporary moment of 2017.

I now turn to the generation of new insights and understandings of an 'aesthetics of production' related to people, the employment infrastructures and the labour organisation of film production.

Notes

1. Note that I make a keen distinction between the genre of 'industrial film' – as explored by Vinzenz Hediger and Patrick Vonderau (2009) which refers to documentary films of different industrial processes. Rather I use the term industrial film to refer to the outputs and processes associated with the 'film industry' as 'an economic system, a way (or ways) of organising the structure of production, distribution and consumption' (Buscombe 1985: 94). Hence I will tend to use the term film production as opposed to filmmaking throughout the book.
2. AHRC project reference AH/L010305/1. This project will be examined in more detail in Chapters 3 and 6.

3. It is important to note (since many of the interviewees refer to its original title) that during production the film was known as *BOMB*, but this was later changed for reasons that will be detailed in Chapter 2.

4. Production Studies is gaining traction as a significant field of study evidenced through a number of publications and events including: a special 'In Focus' section in the 2013 *Cinema Journal* dedicated to the consideration of the field of Media Industries Studies; a dedicated Media Industries Journal; and in the UK in April 2014 a 'New Directions in Film & Television Production Studies' conference was held. The most recent volume about this field is *Production Studies, The Sequel* (Banks, Conor and Mayer, 2016) following on from the original Production Studies volume (Mayer et al., 2009).

5. I use the term craft-based to imply a film that uses traditional, physical and practical techniques wherever possible, in its creation of scenery, props, effects etc. Craft-based films are always location-based where the use of digital VFX are kept to an absolute minimum. Craft-based films are normally those which pertain to realist drama conventions.

6. In an interview with the author, 22 August 2012.

CHAPTER 2

Digital Film Production People

Introduction

This Chapter interrogates the organisation of the people and work of digital film production through the case study of *Ginger & Rosa*, examining how the personnel navigate and negotiate the 'structure of production' (Harbord 2002: 98). In contemporary independent film, I contend that the structure of production is formed under *three inter-linking spheres of labour organisation*: the network, the project and the department.

- **The network** constitutes all film industry practitioners – it is predominantly comprised of individual freelancers pursuing portfolio careers, formed into smaller sub-networks around their particular areas of specialism. The network is the mechanism through which work is sought, publicised and allocated.
- **The project** is 'the film', the framework of organisation within which the production apparatus is constructed and the labour is organised – under which the (horizontal) departments are formed – in this case *Ginger & Rosa*. The project provides the overall legal and contractual parameterisation within which the departments operate.
- **The department** is a hierarchical (vertical) unit of organisation, of a domain of expertise, that is: camera department, costume department, hair and make-up department, and so on. Departments are subject to strict divisions of labour with individuals inhabiting a specific role with tasks allocated to that role by the individual Head of Department.

Within this Chapter, I examine these three spheres of organisation and the relationships between them, through the experiences of the members in four different departments of *Ginger & Rosa*: the Camera Department, the Electrical Department, the Assistant Director Department and the Post-Production Department. I include an examination of how the work of these different departments has been affected through the introduction of digital tools, technologies and techniques. I consider the incremental changes taking effect within departmental production structures in 2012 in response to the introduction of digital media into production processes, through an examination of the intermediary role of the Digital Imaging Technician (DIT) which bridges the liminal space between the analogue and the digital, between the film and data. I begin to establish the various 'aesthetics of production,' through consideration of the challenges and impacts of what can be considered as being three highly contradictory structurations. These challenges and impacts include cross-departmental communication issues, a lacuna in training and development opportunities and the persistent and often conflicting imperatives to work flexibly. I then move on to consider the notion of how collaboration and creativity works across these distinctive departments and established industry hierarchies in relation to *Ginger & Rosa* through the evolution of the notion of 'collaborative auteurship'.

Historical organisational antecedents

Up until the 1960s, the prevailing mode of film production was dominated by the Hollywood Studio system and the organisational and operational principles of Fordism. Within this original system, film workers were employed by a large studio organisation, where all processes and services relating to a film production were contained within the same complex in one geographic location (see page 13 in Chapter 1 which outlines work undertaken in relation to the Film Studio)[1]. These environments fostered strictly delineated working conditions, leading to occupational segregation and the subsequent unionisation of different groups of workers, much of which can still be seen today.[2] As Chanan's study of the establishment of unions within the British film industry revealed: 'the film crew slowly developed a complex hierarchy which is intimately tied up with trade union organisation and history' (1976: 4).

From the 1960s onwards, the dominance of the studio model receded, in a process referred to as 'vertical disintegration' (Christopherson & Storper, 1989). Studios broke down their operations and new forms of 'post-Fordist' labour organisation emerged, which as Harbord describes it, signalled 'a shift from a studio production line to a flexibly organised set of practices orchestrated by major studios' (Harbord, 2002: 97). These new economic and working conditions led to the decrease in permanent employees and the subsequent outsourcing of work, contracting, freelancing, long hours, hard deadlines, problematic and challenging working conditions including temporary employment and a lack of basic benefits such as health care and retirement, which Miller et al. (2005)

conceptualise as a 'New International Division of Cultural Labor'. This, they argue 'divides and reorganizes labor processes, exploiting cost differentials and pitting workers against each other in a relentless competition that is aided and abetted by government policies' (2005: 125). This situation has exacerbated the structures of an industry that have been in place for a long time – this is not just about new technologies impacting on the organisation of work, the film industry has always been buttressed by those inhabiting 'Boundaryless careers' (Jones & DeFillippi, 1996; Arthur & Rousseau, 1996) in the context of 'The project-based organization (PBO)' (DeFillippi & Arthur, 1998; Jones, 1996). Freelancing has always been the dominant model of film-production work. Emily Carman offers a counterpoint to the persistence in framing this as problematic (Randle & Culkin, 2009). She states: '*Independent Stardom* is the term I use to describe this alternative freelance path in 1930s Hollywood. This not only resulted in better salaries for these actresses, but also garnered them more control over their careers' (Carman, 2016: 3). As Carman illuminates in this work: 'These were business-savvy women who challenged the hierarchical and paternalistic structure of the film industry. They took a proactive role in shaping their careers through their freelance labor practices' (Carman, 2016: 4).

Despite the global shifts highlighted above and the increasing 'hyper-mobility of contemporary feature film production' (Goldsmith & O'Regan, 2005: 1) both project and departmental structures have remained the same in the way that work is distributed, organised and managed at both project and departmental level: 'This temporary form of organisation perpetuated, and can be argued in some instances to have accentuated (with respect to the head of departments role), the pre-existing division of labour evident during the studio era (as identified by Staiger 1985)' (Blair, 2001: 151).

The Network

The network or 'Project Network' (Jones, 1996) is a constellation of freelancers and independent workers. A 2012 Skillset census[3] revealed an exceptionally high proportion of freelancers in specific roles associated with film production in comparison to other creative industries. For example, in the UK film industry, the camera department is made up of 70 per cent freelance workers, lighting is 84 per cent, make-up and hair is 70 per cent, and costume wardrobe is 67 per cent (Skillset, 2012:11). Relatively few film industry professionals hold a permanent position within an established organisation; rather they are members of a peripatetic workforce who move from job to job, from production company to production company.

Due to its recognition of pioneering the project-based mode of working[4], the film industry has been the subject of many management studies (Baker & Faulkner, 1991), and has more recently been subject to examination through the lens of precarity (Curtin & Sanson, 2016).

The working conditions of the film industry have often been identified as challenging and sometimes problematic, with no human resource infrastructure in place, workers are vulnerable, with rights unprotected and often open to exploitation. Harassment and inequality of opportunity can go unchecked. One interviewee highlighted their own experiences of uneven recruitment practices and processes:

> A lot of DoPs have a lot of sway over who their DITs are, and that's the way it should be, [. . .] saying that, I get a lot of work from production, and unlike the camera hierarchy where it's solely based on the hierarchy of who gets the job, I can also get a lot of work from the producers. [. . .] I do wonder if I get a lot more work through Producers, as a lot of Producers are female.[5]

The respondent here highlights a number of unconscious practices which are endemic in the film industry, instances of what Rosalind Gill would refer to as 'reasonable' sexism (2014), which are not subject to the conventional checks and balances afforded through a formal human resource management structure. What Keith Randle et al. (2015) identify as a 'web of reciprocity' (2015: 603) in film and television employment, leading to a 'resilient, self-perpetuating habitus' (2015: 603), thus making it difficult for others to access – it is widely acknowledged that the film industry is hard to break into and exclusionary. The following testimonies from a range of production personnel from *Ginger & Rosa* attest to the significance of the network, indeed, the majority of crew members that were interviewed cited that it was their previous connections that secured them the job on this project:

> 'I've done a [. . .] film with her before. We get on very well and she asked me to do this job and I said Yes.'
> 'I'd worked with the [. . .] before a couple of times who gave me a call about this film. You're always relying generally on first ADs or line producers, production managers who have worked with you before to give you a call and get you involved.'
> 'We worked with [. . .] before, so it's keeping the same team together, really.'
> 'He's brought me on a couple jobs. We've ended up here after a couple of features with [. . .]. He's been very good to me.'
> 'we've been doing maybe six or seven films now. So it works out quite well, because we know what we need, I know what he needs, and so he doesn't have to explain things and it saves time and effort, really.'

Many also used the 'You're only as good as your last job' maxim:

> 'You're only as good as your last job. Therefore, you have to be on the ball at all times because the first time you drop the ball is probably the first time you don't get a call for a new job.'
>
> 'You very rarely get a job from someone you don't know. It generally tends to be people want to work with people they know and trust and can use, so you always have just got to do your best job and then hope people ask you back for the next project.'[6]

As most of those interviewed as part of this research were ostensibly in position through their prior network connections, it illuminates the notion of 'Serial collaboration' (Zuckerman, 2004) – a defining characteristic of the project network – and also of Potter's own work and her choices to repeatedly work with the same Heads of Department across her film work.

There were two exceptions in the case of the crew members of *Ginger & Rosa*: 'I didn't know anyone in London, so I started from the very bottom and just got pen and paper out' (Third Assistant Director), and the Director's Assistant who stated: 'I actually saw the role on Mandy[7]. It was advertised in there and I couldn't believe it because there's never roles like that advertised on there.'[8]

The Network Organisation has also been conceptualised as the Latent Organisation which Starkey et al. define as: 'forms of organization that bind together configurations of key actors in ongoing relationships that become active/manifest as and when projects demand' (Starkey et al., 2000: 299).' The notion of the Latent Organisation which is attributed to account for a defining characteristic of the project network, can also be seen to account for the prevailing affective structure on-set – there is a layering of crew members across the different departments who are assigned 'standby' roles. These crew members are literally required to stand by and wait until the moments in which they are needed to spring into action and undertake their role, as the standby costume explains: 'I'm quite literally standing by if anybody needs anything and to keep actors warm.'[9] This latency within the film-production workflow will be examined in more detail in the following Chapter.

The Project

The project is the holistic unit of organisation for the production of a film, shaped by legal and contractual mechanisms that govern exchanges and relations between the film and its workers. As the Producer of *Ginger & Rosa* explains:

There are two aspects to making a film. One is artistic and one is business, because cinema is unique as an art form because it's an industrial medium. Therefore, you need a business structure in order to support the filmmaking, the artistic process of the filmmaking. My job consists of taking care of all the business elements, which is financing, budget, schedule, the hiring, the firing, and then the day-to-day running of the film production as a business. I always say that making a film is like having to construct a factory and equip a factory and staff a factory and then build one object and take it all apart again. In that sense, I'm a factory manager, I suppose, as well as chairman of the board who creates this thing that makes the film and then take it apart again.[10]

Here the Producer outlines the two clear and distinct lines of activity in film production – the creative and logistical. The driving principle of the project is the management of the project and becomes one of efficiency, in terms of time, resource and cost.

The project is the mechanism through which cast and crew are recruited, contracted and remunerated, and through which all legal and contractual concerns are managed.

The project process (both creative and logistical) is examined in depth, in the following Chapter.

The Department

The film-production process is formed as a fragmented set of specific, detailed practices assigned to a distinct set of departments. The department is the core unit of organisation during the project period – there are multiple departments which operate within a flattened hierarchy. In the case of *Ginger & Rosa*, these departments were specified in the production phase[11] as: Director/Writer, Producers, Production, Accounts, Art Department, Assistant Directors, Camera, Casting, Catering, Chaperones, Construction, Continuity, Costume, Dialect Coach, Editing, Electrical, Facilities, Financiers, Hair and Make-up, Health and Safety, Locations, Medic, Music, Post-production, Property Department, Publicity, Security, Sound, Special Effects, Stand In, Stills, Stunts, Transport and Tutor (for Elle Fanning). The size of departments varies dependent on different projects and their respective budgets, some roles may be doubled up in cases where efficiency measures are necessary.[12]

The opening and closing credits of a feature film provide a clearer indication of the hierarchies in place within a film production[13]. Structured through protracted contractual negotiations which link back to the initial contracts that were issued to all cast and crew members – it is one form of industry representation (along with other industry-created and industry-sanctioned representational paratexts that will be discussed more fully in Chapter 5.) Lovell & Sergi highlight the political dimension of the film credits: 'Far from being just a means of arranging the names of the various collaborators, credits become a tool to ensure that a hierarchy of roles is maintained'. (Lovell & Sergi, 2005: 56). As one of the producers of *Ginger & Rosa* explains:

> The credit roll, which is the end roll that most people leave the cinema for, a lot of time is spent on that because you want it perfect [. . .]. All the finances have to have a look at it, sign off on it, we send it to the HoDs and the crew to make sure they're happy with their departments who's being credited. Contractually, there's lots of things you have to make sure that happen in a certain place on the end roller. Normally that document then goes around, I think on this film, probably about twenty to thirty times. [. . .], it's kind of lots of chefs, but that happens on every film.[14]

The structure of the credits does not always present the departments in their original organisational structure, and so to the untrained eye, it is not possible to ascertain the original workaday hierarchies of the different departments. For example, the creative HoDs each have their own static title in the opening and closing sequences, their names are not listed again above their respective departments within the rolling credits.

Taking a sample of four departments which exemplify the three different skill sets of film production which I have framed as: creative (camera), technical (electric) and logistical (Assistant Director), and the post-production represents all three – creative, technical and logistical – I explore in depth their structures and politics. The departments also show the different aspects of film-production work that are at varying stages in their film-to-data transition – the camera and electric departments have been subject to the most recent and profound changes, the Assistant Director Department, as examined within the context of *Ginger & Rosa*, has remained relatively unchanged, and the Post-Production Department has already been subject to huge change. These changes, I argue, all relate to the integration and take-up of the new technologies and tools of production and how they have impacted upon the nature of work. The different departments also provide insights into the different conditions of work – with the Assistant Director and Camera/Electrical still being very unionised and subject to the same conditions of work organisation, whereas post-production personnel tend to sit outside union structures and in some cases may have more permanent, and stable conditions of work (but not always, see Curtin & Vanderhoef, 2014 and Atkinson, 2015a). Despite this, all departments under consideration are still deemed to be 'semi-permanent work groups (SPWG) [. . .] working together on a repeated basis' (Blair, 2001: 154), on temporary projects. The department is modular in both its wider project context and in its strict delineation of roles, which works to avoid entropic encounters as workers frequently move from project to project.

Camera

The structure of the Camera Department hierarchy has remained the same for decades and is widely understood to be structured hierarchically thus:

> Director of Photography
> Camera Operator
> Focus Puller (1st Assistant Camera)
> Clapper Loader (2nd Assistant Camera)
> Camera Assistant
> Key Grip
>
> [Digital Imaging Technician (DIT)]

In their book entitled *The Work of the Motion Picture Cameraman*, Freddie Young & Paul Petzold describe the team, led by the Director of Photography (DoP) (previously known as the Lighting Cameraman), as being comprised of the operator, the Focus Puller, the Clapper Loader, and the Dolly Pusher (1972: 26–28). The Dolly Pusher is now referred to as the Key Grip, which is likely to cover numerous handlings of grip equipment (Dollys, tracks, Jibs, etc.) Two of these original role titles – Focus Puller and Clapper Loader – specifically refer to the celluloid practices of operating an analogue-film camera and handling and loading film into the camera, respectively. Focus Pulling was once a dedicated role, as the 1st Assistant Camera/Focus Puller explains his role: 'the principal responsibility is to keep things sharp, so there's also looking after the gear, assisting the cameraman, it's basically a cameraman assistant position' [. . .] 'it's about judging the distance and setting it on the lens.'[15]

These roles have been subject to changes in emphasis and responsibilities wrought by the introduction of digital cameras and the introduction of a new role, the Digital Imaging Technician, but as we shall see in a moment, camera crew members continue to use the prior titles with the new appellations interchangeably.

In *Ginger & Rosa*, the camera department was structured (and named, as per the film's credits) thus:

Director of Photography
1st Assistant Camera
2nd Assistant Camera
Camera Assistant
Key Grip
Camera Trainee

The camera department was comparatively small compared with larger-scale productions with individuals taking on two roles – effectively 'doubling up' responsibilities. In this case, the Director of Photography also worked as the Camera Operator and the Camera Assistant also performed the role of the Digital Imaging Technician.

When the department members are describing their roles, the previous 'film-based' names are retained, as we see here in the words of the Camera Assistant:

> Robbie the DoP, Andrew the Focus Puller, Sean is a Clapper Loader and James is the Video Assistant,'[16] he then goes on to clearly indicate the hierarchy in relation to his own position: 'I'm basically, under the Clapper Loader, and under his supervision I download the footage and I just generally give him a hand on-set.[17]

The Electrical Department also falls under the Director of Photography's responsibility and in *Ginger & Rosa*, maintained the traditional industry structure:

Gaffer
Best Boy
Electricians
Rigger

The Gaffer on *Ginger & Rosa* explained the purpose and roles of the Electrical Department: 'it's all about controlling levels of light.' And to 'push light further into buildings and into rooms.'[18]

The camera department is anecdotally known for its ossified structure and protracted periods of 'probation' in each of the roles. As Young and Petzold noted in 1972: 'Promotion is a slow process. There are very few lighting cameramen in the business who have not been at it for at least ten years and there are very few operators who have not also been focus pullers for at least five or six years' (1972: 29). It is also the department which is least-represented in terms of gender, the one going through the most significant changes at the time and the one where new opportunities for entry beyond the restricted traditional structure were emerging. On-set, the gradual and incremental emergence of the new tools, formats, hardware

and software of digital film production were leading to fissures in the knowledge and expertise not covered by traditional film-production disciplinary
practice. Just as the intermediary processes of film-to-data transfer were the
first digital interventions into celluloid production workflow, so intermediary people took the first steps in personnel intervention to manage implications of this transition – and that was through the role of the Digital Imaging
Technician (DIT). This position exemplifies transitional approaches to
addressing the challenges of an industry in transformation. The job straddles
two distinct production departments – the camera/electrical department and
the Post-Production Department. DITs tend to graduate from either one or
the other to inhabit this individual role.

This is a relatively new and I would argue, highly significant role
(which has been seen as marginal by others – defined briefly by David
Bordwell and Kirstin Thompson with no additional detail as 'Specialist
who assists the cinematographer on image capture in digital formats.
Also known as video controller' (Bordwell & Thompson, 2013: 24), but
I argue that is hugely significant for a number of reasons. On *Ginger &
Rosa*, there wasn't a dedicated DIT, rather the Second Assistant Camera undertook the tasks that would now be attributed to a DIT. This is a
corollary of the intensification of workloads in the doubling up of some
of these roles on lower-budget productions, as the Second Assistant
Camera stated:

> I could be in a three-man team where we can afford to sit around and we can put
> metadata in, and we can create the image, and we can transcode. But for a medium
> to low budget shoot, they just won't pay for that, like putting the clapper board
> on, and then running back to download, like I did on *Ginger & Rosa*, I was doing
> everything, I was more of a Camera Assistant than a DIT.[19]

My observations which follow around the work of the DIT are informed
through a number of questionnaires and interviews with a practising cadre
of DITs working within the UK, USA and Canada, in 2012 and 2013. As
with all camera crew vocations, DIT work is a male-dominated profession
in which, of the forty listed in the 2012 edition of 'The Knowledge',[20] only
two were female. Although the number of women identifying themselves
as DITs is still comparatively low, those that have been interviewed as part
of my research appear to be thriving in this vocation.

The work of a DIT can encompass a range of duties and responsibilities. First, there is Data wrangling. This is the term used to describe the
management, copying, transfer and conversion of files generated on-set,
from the storage media of the digital film cameras to the computers and
hard drives of the editors and post-houses. Data wrangling is not always a

distinctive role or profession *per se*, allocated to one person in the production credits, rather it is a set of responsibilities that may be allocated to a specific member of the camera department dependent on the film's budget. In many cases, although this role can fall to the Clapper Loader in more modest productions, in more high-end films this role is undertaken by the DIT. DITs also oversee and maintain the image quality and require refined communication skills to be able to translate and articulate complex processes to other less-technical members of the crew (such as the Director, Producer, DoP and so on).

The use of the Arri Alexa on *Ginger & Rosa* reflects the wider trends of the time in 2012 – the widespread use of digital motion-picture-style cameras on film sets throughout the world. This has inevitably led to the need to contend with the data complexity that the new technologies bring. As post-production evolved before this, in order to accommodate intermediate digital processes within the photochemical workflow, the camera department, recently subsumed by digital practice and process followed suit.

It was the widespread adoption of the RED ONE digital cinema camera in 2007 that is often cited as the watershed moment which revolutionised film production, and was one of the first instances where a technician was needed on-set to manage the complexity of the camera and the data that it produces. Such cameras are now commonplace on both independent and commercial film shoots, with one of the most popular being the Alexa. These cameras are capable of capturing 4K data – a resolution now demanded by cinema exhibition but one which is increasingly being adopted by television broadcast as well as by streaming services.[21] As *Ginger & Rosa's* Second Assistant Camera observes: 'I thought cameras would simplify themselves, instead they've got more complicated, the resolutions got higher, the technical aspects have got more difficult and more complicated [. . .] the job just needs to be dedicated to handling the media and the workflow.'[22]

One DIT succinctly captures the essence of their work:

> The DIT is specifically responsible for ensuring that all the technical aspects of image acquisition are correct, that metadata and grading information is passed to post and that all display devices are correctly calibrated.[23]

As an emergent role, there is a lack of clarity around the DIT position and what they actually do, which is compounded by the different nomenclature that is used in the UK, US and Canadian film industries where, amongst others, they can be credited as Digital Intermediates, Video

Controllers, Workflow Supervisors, Digital Loaders, Dailies Colourists, Utilities, Dailies Technicians or Data Management Technicians. As one DIT explains the nuanced complexities:

> Data Management Technician – sometimes DITs fulfil this role, other times they're called Digital Loaders or Utilities and they have no DIT experience. On bigger shows they'll handle the media ingestion/backup and occasionally dailies creation, leaving the DIT free to focus solely on color/exposure management with the DP. On smaller projects the DIT comprises all DIT and DMT functions.[24]

Whatever their title, these individuals are always based within the camera department working alongside the Director of Photography, and are pivotal to the management of the complex workflow. This is in addition to copying and cloning camera data, data handling, file transfers, ensuring the accurate recording of crucial metadata and on-set colour correction. In the case of *Ginger & Rosa*, the Camera Assistant talked about their data management strategy:

> Back then – the Alexa was relatively new [. . .] We shot ProRes444 on 32GB SbyS cards, roughly 15 minutes of footage at 24 Frames Per Second [. . .]
>
> And my job was to basically make a clone of the footage, there was no transcoding done on set – that was all done at editorial later that night, so we had three copies in circulation at all-times. Cards would come out of the camera, they'd be taken to the camera truck, be backed up onto hard-drives, we would have 2 3TB drives, one as a backup and one as a rushes-shuttle drive, and then editorial would make an additional copy that night, and transcode to DNX36.[25]

> On larger shoots, whilst the more routine of these tasks are the responsibility of the Data Wrangler, the DIT inhabits a senior role comparative to that of the DoP, with many DITs claiming that they earn more than DoPs, such is their demand and perceived value. It is a hybridised role – a combination of creativity, logistical and high-level technical skills. Traditionally technical jobs are below the line, however DITs represent a new hybrid role – technical and art – but are classed as 'below the line' on most film budgets.'[26]

There was a common thread that ran amongst many of the responses attempting to express the importance of the role and that related to the 'bridging' nature of the work. One described themselves as 'the bridge between production and post-production.'[27] Another emphasised the technical emphasis of their work: 'The DIT is a bridge between the cinematographer and an ever-evolving landscape of digital tools.'[28] A female DIT emphasises the importance of the communicative aspects, the DIT as interlocutor: 'my job is to be the bridge between the DP/Camera and all departments, thus promoting a steady workflow on set.'[29] This could be in part attributed to the 'feminised' labour (as in the way Hill, 2014 applies the term above), the quality and features which characterise their work (and not the volume of women who inhabit those roles as implied by the theory proposed by Hesmondhalgh & Baker, 2008), as DITs oversee and maintain the image quality, and require refined communication skills to be able to translate and articulate complex processes to other less-technical members of the crew (such as the Director, Producer, DoP, and so on).

Since the DIT role bridges production and post-production, it opens up a more accessible career progression opportunity: DITs tend to graduate either from the camera department or from the Post-Production Department (where there is a higher representation of women). It provides a window of opportunity for the gender imbalance and inequality of opportunity to be addressed. In the traditional camera crew hierarchy, as described above, people would start off as Film Loader, Camera Assistant, before graduating to Clapper Loader (2nd Assistant). There is no clear career trajectory mapped with DITs aspiring to become DoPs or post-production colourists.

It provides a new opportunity for working within the camera crew which doesn't necessitate having to work through the staid hierarchy. One respondent invokes the highly adaptive nature of the role and the need to respond to a high level of flexibility:

> Camera prep (setting management, matching), pipeline setup and management (legal to extended, legal to legal, all transformation paths), exposure monitoring, LUT[30] creation (CDL, RMD, etc.), data archival and backup, checksum verification, audio sync, quality control passes, LUT application dailies creation (for editorial and for on-set viewing), communication with the laboratory, communication with production and communication with editorial. Specific tasks and timeline vary from project to project – there's not one set workflow, it's highly modular depending on what's going on.[31]

This relatively new role represents an invisible and emergent form of below-the-line labour in the film/media industries and is endemic of the new data economy within the film industry, with Data Wranglers and DITs – engaging in new forms of data and digital labour. Whether it is a transitional role, whilst the film-production industry and life cycle completes the full transition, remains to be seen.

Assistant Director's Department

The Assistant Director's Department is traditionally structured thus:

First Assistant Director (1st AD)
Second Assistant Director (2nd AD)
Third Assistant Director (3rd AD)
Floor Runners

The *Ginger & Rosa* AD Department was structured as above, with two Second Assistant Directors and five floor runners who worked at different stages throughout the production. The hierarchy of this department is described in different ways by its constituent members. The 2nd Assistant Director explains the distinctions between the different roles:

'Our department is made up of the first Assistant Director. He's my sort of boss. He schedules the film and who then runs the set. He's on set throughout the day. I'm the second AD. I work back at base, the base camp where all the trailers are and the costume and make-up areas. We've got a Third Assistant Director who assists the first AD on set, and then we've got two runners.'[32]

The Third Assistant Director describes the nature of the department's work:

a first's responsibility really is to take all the pressures off the director of the technicalities of filming on the floor so the director, if that's her or his desire, can just concentrate solely on the artists and the performance.[33]

As one of the Floor Runners describes the hierarchy:

'There's the first, the second, the third and the runners. First calls all the shots, and controls the set, the second controls the base and does the call sheets and the third is kind of the little minion, runners like us are the other minions.'[34]

The Assistant Director (AD) department provides the logistical support and the infrastructure through which action can take place – in short they create and sustain the 'conceptual' framework for production (as opposed to the physical space which is provided by the Production Department). This is described most clearly by the Third Assistant Director on *Ginger & Rosa*:

The actual filming is down to the first to coordinate. Obviously one person cannot control five or six Heads of Department on the floor, so they need additional help. On this we have one third.[. . .] That's basically the dissemination of the information for what the shot is requiring in terms of the dressing, the props, which artists need radio micing. Are we going to radio mic with a boom, for instance. For the camera, where the camera is going to be set up so we know which way we're looking, so then we can find the dead spots to put the rest of the crew and the monitor. [. . .] I then assimilate various tasks for the runners or myself to carry out in order to basically prep the floor so it's in a state of readiness for when the artists arrive to shoot on straight away. As is in every industry now, time is money, so you don't really want to call artists down to have them waiting around.[35]

In practical terms the Assistant Director Department provides the support necessary for creativity, ensuring that all of the resources required (personnel, physical and temporal) are in place for the Director to draw upon. These include the extras, who form part of the precariat film economy (Mayer, 2016) or 'background' as they're sometimes referred to; these are marshalled and separated from the main action by the AD Department. They are then 'creatively' overseen by some of the on-set standby roles, most keenly the costume and hair and make-up who are on hand to make physical adjustments and alterations to their appearance.

The AD Department devises the schedule and then are responsible for ensuring that it all runs smoothly and everything is achieved on a daily basis through a process of monitoring and reporting.

The AD Department forms a key part of a chain of communication which moves through the various annulated layers of the production, as the Second Assistant Director states: 'I'm the point of contact back at base here with the costume truck and the make-up truck and passing on information here.'[36] And the Third Assistant Director talks about themselves as being a '. . . conduit to make sure that all information is received and it's actioned on.'[37]

Post-production

The least hierarchical of all the departments is arguably the Post-Production Department, the newest and flattest in its organisational structure. There is an equitability across the different post roles, facilitated by new digital systems and the simultaneous access afforded to the assets of production, where the materials of work can be accessed and worked upon simultaneously. This is very different to work on-set, where it feels as if tasks are passed up and down a hierarchical chain. This is not actually the case in large VFX productions where a hierarchy of roles and organisations emerge, but was certainly the case in my observations of *Ginger & Rosa*. The flattened structures of the Post-Production Department illuminate an unresolved duality – it is the department where the most opportunities for diversification of the workforce are available, but conversely, it is the department that is recognised as having the most problems because it lacks the union structures and protections afforded to the other departments (in relation to VFX artists see Curtin & Vanderhoef, 2014). Post-production does not work to the 'daily' rate mode and is subject to fixed rates breaking the mould of union-ised production organisation. Thus the paradox of the Post-Production Department – on the one hand it offers new and exciting opportunities and a gateway in. On the other hand, it is one of the most open to exploitation in its non-unionisation, and reportedly punishing working conditions. The Post-Production Department is normally externally sourced and contracted into the production, indeed the VFX sector has been referred to as a 'ser-vices industry' (Mukherjee et al.: 2013). Post-production services are subject to fixed-price bidding models and contracted to deliver a specific number of shots (regardless of any directorial changes) and since post-production workers are not always paid hourly or daily rates like others in the industry, they can be subjected to long working hours and extended working weeks. This is compounded by the phenomena of 'runaway productions' whereby a system of government-funded subsidies and tax breaks attract work to different countries, meaning that post-production workers have to travel from country to country to follow the work. Miller et al. cite the animation industry as a precursor, saying that it has outsourced labour operations since at least the early 1960s, a noteworthy comparison to what is happening now in VFX (2005, 125). The VFX industry in London is particularly buoyant. This of course is the broader global picture, and not so pertinent to the Dan-ish post-production context in which *Ginger & Rosa* was post-produced, in which the team were structured thus:

> Post-production Coordinator
> Digital Production Manager
> Digital Intermediate
> Online Technician
> Visual Effect Supervisor
> Compositors (3)
> Digital Colour Grading
> Graphics (2)
> DCP Mastering
> Mastering
> Colour Timer
> Laboratory Production Manager
>
> Supervising Sound Editor
> Re-recording Mixer
> Sound Assistant
> Foley Artist
> Additional Dialogue Editor

Within post-production there is more equitability across the different skill sets and more potential for movement as opposed to the inflexibility noted

in the production departments: for example, in *Ginger & Rosa*, the graphics operator also worked as a compositor.

Post-production was undertaken in Copenhagen in Denmark using
two different facilities – *Shortcut* for picture and *Mainstream* for sound.
As the Digital Production Manager for *Shortcut*[38] said: 'Shortcut is the
largest post-production company in Copenhagen and Denmark. We have
done around 40 feature films a year.'[39] What is key to this department, in
relation to the research questions underpinning this book – is the crossover between analogue and digital skills and technologies.

Having considered these different departmental units of organisation,
I now move on to consider the creative organisation of the project and
the interrelations, interactions and communication strategies between the
departments.

Cross-department communications

Despite the close intra-department working relations – there is a disconnect in cross-departmental liaison and communication within craft film
production, particularly at different temporal moments in the production
chain, when the work of one department has reached its conclusion. This
is not true in all cases – the Production Department liaises with all departments – and there are highly effective and established norms and mores
of communication – nonetheless, cross-department communication, apart
from that which sits within the rigid on-set procedural communication
protocols, is generally minimal. As one of the crew members tellingly
reveals: 'The crew sometimes don't know who I am because I never bump
into them until the wrap party.'[40]

One example which wonderfully illuminates the lack of communication between different departments, as a result of the detached departments and temporal ordering of production – which in this case led to
a problem arising in a shot that is the final scene of the film – was an
exchange between Ginger and her father (see Figure 2.1). Robbie Ryan,
the Director of Photography, explains the artistic rationale behind this
creative decision, and Potter's desire to achieve a:

> defined depth of field so somebody in the fore ground would be the same focus
> as somebody in the background. We used a 'split [focus] dioptre' which is like a
> magnifying glass and half of it goes over half of the lens and the other bit of lens is
> clean; the background is in focus, but also if you can imagine the focus in the fore-
> ground is in focus. It's nice. It's a good effect [. . .] It's good if you have a vertical
> line to kind of hide . . . There's always a little bit of a soft focus blur of a line so it's
> good to kind of have a vertical to help hide that.[41]

In this case, illustrated in Figure 2.1, the line that split the lens across the centre of the frame cut across Ginger's hair. This choice unfortunately resulted in an increase in the time and complexity of the work required in the post-production phase to visually correct the results of this decision. There is a visible line, where the hair of Elle Fanning and part of her shoulder moved in and out of frame, as the compositor responsible for this explains whilst showing me his work space on the computer:

> it's a 4,000 frame shot, so it's three and a half minutes. You see this reflection of the window that doesn't make any sense? Also, his back was so messed up, her shoulder's transparent? [. . .] the quick observer will notice that they're both in focus which is odd, right? I suspect they may have been using some sort of a tilt focus camera or something like that. Anyway, it's really badly messed up, so I fixed that so it turns out like this. Basically, that's done with a huge number of patches. [. . .] There's so many fixes in this shot, it's unbelievable. I think it took me probably five days to repair it into a state where you would not notice it.[42]

This is clearly not something that was necessarily seen and *accounted* for in the original planning and budget. As Ryan quipped: 'What I say with visual effects is it's a second of the lips forever on the hips because it's very quick for me to shoot it.'[43]

This creative disconnect between the two departments – camera and post-production – is widely understood, as are the tensions and conflicts between what they prioritise within their decision-making processes. Mike Figgis discusses the sometimes problematic role of the editor: 'They will make decisions – as a cinematographer would on-set – to give the best possible technical cut, which nevertheless may not use the take that contains what is, emotionally, the best performance' (2007: 119).

Figure 2.1 The final frame of *Ginger & Rosa* which was subject to extensive correctional work by the compositor. (*Ginger & Rosa*, 2012, Dir. Sally Potter)

This conflict runs throughout, in practices of continuity, which are meticulous detailed decisions over creativity. I argue that, in many cases, it is not the tension and conflicts that arise between film and data processes, but those which arise between logistics and creativity. I will now proceed to examine how these tensions arose through the structuring of the labour organisation specific to *Ginger & Rosa*.

The Creative Core Personnel Structure and Working Relations model

The Creative Core Personnel Structure and Working Relations model (Figure 2.2) has been created to show how the different departments and individuals were structured through the entirety of the film's production. This structure would have started to evolve and manifest in the development phase when the Director would start to make decisions about her key creative collaborators; it would then be finalised in the pre-production phase through the hiring and contracting of all production personnel. The Personnel Structure and Working Relations model is conceived as an orbicular diagram as opposed to the standard organisational hierarchical flow chart model in order to more effectively convey the persistent points of connection, types of influence, and the varying levels of proximity that the different agents of production have to the 'creative core' at which the Director is central.

> Sally, she's so hands on. It was one of the first things that I noticed. Some directors will ask someone to move that or fix this, but Sally will actually get up. She'll move it and fix it. She will do it herself because she has such a vision. (Elle Fanning)[44]

The diagram also usefully details the order in which the different individuals and departments were recruited to the project which, it is important to note, are specific to the auteur/director-led approach to film production. These would clearly be of a different nature in other types of production such as in studio-based films where directors are 'hired in' to the process.

In this production, the Director chooses her Heads of Department on a creative basis. The Department Heads would then select the crew members they want to work with. The Producers are more likely to select and organise the location infrastructure logistics (Construction, Facilities, Security, Catering, Health & Safety, Accommodation, Medics, Transport, and so on), as these non-creative decisions would be taken away from the creative core – aside from the selection of the locations themselves which are obviously a key part of the creative process. Some are hired (sub-contracted) via other organisations, i.e. 'The Movie Lot' (for unit security) or 'TLO Film Services' (for action vehicle hire).

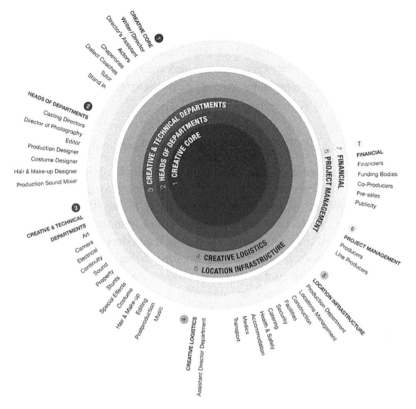

Figure 2.2 Creative Core Personnel Structure and Working Relations model.
(Author's own, graphic design by Bullet Creative, bulletcreative.com)

Creative Core Personnel Structure and Working Relations Model key:

1. **Creative Core**: Writer/Director (Director's Assistant) and Actors (Chaperones, Dialect Coaches, Tutor, Stand in).
2. **Heads of Departments**: Casting Directors, Director of Photography, Editor, Production Designer, Costume Designer, Hair and Make-up Designer, Production Sound Mixer.
3. **Creative & Technical Departments**: Art, Camera, Electrical, Continuity, Sound, Property, Stunts, Special Effects, Costume, Hair and Make-up, Editing, Post-production, Music.
4. **Creative Logistics**: Assistant Director Department.
5. **Location Infrastructure**: Production Department, Locations Management, Construction, Facilities, Security, Catering, Health & Safety, Accommodation, Medics, Transport.
6. **Project Management**: Producers and Line Producers.
7. **Financial**: Financiers, Funding Bodies, Co-Producers, Pre-sales and Publicity.

The diagram helps to illustrate these bi-directional flows of influence, which continually emit both from the centre outwards, and from the outwards inwards. This relationship is specific to a film that is creatively led by the Writer-Director and is funded by a complex range of both public and commercial sources.

One could look at this in two ways – as a centrifugal model – the writer/director along with their core creative team are the dominant source of influence, making creative decisions which emanate radially outwards to the peripheries in a cause-and-effect chain of events across the different areas of production; or as a centripetal configuration – in which the outer ring of the financiers drive key decisions which inwardly affect the activities, size and influence of the concentric layers on the creative process and final output.

Of course, in reality, this is a dynamically shifting and fluctuating process which is contextually dependent on the different points and moments in the process where at one point the outer influences may dominate a particular budgetary allocation, and at another a creative casting decision is paramount, and the budget has to be changed accordingly. It is an ongoing process of negotiation and compromise between these two dominant circles of influence. As noted by Alan Lovell & Gianluca Sergi: 'Making a film is a dynamic process. At different stages in the production of a film the relationship between the director and the other filmmakers changes' (2005: 13). As the Producer describes:

> it's like a chain. If one person doesn't do their job right, everything stops. If that means that the costume department have forgotten a costume or the driver has fallen asleep and not picked the actors up, or the producer hasn't signed a contract, it takes one person to make one mistake and everything grinds to a halt. There's bigger quality in that. Part of it is everyone is just as important as everyone else.[45]

The Line Producer in the Production Department explains his remit as overseeing: 'The budget, the schedule, and breakdowns of the script, which essentially is the schedule, and then the budget comes from that. Then all the departments do their own breakdowns, so costume, art department, etc.'[46]

This role of Line Producer is the literal 'line' and logistical membrane between the rest of the production's producers and their concomitant financial and contractual priorities – to ensure these are followed through and monitored 'on the floor' during the production phase. Location management provides and ensures the physical infrastructure, ensuring the safety of the production personnel.

This annulated model is proposed as an antonym to the usual tiered linear structures and is more indicative of the organisation of work and work flow on-set, showing the distance between the pure creative work of the epicentre and the pure logistical work at the perimeter. It is also indicative of the spheres of influence that can shape and govern the project. The 'creative core' also works as an analogy to the protection of the Director and the performers in the central and frenetic creative hub. The Director tends to communicate directly with the Heads of Department, who are responsible for liaising with their own teams: the Director tends to have minimal direct contact with other members of the departmental teams. The Director's Assistant from *Ginger & Rosa*, the conduit for much of these communications, reflects on their complexity and coherence:

> My role was basically to be the point of contact between everyone and Sally because you can imagine, she has between a hundred and hundred and fifty people. All of the crew always wanting her and needing answers. Sally's very involved so she will have scheduled meetings throughout pre-production with all the heads of department, with everyone involved to see fine details. Everything that's in the film basically she signed off on, she discussed. She had complete control over all the departments [. . .] Even during the shoot, I would catch her for maybe two minutes between traveling in between two sets and then I'd have to show her the pictures coming in from the light department for tomorrow's shoot, what do you think of this? Discuss things like that and pass those messages on directly to her. (Director's Assistant)[47]

Despite the fact that the Creative Core Personnel Structure and Working Relations Model has been conceived to effectively translate a structure which facilitated collaborative production, it is also one which clearly communicates a strict delineation of work and a rigid specification of appropriate channels of communication. This leads to considerations of the conflicting expectations of film-production workers when functioning across and within the contexts of network, project and department.

Flexibility

Throughout the discussions around modes of film-production work, a discourse of flexibility pervades. Flexibility is the defining rubric of the network and the project-based organisation (DeFillippi & Arthur, 1998; Jones, 1996; (Ebbers & Wijnberg, 2009: 988–9). There is a need for the workforce to be flexible in their interactions and engagements with the network, while the working practices in the project and the department, once the project is established, are fixed, immovable and entirely inflexible. Indeed, Diane Perrons (1999) had previously noted, 'a flexible discourse of flexibility.'

The most pervasive of these discourses is the need for '*flexible specialization*' (Harbord 2002: 98) – which, Janet Harbord argues, 'represents the shift from a product-based industry to a *process-based practice*' (2002: 98, emphasis added). This process-based practice is manifest in an arguably affective paradox in which the worker must have an acute specialisation but is deftly able to apply this from project to project, from environment to environment and context to context, demonstrating high levels of portability. This contradiction is also endemic within the film-production departmental structure and the prevalent tensions between creativity and logistics, as noted in the previous Chapter: 'On the one side, there is an artistic mode relying on *flexible* and decentralized expertise held by distinct creative communities of specialists; on the other side, is a strict managerial attitude looking for the advantages of tight integration of these activities within time, cost and market constraints' (Cohendet & Simon, 2007: 588, emphasis added).

The expectation and requirement to be flexible was manifested in a number of ways in the production of *Ginger & Rosa* – logistically, spatially, communicatively and creatively.

The Unit Manager also reflects upon this from a *logistical flexibility* perspective: 'We have to adapt well, for me especially because I have to deal with a different problem on a daily basis.'[48] The Unit Security Guard reflected upon the challenges of managing a peripatetic workforce and the complexities of location-shooting:

> You really need awareness. Let's say, it looks like there's really a lot of people really standing around doing nothing. [. . .] You've basically got to keep an eye out on everything that's going on, at all times. You just sort of keeping a level of concentration on your surroundings, which is quite difficult.[49]

The Set Decorator highlighted the need for flexibility of space and the adaptability of work processes:

> My workspace can be anything from the inside of my car to a massive church hall to a leaky building to a prop store to a car park to an exterior of a waste ground to inside a school laboratory. My workspace is wherever the set is so I kind of go beforehand and create in whatever space is thrown at me.[50]

Workspace flexibility was also paramount for the Assistant Production Coordinator, who reflected on the location of their interview: 'Make shift office at the back of the bus. So we're going to work from here, which is going to be a bit difficult because I'm presuming internet access is going to be limited.'[51]

Communications was a key area where flexibility was also expected. One of the floor runners emphasises how time pressures impacted on on-set communications:

> Good to be clear in communication, especially when you're talking on the radio and time is of the essence. Sometimes there is a tendency to maybe use too many words, especially for me, but you have to be clear and concise.[52]

The Production Coordinator also emphasised the importance of these skills in response to the high-pressured environment:

> You need to be an excellent communicator. You need to have great people skills. You need to be very organised. You need to be able to manage your time very well. You need to have a brilliant sense of humour.[53]

Time and time again, production personnel were both tacitly and explicitly required to willingly demonstrate flexibility, adaptability and chameleon-like qualities in relation to their surroundings – having to move from space to space and period to period. As the Assistant Costume Designer reflects on the appreciation of *creative flexibility* afforded by the contextual period richness of *Ginger & Rosa*:

> Each project is different and has a different knowledge base and you learn with every job. Because it might be a different period in time. [. . .] I'm very excited about getting the opportunity to do a couple of teds. So you've got Teddy boys, you've got the early rockers, you've got the mod kind of just about starting to happen, you've got the beatniks, then you've got the sort of CND movement with its earnest kind of duffle coat look. So, in terms of all of those, they're really costumes to create. And that really sort of floats my boat back, so to speak, because of my interest in youth subcultures and reproducing that. So I'm finding this film particularly exciting to work on.[54]

However, flexibility and temporality do not always imply instability according to some Organisation and Management studies perspectives. Beth Bechky has proposed 'that common portrayals of temporary organizations as ephemeral and unstable are inaccurate' (Bechky, 2006: 3), and according to Joris Ebbers and Nachoem Wijnberg, the 'latent organisation' 'provides the organizational continuity in which relational contracts, organizational citizenship behavior, and *flexible* rewarding can flourish' (Ebbers and Wijnberg, 2009: 989, emphasis added).

> Studies of team-based organizational structures indicate that organizational flexibility does not necessarily occasion unstructured work organization. For example,

Figure 2.3 Illustrative promotional still showing some of the various different periods of costume described by the Assistant Costume Designer. (*Ginger & Rosa*, 2012, Dir. Sally Potter)

> although self-managed teams lack the controls of bureaucracy and hierarchy, they tend to develop alternative control mechanisms. With these less centralized control tactics, normative control constrains and structures the behavior of team members. (Bechky, 2006: 5)

This particular article is silent on how skills development and knowledge exchange takes place within these structures. There seem to be no mechanisms for sustaining, growing and developing the network: 'The first challenge of maintaining the project network's viability as an organizational form is comprised of three tasks: Identifying and training new members; establishing workshops that develop talent in the field; and coordinating events such as film festivals' (Jones, 1996: 66).

Pedagogic problems

Key to the progress of the industry is professional development and training. Unfortunately, this has become inhibited by the project-based nature of the industry (and applies to other industries who may be looking to favour this model). Workers go from job to job with no time or resources to develop, or moreover, to change practices. The fact remains that working processes and cultures are evolving at a much slower rate, and there are inefficiencies in practice as a result.

As noted above, the multi-layered and fractured organisational mechanisms of film production such as the network, the project and the department, lead to developmental challenges, as captured by Irena Grugulis and Dimitrinka Stoyanova's work into the 'missing middle'. They have undertaken a number of studies concerned with skills development, or the lack thereof, in the film industry (2009 and 2011), and the limitations of professional film networks (2012) concluding that: 'It is not clear how the industry's current cohort of novices will ever acquire the skills taken for granted by previous generations of workers' (Grugulis and Stoyanova, 2011: 350).

The Creative Core model illuminates what Grugulis and Stoyanova refer to as 'legitimate peripheral participation' (2011: 344) and the limited opportunities there are for observation and heuristic approaches to learning which is stymieing the professional development of novices. Such are the pressures of this framework, it is difficult to see a resolution.

The *Ginger & Rosa* crew constituted a diverse mix of established and experienced film professionals and new, emerging practitioners.[55] They were from contrasting backgrounds – some had been through film school and others had worked their way through the industry learning on-the-job. According to the 2012 report conducted by Oxford Economics, 70 per cent of the production workforce were university-educated (2012: 10).

Film school traditions led to a number of above-the-line successes and privileges whereas the learning on-the-job approach has led to slower progress through the ranks. Some of the main creative HoDs attended film school (the DoP, Sound and Art). For instance Jean-Paul Mugel, a long-term collaborator who has worked on five of Potter's films, attended L'école Vaugirard[56]. Ander Refn, *Ginger and Rosa's* editor, attended film school in Denmark as he explains:

> I'm educated as a director in the Danish film school, but the Danish film industry is so small so you cannot survive being a director all the time so it's very typical for Danish directors if they have a lot of skills, for example script writing, editing, or working as assistant directors to each other, so we have a very flexible structure in the Danish film industry. This has been maybe one of the successes of Danish film internationally that we are flexible and moving along and inspiring each other.[57]

In Duncan Petrie and Rod Stoneman's study (2014) of film school education in the UK, EU and US, in consideration of continental film schools and in particular around the approaches taken by the National Film School of Denmark, which are pertinent to *Ginger & Rosa* as an international co-production between the UK and Denmark, they noted a move away from auteur approaches in 1975, and an 'industrial turn that came to dominate European film schools (. . .) from the 1980s onwards' (2014: 39). Refn's account above is emblematic of the traditional film school approach.

Ryan, DoP, describes his own experiences of attending film school:

> . . . it gives you a belief that you can do something [. . .] because in this business a lot of times what happens is maybe you start as a trainee in a camera department and you go up the ranks and there's a lot of hierarchy. So sometimes you don't believe in yourself that you can do it whereas college is a lot more open and they instil in you the belief that you can do something [. . .] I believe that is true so I had a great time in college and I came out and I didn't want to be a loader or a trainee. I just wanted to be filming stuff and I was lucky enough to be able to do that and I was with friends and we just kept shooting all the time and then two of my friends came over here to England and they got work as commercial directors and they brought me and another cameraman.[58]

Aside from The Production Designer, all key above-the-line personnel were educated in film school. The Production Designer explains: 'I think it's the experience. That's how I started as a runner and I just did it all, from Runner for second assistant, art director, and I did set decoration, also. That gave lots of experience.'[59]

One of the responses from a junior member of the sound department demonstrates how film school graduates appear to be making quicker inroads into the industry through elite film school credentials and connections:

> Got into the NFTS [National Film and Television School], really lucky to do that, and I did a year and a half in sound recording for film and TV. And here I am, I graduated February, 2011. Here I am, doing the big one.[60]

These film school experiences sit in direct contrast to the experience of many of those in below-the-line roles, many of whom do hold university degrees. The Second Assistant Director explained:

> I ended up doing a film degree [. . .] It's useless, but then I did some work experience over a summer at production companies and working student films. The thing about working in the film industry is you can't really get trained for it very well, so you tend to have to get experience. That often means unpaid work and unpaid work experience. After a while you can build up a CV and you've got some stuff to show people.[61]

There is a tacit acceptance that workers are expected to initially work for free to build up CV credits and longitudinal levels of experience, in an industry built on an economy of 'hope' labour (Horne, 2010; Kuehn, 2013).

The degree qualifications are often belittled or demeaned as being irrelevant in comparison to the quality and authenticity of on-the-job learning and accumulation of experience. (The following are purposefully anonymised):

> I have a degree in film, but I don't think my degree really means anything in that kind of film workplace because afterwards . . . After I've kind of worked in the industry for quite a long while in the location department I think business management would've really been the kind of part where it could've helped me a hell of lot in the future, what I'm doing for my job anyway.
>
> I do have a degree in drama and English, but you don't really need a degree. I would say it's more about the tools of the trade. It's such a different job and a lot of people don't even realise that a location department exists. It's such a different criteria of job that you can only really learn it by hands-on experience and work with what's needed on the floor. It's *more time than anything*. (emphasis added)

The Stunt Coordinator is one of the exceptions where professional skills training is a requirement and accreditation is essential to progress:

> It's about 15 years to stunt coordinator. To get on the UK stunt register, you need six skills. There's seven categories. You have a fighting category, a water category, a falling category, an agility and strength, and there are things like gymnastics, trampolining, martial arts, fencing, horse-riding, motor-riding and driving. You have to have six skills to a prescribed standard and get an equity card. Then you apply to the stunt register to be accepted, and then you spend time as a probationary stuntman for a number of years. Then you become an intermediate, then a full member, and then a stunt action coordinator.[62]

Similarly, in the following response, the highly-specific skills identified can only be accessed and learned through on-set experience, as the Special Effects Supervisor surmises:

> So if you've done one or many different trades, you'll see it makes it easier for you to get in. But, a lot of special effects are basically unique to the film industry so you have to learn that to be in the film industry.[63]

As Heidi Philiphsen contends of this collaborative 'turn' in film school education:

> [r]ather than speaking of phasing out the notion of the auteur, one could think of it as an enhancement of the auteur notion where the film school has sought to train people to work within film teams where everyone leaves a personal imprint on the film. (Philiphsen 2009: 12)

This leads to considerations of the specific notion of the auteur embodied and practiced by Potter in her approach to collaboration.

Collaborative auteurship

Deliberately and consciously designed, the Personnel Structure and Working Relations model diagram, Figure 2.2, lends itself not to a hierarchical but to a concentric circle model of organisation in order to capture and illuminate the close working relationships between the crew and the social dimensions that persist between them. I use the term collaborative auteurship to capture the essence of the Creative Core approach. This juxtaposition of seemingly contradictory concepts may seem oxymoronic, but I propose that it is a unifying principle, which accommodates for a distinctive authorial signature, whilst also acknowledging and understanding collaboration, and the creative value and impact that brings to bear on the qualities and aesthetics of the final film product. Potter herself embodies hybrid dispositions of auteur and collaborator, as she works within delineated and separated structures – which do not necessarily easily lend themselves to creative collaboration.

The production of film has traditionally been conceptualised and narrativised by a number of discourses. Arguably, the most dominant, compelling and romanticised of these has been auteurship, which places the Director as the dominant creative figure.

> The reasons for the persistence of auteurist approaches to the cinema are not hard to understand. The idea that the director is solely responsible for a film's meaning is a comforting fantasy, restricting a potentially threatening diversity of interpretation, and giving secondary status to other analytical frameworks, such as production context, genre, audience, or ideology, which might put spanners in the works. (Medhurst, 1991: 370)

Auteur theory originated in François Truffaut's 'La politique des auteurs' (1954), and was taken forward by André Bazin, *On the Auteur Theory* (1957) and subsequently work by Andrew Sarris took it into the USA (2007, originally published in 1962). Contemporary theorists have expanded this concept to account for emergent notions of auteurship such as the 'blockbuster auteur' (Flanagan, 2004) and the 'industrial auteur' (Tzioumakis, 2006).

Despite the dominance of Alfred Hitchcock in auteur studies, his own viewpoint was:

'Of course there must be co-operation, division of labour, all the time. The old saying, "No one man ever made a picture," is entirely true' (Hitchcock in Davy, 1938: 12). As Robert Carringer points out: 'More recently, the model of the author of a film has been replaced by the model of the *authors* of a film, in recognition of the collaborative nature of the enterprise.

Ironically, Truffaut's ideal model of the film auteur was Hitchcock – a director whose almost unbending insistence on regularity of procedure extended
to his use of collaborators' (2001: 374). The auteur is a construct in final film
– but cannot necessarily be consigned to an *approach or* a *work ethic* adopted
by the Director. As Michele Hilmes contends:

> the nomination of the individual *auteur* figure works against the complexity and
> interdependence of a media industries approach, and thus efforts to isolate the
> contributions of a particular figure must always fundamentally distort the realities
> of media authorship. (2009: 1988, original emphasis)

There have been several calls to acknowledge the collaborative nature of
film production, within film studies in particular:

> Rather than rigidly categorizing films by their directors, films should be multiply
> classified: by actors, cameramen, editors, composers, and so on. The career paths
> of all cinematic artists need to be traced, showing how their work adapts to new
> contexts, demonstrating how each interaction alters the ingredients and flavours
> of the cinematic pot-pourri. (Gaut, 1997, p. 165)

The notion of collaboration has become growing thematic concern in
studies of media work (Deuze, 2006), and in Media Industry Studies looking at complex cross-platform production (Johnson, 2014). Yet there have
been relatively few studies in film studies of the collaborative endeavour
of the form in comparison to the volumes dedicated to that of Director,
and there is a notable absence of female directors within auteur discourse.
This is not least because, as Judith Mayne states, 'it can be argued that
the privileging of female authorship risks appropriating, for women, an
extremely patriarchal notion of cinematic creation' (1990: 98).

Paul Sellors coined the term 'collective authorship' (Sellors, 2007), in
relation to film. It does not adequately account for the processes and relations that I witnessed in this particular example – collective authorship
and equality throughout – that implies a co-production. Potter is both
author (as writer) and auteur (as the Director) and perhaps it is in this
inhabitation – her signature, her style, the confidence in her work is writ
throughout, that enables her to 'let go'. She illuminates how creativity can
be enabled to flourish within the structures described above and to over-
come the inherent tensions between departments and overall pressures of
film production.

'Collaborative auteurship' most usefully captures the approach and
the resultant text, collaborative relations between an auteur and creatives
more fully accounts for Potter and her collaborators, and how multiple

auteur signatures were enacted and imprinted upon the final text, and then the number of collaborative encounters that were enacted throughout the process. Collaborative auteurship is an activity, a process, and an understanding and reflexivity on the part of the Director to enrich and augment their vision and craft. Potter is considered to be an auteur in her creative style and output, her working practices are notably highly collaborative and inclusive, and the 'creative core' derived from her practice and approach and through my observations of *Ginger & Rosa* may not be applicable upon the close analysis of, say a Hollywood Studio production. However, in her process and practice she is famously open and, as we will go on to consider in Chapter 6, through the release of all of the production materials in SP-ARK. The Unit Publicist who holds a privileged position of attentive observer of the production process commented: 'it definitely felt like an intimate production and a sort of family atmosphere.'[64] He went onto recount Potter's responses to the test screening:

> For someone as visionary as Sally that really amazed me that she was prepared to do that and to actually alter the film based on what other people said. I understand that she made some changes based on the questionnaire and that discussion, so that was a fascinating experience to be part of.[65]

Casper Tyberj points to the resistances of such approaches: – 'The problem with this approach [a collaborative one] is that it would produce a proliferation of little authorial personalities whose individual contributions would then have to be extracted from the fabric of the films' (2004: 45). Here, collaborative auterism is seen as a problem, not as an opportunity or inevitability, evidence of contributions are interwoven in the warp and weft of the film. They cannot solely be extracted from the fabric of the film, therefore deeper understandings of process and practice are required.

Technology has played a key part in the collaborative production process, making it accessible: 'Suddenly the private world of the viewfinder was a public property and the sightlines of cinema changed' (Ganz & Khatib, 2006: 23); it also opens up a chance for new types of contribution.

There is an attempted separation between Potter and the concerns of the Producers in a process of 'buffering' (Bilton, 2007). Rather than there being a separation of creative processes and management (Bilton, 2007), I would propose that these are always in constant dialogue and inseparable. This is a community and not a conflict. Potter explains her vision of collaboration:

> My goal is that every single person I'm collaborating with is working on the same film. But they need to feel also as if it is theirs. They need to own it, in a way, but not take it off in the wrong direction. They can give input and all kinds of things, and they continuously do. They enrich it, so I'm always open to that. But I have to guide it, because I'm the only one that has the whole picture in my head. Everyone else has part of it. [. . .] All that energy, all that collaborative energy, all that input, it becomes a kind of organic evolution, really. That's the sort of magic, the alchemy that as a director you work through the work of others. You're curiously hands-off in the end. If you're a writer/director you start totally hands-on. It's all yours. It's all your idea. Then you have to, in a way, back away, and learn how to inspire, generate this kind of energy and enthusiasm, this embodiment, really, in this enormous group of other people, and let go. Sort of guide and let go at the same time.[66]

Here, Potter touches on her own perception of her subjectivity as a guide. It is through her transitional virtuosity, her ability to bridge the gaps between practitioners, and between the film and data domains that resonates with Seung-hoon Jeong and Jeremy Szaniawski's conception of 'Transitional auteurship' (2016: 16). They use this term to characterise the canon of film directors working in 2000–15, although Potter is not included in this particular canon. I would extend their notion, which they use to temporally frame the directors working in this epoch, to account for Potter's particular approach to her working practices. She describes the pragmatic dimensions of her approach:

> In preparation, I work again and again and again through the whole film, patiently, from beginning to end, on every detail, with every head of department, every actor, and sometimes other people in the departments. If I can get each head of department totally clued in to, inspired by, energized by the vision and clear about the vision and what they need to do to achieve it, even if they don't know exactly there and then, they know where they're trying to get to, that will then funnel out to all of the people in each of their departments. I try and set a tone and a relationship and clarity of information and purpose and make myself available to answer their questions when they're in doubt or there's choices to be made at any point, all the time.
>
> Having established the groundwork of the preparation in that way, by the time you come to the shoot, you've already got a short hand with each of the heads of department, who in turn have got a short hand with their people, and you've built relationships with the actors in parallel. I've been building one-on-one relationships and trust and openness and working through the ideas so that by the time we come to shoot, we know what we're talking about, we know why things are happening, and they know and understand what I'm pulling out of them.[67]

Potter had a number of different collaborative relationships across and within the different aspects of production and post-production. It transpired most noticeably in her work with Ryan as noted by the actors in the film:

Together they would spontaneously decide what they wanted to shoot right then and there. The main overarching feeling that I had was of freedom, of a messiness that totally went against everything that I had anticipated from Sally. (Alessandro Nivola)[68]

I think with Sally, she worked very well with Robbie. They had a very keen relationship. We would often do the scenes a few times through and then just feel how that was going, just to get what it was all looking like and see what you're catching. Then sometimes we'd change it up.

What was really great is this has been an extremely quick shoot, but Sally always would make time to be able to give us all the time we needed to do scenes. (Alice Englert)[69]

Her directing style combined with the cinematographer, who has a very unique way of working. He holds the camera. Usually as an actor, you're used to hitting marks, and you're used to being on a specific spot in order for it to be in focus or in order for the frame of the camera to capture a certain something, but they're very free that way, both of them, maybe particularly on this movie for her. I don't know. That affords all of us acting enormous freedom that we are not stuck and you have to be in one spot. I've worked with people, very good people, who were detailed down to is your head turned this way or is it turned this way, and the difference between that and that, so this is very free. (Annette Bening)[70]

Every single thing, she's got an eye on the whole pallet and the whole imagery of it. It's a lovely feeling of being in a collaborative experience, but in the hands of someone who knows exactly what they want. (Timothy Spall)[71]

The Focus Puller/First Assistant Camera described the challenges that Ryan's approach posed for his work:

Robbie's very organic, I mean one of the things about my job is there are a lot of variables that make it tough. The more variables, the tougher it is. You control the variables but here with Robbie, there's no control. And you wouldn't want to control him because he's kind of, very organic, could go anywhere, kind of cameraman so it's, it's tough. It's actually as tough as it gets really.[72]

Another significant creative collaboration is described in Potter's reflection of her working relationship with Andres Refn:

Working with Anders was quite revelatory, the most experienced editor I've ever worked with. Coming from working a lot with Lars von Trier and others and quite a very strong sort of point of view and strong sensibility, we had a quite combative, very creatively combative relationship in the cutting room. He made a lot of suggestions which I resisted initially, but which he was absolutely right, so it was really good for the film.[73]

Potter's characteristic openness and collaborative approach to her work was noted by many others. The colour grader stated that:

> Obviously Sally is a director who has a finger on everything. She likes to be here as much as possible. That's been a really great experience for me working with someone that's so focused. She can literally see anything, everything. She remembers everything. It's really, really great. It's been, how do you say it? Opposite of typical.[74]

Her approach was clearly appreciated and recognised as distinctive. The Post-production Coordinator similarly commented that:

> I don't know if that's especially for Sally or if it's a British thing, but it's very much all fingers into all parts of the production, whereas in Denmark the director would come in and say go ahead, and sit in a few hours. I know Sally spends a lot of time in both the sound and picture department, and the post production. She's very hands on, which I like a lot.[75]

The US Casting Director observes the effect of Potter's meticulous nature and her persistently disarming approach:

> Bomb or now Ginger and Rosa was very, very much running the marathon. I'm sure many people . . . I worked with them, I don't know how long. I think it's been a good two years or more this movie. It just became this obsession. I think Sally's passion and her desire to get it right, somehow I would think that it would become more frustrating, but I just kept wanting to dig deeper and keep pushing it, and I did. She's infectious that way.[76]

Through this lens of the 'social' of production (Szczepanik & Vonderau, 2013: 6) we can appreciate Potter's inhabitation of the collaborative auteur approach – the free-flowing hand-held camera work, the fact that there is no non-diegetic music, the use of naturalistic locations all bear the hallmarks of the Danish dogma 95 movement. It is only through the analysis of the completed film that these became apparent. As Torben Grodal et al. contend:

> If an author is defined as a creative human agency, a given film may be produced by many different agencies: authors, directors, scriptwriters, actors, cinematographers et al. who sometimes work after a centrally conceived and negotiated plan, but sometimes also just improvise 'in concert' so that the individual also creates with an explicit or, just as often, an intuitive understanding of how their individual creativity may contribute to the work in progress. In such 'jam session' cases, the intentions of the work can only be established *a posteriori*, when the artwork has been completed.
>
> (Grodal et al., 2004: 7).

This quotation also invokes an orchestral-surround analogy, which can be aligned to the circular Creative Core conceptualisation, presented in figuer 2.2, in which the Director is situated in the centre of the process.

Conclusion

I have argued that the three organisational axes upon which a film industry professional is expected to operate, are at odds with one another. Where the network's guiding principle is flexibility, the project's are efficiency and creativity and the department's are strict delineation and rigidity. These conflicting expectations have led to inefficiencies in process, to a lack of opportunity to innovate and experiment, and to limited training and developmental opportunities. Across and within these three organisational structures a clear contradiction exists – we see a fragmented workforce which is expected to be flexible, responsive, and on–standby, but where practitioners work within stilted departmental structures which offer limited opportunity for progression and promotion. There is a high frequency of horizontal progression – from project to project – but a highly infrequent opportunity for vertical progression and promotion within and across the departments. Identifying these challenges is not to undermine or understate the affective pleasures that film-production workers clearly derive from their work and their inhabitancies and experience of these structures – as evidenced by the many emphatic accounts to the contrary. Film production, as with other creative endeavours is very often conceived as a passion project in 'addictive environments' (Rowlands and Handy, 2012).

Research suggests that understanding the project-based nature of industrial film production is helpful in understanding how these practices are continually influencing new industrial paradigms (Davidson, 2015), as Helen Blair also observed: 'Numerous commentators, both academic and national and international policymakers, view the forms of organization evident in the film industry as typifying those emerging in the 'information economy' of the twenty-first century' (Blair, 2001: 149). The emergent interstitial processes between film and data practice are also insightful in this regard, in particular, the role of DIT, which acts as both suture and translator to the complexities of digital film production. This particular role is also a useful lens through which to examine responses to other issues identified in this Chapter – such as work mobility, cross-department communications, diversification of the workforce including addressing gender inequality, and training and development.

Having activated the production paradigms of 'collective and transitional auteurship,' I now turn my attention to considerations of workflow and process in my continued examination of the political and discursive apparatus which frames film production

Notes

1. The UK studio economy is shaped by the expansive purpose-built complexes clustered around the western edges of London: Pinewood, Shepperton, Denham and Borehamwood. There are also the smaller studios of Ealing and Elstree and smaller complexes based at the aircraft manufacturing plant at Leavesden and Three Mills at London's Docklands. *Ginger & Rosa* was shot entirely on location, so considerations of studio-based working practices and personnel structures are beyond the purview of this book.

2. There are numerous unions and guilds in operation in both the UK and the US. As can be seen by the different titles of the unions, this unionisation of individual roles is most potent in the US, representing the interests of various different workers by role. These include: Hollywood's principal trade organisation – the Motion Picture Association (MPA); Director's Guild of America (DGA); The Writer's Guild of America (WGA); The Alliance of Motion Picture & Television Producers (AMPTP); Motion Picture Sound Editors (MPSE); The Screen Actors Guild-American Federation of Television and Radio Artists (SGA-AFTRA); The International Alliance of Theatrical and Stage Employees and Casting Society of America (IATSE); The International Association of Theatrical Stage Employees (IATSE); The Society of Operating Cameramen (SOC) and The Motion Pictures Editors Guild (MPEG). In the UK, the union organisations are less 'role specific,' they include: The Broadcasting, Entertainment, Cinematograph and Theatre Union (BECTU); The National Union of Journalists (NUJ); The Association of Cinematograph, Television and Allied Technicians (ACTT) and The Broadcasting and Entertainment's Trades Alliance (BETA).

3. The census which covered TV, Game, Interactive Media, Radio, Animation, Corporate Production and Games found that 24 per cent of this overall sector were freelancers (Skillset 2012), but this only accounted for permanent roles within film production.

4. According to Blair 'non-standard forms of employment have, especially in the United States, used the film industry as an exemplar and signifier of future industrial change' (2001: 149).

5. In an interview with the author, 28 January 2015 (female respondent F001).

6. In an interview with Kurban Kasssam, March 2012. Kurban Kassam worked as the Associate Producer on *Ginger & Rosa*. He was also assigned the task of assisting me with the interviews, given that he was present on the film set for most of the shooting days and therefore able to access crew members for interview at short notice during their moments of downtime.

7. *Mandy* – http://www.mandy.com/ is one of a number of established online websites used to publicise job opportunities in the film and television industries.

8. In an interview with the author, 23 July 2012.

9. In an interview with Kurban Kasssam, March 2012.

10. In an interview with Kurban Kasssam, 28 March 2012.

11. In a document referred to as the 'One Line Unit List,' produced on 21 February 2012.

12. The full list of departments and their constituent members of *Ginger & Rosa* are listed in the appendix.
13. The full on-screen credit listing of *Ginger & Rosa* is provided as an appendix to this book.
14. In an interview with the author, 22 August 2012.
15. In an interview with Kurban Kasssam, March 2012.
16. In an interview with Kurban Kasssam, March 2012.
17. Ibid.
18. In an interview with Kurban Kasssam, March 2012.
19. In an interview with the author, 15 October 2014.
20. The Knowledge is an industry produced directory listing the names and contact details of individual freelancers and organisations working within the Film and Television industry http://www.theknowledgeonline.com
21. Amazon and Netflix both offer UHD streaming- http://www.digitaltrends.com/home-theater/amazon-launch-4k-uhd-find-available-free/
22. In an interview with the author, 15 October 2014
23. In a questionnaire response (male respondent M002).
24. In a questionnaire response (male respondent M004).
25. Ibid.
26. In a questionnaire response (male respondent M001)
27. In a questionnaire response (male respondent M002).
28. In a questionnaire response (male respondent M006).
29. In an interview with the author, 28 January 2015 (female respondent F001).
30. A look-up table (LUT) is a tool through which the colours being captured by a recording device are transformed and output into an alternative colour palette. A LUT can take the form of either a hardware imaging system function or an image processing software application feature.
31. Ibid. (male respondent M004).
32. In an interview with Kurban Kasssam, March 2012.
33. In an interview with Kurban Kasssam, March 2012.
34. In an interview with Kurban Kasssam, March 2012.
35. In an interview with Kurban Kasssam, March 2012.
36. In an interview with Kurban Kasssam, March 2012.
37. In an interview with Kurban Kasssam, March 2012.
38. The posthouse is part of Nordisk Film: Egmont Group.
39. In an interview with the author, Mia.
40. In an interview with Kurban Kasssam, March 2012.
41. In an interview with the author, 26 October 2012.
42. In an interview with the author, 9 August 2012.
43. Ibid.
44. *Ginger & Rosa* EPK interviews.
45. Ibid.
46. In an interview with Kurban Kasssam, March 2012.
47. In an interview with the author, 23 July 2012.
48. In an interview with Kurban Kasssam, March 2012.
49. In an interview with Kurban Kasssam, March 2012.

50. In an interview with Kurban Kasssam, March 2012.
51. In an interview with Kurban Kasssam, March 2012.
52. In an interview with Kurban Kassam, March 2012.
53. In an interview with Kurban Kasssam, March 2012.
54. In an interview with Kurban Kasssam, March 2012.
55. A practitioner filmography, which provides illustrative lists of all the different films that *Ginger & Rosa* crew members have worked on, is provided in the endmatter.
56. 'L'école Vaugirard' that Mugel refers to was founded in 1926 as 'l'École Nationale de la Cinématographie et la Photographie', and is currently known as 'École nationale supérieure Louis-Lumière'.
57. In an interview with the author, 30 April 2012.
58. In an interview with the author, 26 October 2012.
59. In an interview with Kurban Kasssam, March 2012.
60. In an interview with Kurban Kasssam, March 2012.
61. In an interview with Kurban Kasssam, March 2012.
62. In an interview with Kurban Kasssam, March 2012.
63. In an interview with Kurban Kasssam, March 2012.
64. In an interview with the author, 6 June 2012.
65. Ibid.
66. In an interview with the author, 12 October 2012.
67. Ibid.
68. Ginger & Rosa EPK interviews.
69. Ibid.
70. Ibid.
71. Ibid.
72. In an interview with Kurban Kasssam, March 2012.
73. Ibid.
74. In an interview with the author, 9 August 2012.
75. In an interview with the author, 9 August 2012.
76. In an interview with the author, 3 July 2012.

CHAPTER 3

Digital Film Production Time

Introduction

This Chapter is concerned with the film production *process* and the shifting temporalities of production within the film-to-data transitional moment. Much has been written about cinematic on-screen temporalities (Mulvey, 2006; Stewart, 2007; Mroz, 2012; Corrigan 2016, Kendall, 2016), in particular, there has been a renewed interest in slow cinema within Film Studies scholarship (James 2010; Sandhu 2012; Schoonover 2012; Koepnick 2014; Tiago and Barradas 2015; Andrew 2016; Archer 2016; Beckman 2016) but in contrast, there has been limited consideration of film production *time:* the temporalities and speed of film production.

Film is a time-based medium in every sense of the term and in every aspect of production; it is a temporal register which can both expand and compress time. Similarly, film production is a time-based and time-bound process. As Babette Mangolte states: 'For a filmmaker, you could say that time is of the essence and is everywhere inscribed into film in a complex and metaphorical manner. Time is appended with an adjective and to name a few, filmmakers speak of running time, screen time, performance time, shooting time, real time and a sense of time' (2003: 262).

Time is literally imprinted on all aspects of the production process via the ubiquitous time code – the eight-digit numerical code which displays hours, minutes, seconds and frames, and is used to both identify and subsequently synchronise every single frame of film or digital film: it is 'a unique, searchable identifier' (Brown, 2015: 264). Both celluloid and digital film production semantics are steeped in time-based analogies and metaphors which allude to the procedural and processual, from celluloid film being *processed* at a laboratory and being subjected to careful timing of exposures, to the delivery of the Digital Cinema Package which can only be projected in cinemas with its accompanying *time*-based access key.

This Chapter's considerations of the structures, patterns and work-flows of industrial, location-based[1] digital feature-film production through the primary case study of *Ginger & Rosa* reveals that time shifting is manifesting in two key ways within the industrial digital film production cycle.

Firstly, through procedural anachronism: by that I refer to the temporal reordering of film production processes. Although this is not as radical as some would have us believe with simultaneous instances of pre-production, production and post-production, there is certainly an emergent overlapping, slippage and a change in ordering of processes in the craft-based[2] film production chain. Secondly, there are emergent production temporalities, that is, there is a notable speeding up *and* slowing down of certain processes and tasks at various stages in the film production process. The rhythms of work have changed and continue to change. I examine these two temporal phenomena innate to the film-to-data transitional moment, through a detailed 'production analysis'[3] and 'labour process'[4] approach. I explore how a smooth and fluid workflow was achieved and textual coherence was ensured in what is essentially a highly-fractured workflow. I draw from interview transcripts and my own observational field notes as well as analyses of production documentation generated by *Ginger & Rosa*. As well as revealing the time shifting, many of these reveal the prevailing archetypes and 'aesthetics of production' and their continuities, discontinuities and ruptures.

This Chapter will firstly provide a synoptic account of the historical legacies of current film production temporalities, particularly in relation to film production management. As discussed in Chapter 2, there has always been a tension between the managing and making of a film, between art and business, between the logistical and the creative – there is always a constant dialogue between the two, and no creative or logistical decision is made in isolation. In addition to a consideration of the histories and legacies of film production, I will also be examining the various impacts upon film production practice that the digital, the economical, and labour relations have had, acknowledging that there is not one singular dimension at play within the film-to-data transitional period.

Finally, I will detail how the results of these conflicting innovations and resistances has led to a paradoxical film production logic which I refer to as *workflow-warp*. In short, this is the phenomena caused by the affordances germane to digital technologies that have enabled the creative domain of film production (mainly camera, sound and post-production) to be free flowing, responsive and dynamic, while the economical and logistical frameworks have restricted these potentialities.

Historical legacies of film production: managing making

Whilst digital developments and innovations have most visibly impacted upon the working practices and pace of work of creative agents within the film production process, such as Directors of Photography and Visual Effects (VFX) artists, what does not appear to have been effected is the approach to production management during development, pre-production and production phases. These practices of *organising* or *managing* have remained largely unchanged since post-sound early cinematic practice, following the establishment of a blueprint of stringent record-keeping and a fine-grained division of labour (Bordwell & Thompson, 2013: 29) creating an environment where 'the film essentially makes itself' (Geuens, 2007: 418). This production blueprint has also been replicated in television production (see for example Elana Levine's 2001 study of a US television series). The very notion of a film 'industry' of course connotes a mechanised process, but this is normally aligned to the mass production and reception of undifferentiated outputs, not in the initial creation of the individual film output which is considered and represented as a highly artistic process.

The structure of the production life cycle has been widely attributed to the work of silent film pioneer Thomas Harper Ince who introduced the routinised film production model in 1913 – 14, which was, and remains, in place across a number of key periods of film production activity which are often likened to those of a factory production line. This is unsurprising, since it was a process born in the context of industrialisation – it was also in 1913 that Henry Ford installed the first car production moving assembly line. This analogy has resonated throughout critical theory discourse, as Michael Chanan observed 'In the early days, film production was called manufacture' (1976: 1). Theodor Adorno and Max Horkheimer famously aligned car manufacture with film production: '. . .for automobiles, there are such differences as the number of cylinders, cubic capacity, details of patented gadgets; and for films there are the number of stars, the extravagant use of technology, labor, and equipment, and the introduction of the latest psychological formulas' (1997: 123–124).

This alignment was made most explicit by the Ford organisation themselves who documented their car manufacturing process through the medium of film. Through an examination of the Ford Motor Company's extensive use of film in the 1910s and 1920s, Lee Grieveson noted: '. . . its establishment of the Motion Picture Department positioned cinema itself as an exemplar of new practices of mass assembly and thus in some respects as a Fordist cultural form. In an early account of the functioning of the new department, published in the Ford Times, emphasis was placed on the "high degree of manufacturing efficiency" needed in the "production of moving pictures" – Ford Times, July 1916' (2012: 31). Grieveson goes on to state that: 'The most intriguing of these images in the Ford Times, titled Assembling the Film, shows film "assemblers" working together in a line – a literal illustration of a mass assembly line for film, of the work of cinema in the age of mechanical reproduction' (2012: 32).

In addition to a continuation of these structures of film production management and process within contemporary film production practice, albeit to a lessening extent, a similar Fordist nomenclature continues to persist. For example, 'assembly' is still the term used to refer to the first step in the editing process when all of the scenes are 'assembled' into the order in which they are written in the script in the editing suite. 'Assembly' is a key editing term and the concept also frequently features in editing tuition materials and associated digital editing software. This is also evident in the language used by the Assistant Editor on *Ginger & Rosa*:

> The job on this film, as an Assistant Editor, is to be a technical assistant to the editor. Sometimes you might have more *cutting* than other things. I *cut* a first pass of a trailer and did *assemblies* of scenes [. . .] And with this film since we are shooting on the Alexa, which is a digital camera there's not a lab that looks at the *rushes*. So I'm in a sense, the *lab*, as well, when I make these day's DVDs, I also look at the *rushes* for a technical check.[5] (emphasis added)

Despite now dealing with a purely digital medium, it is clear, in the Assistant Editor's chosen semantics of 'cut', 'rushes', 'assemble' and 'laboratory', that the materiality of film continues to resonate and infuse current production nomenclature.

Film production process

As I have noted, there are two key tracks of activity which span all phases of the film production process – the creative and the logistical – although these are not always mutually exclusive – they overlap and intertwine – they can exist in harmony, as well as engaging in conflict. One can suffuse the aesthetics of the other – as we will see in this Chapter – the mechanisation of film production apparatus can become inflected on the creative choices and decisions that are made within the film production process, and vice versa, creativity is imbued in the pervasion of a creative discourse around the logistical – as seen in the linguistic conflation of the terms that are often seen in film industry accounts and academic discourse: for example, 'The Fine Art of Co-Producing' (Neumann & Appelgren, 2007) and 'Creative Accounting.'[6]

Since there are already many practical books which comprehensively map the film production process and its traditional chronology, including Bruce Kawin (1987), Eve Light Honthaner (2001); Steven Bernstein (2004); Stephen Greenwald and Paula Landry (2009); Bernard F. Dick (2010); Bastian Clevé (2005) and David Bordwell & Kristin Thompson (2013, now in its tenth edition); this Chapter will not seek to replicate the materials covered within such comprehensive volumes. Instead, by moving through the production process as it ran within *Ginger & Rosa*, I expound and explore instances of procedural anachronism and the emergent temporalities of digital film production. I pay particular attention to the hybrid film and data processes and protocols that were seen to emerge. During my observations and interviews, I witnessed a complex interplay between established and experienced film professionals who were working alongside new, emerging practitioners.[7] This meant that departments were often simultaneously engaged with the craft processes of traditional classical narrative film production, alongside new digital technological practices. Many of the more experienced practitioners had lived through significant economic, social and industrial transitional changes and are able to reflect back on prior experience and to provide comparisons to current practice. Take for example, Irene Lamb who recalls:

> When I was still 19, they had a lot of people under contract, like Maggie Smith which would hire in some various stars. Because it was the end of that 'Rank' era where you had contract stars.[8]

The examination of digital film processes was a complex endeavour, such is the hybrid nature of current film practice which is a blend of both analogue and digital, film and data, mechanisation and datafication. As Janet Harbord has noted, there has not been a clean break between the analogue-to-digital, film-to-data transition – 'Digitalization has entered the world of film largely through the back door' (Harbord, 2002: 139). Instead, there has been a phased transition within the different departments of the film production chain, with the intermediaries (the processes that first initiated this transition, such as digitising and encoding, and post-production) being first to digitally transform, followed, next, by exhibition, with the widespread installation of digital projectors into cinemas, and finally by the camera department in its move to digital film format cameras (which, along with the other materialities of film production apparatus will be more fully examined in Chapter 4). As Bordwell noted:

> By 1999, post-production was on its way to a completely digital workflow, incorporating special effects, sound, editing, and DI reworking of the footage. Pre-production

had also been digitized, with screenplay programs used to format scripts and animation permitting previsualization of sequences or entire films [. . .] Only three areas
of creative work remained stubbornly analog: shooting the film, distributing it, and
showing it. (2012: 27).

In order to ensure a consistent and settled set of terminologies, the Chapter
(as do other Chapters in this book) draws on the research of the AHRC –
funded Deep Film Access Project (DFAP 2013–2014). The DFAP took the
case study of both the making and subsequent archiving of *Ginger & Rosa* as
its focus. The project involved working with the entire *Ginger & Rosa* data
set generated by the film to develop an 'ontology'[9] for the organisation of all
of the materials (and their associated metadata) of production, from development through to delivery. The project sought to explore the potential role of
semantic technology in film production processes, focusing on how a semantic infrastructure could contribute to the integration of the data and metadata generated during the film production lifecycle. The project presented
a preliminary development of a knowledge framework to support the auto-
matic management of feature-film digital assets (see Lehmann, Atkinson and
Evans, 2015). The ultimate aim of the DFAP was to inform future archival
access to the materials of film production. As Principal Investigator on the
project, I was responsible for the complex task of writing natural language
descriptions for all aspects of the film production process, people, materials of production and metadata. This task was undertaken in collaboration
with film industry practitioners and film archivists, and included all analogue
(film) and digital (data) processes as well as conflations of the two, between
these different agents. In effect, I became the mediating interlocutor, to make
legible the different disciplinary discourses.

The terms used within the DFAP project break down into a number (of
what used to be mutually exclusive, but are increasingly interrelated and
overlapping) phases: Development, Pre-prep, Pre-production, Pre-shoot-
prep, Production, Post-production, Delivery, Marketing, Distribution and
Reception, and Archiving. These phases are based on the *Ginger & Rosa*
model, in a different type of shoot, one which included Computer Generated Imagery (CGI), studio-based special effects, or one being shot in stereoscopic 3D which would obviously have different phases relating to other
digitally specific processes such as pre-visualisation. Those listed here are
considered to be the core, baseline, requisite stages of any industrial feature-film production. Each phase includes a number of interdependent
operations which, in traditional film production are normally undertaken
in a chronological sequential order. Table 3.1 clearly illuminates how craft-
based digital film production sustains the fragmented and modularised
process founded upon the principles of celluloid film production.

Table 3.1 The key phases and operations of the film production process. Operations tend to be stand-alone activities undertaken by different departments. (Author's own in collaboration with Adventure Pictures)

Phases	Operations
Development	**Creative:** Idea Storywriting Scriptwriting Research Casting Storyboarding **Logistical:** Rights acquisition Budgeting Scheduling Sales estimation Financial planning Financing Pre-sales
Pre-prep	**Creative:** Scriptwriting **Logistical:** Company formation Recees (tax incentives) Crew research/expansion of crew Insurances
Pre-production	**Creative:** Rehearsals Cast voice and dialect coaching Cast skills development (i.e. choreography, singing, learning musical instruments, martial arts) Production design Hair and make-up tests Wig-making Prosthetics Camera tests Casting extras Property construction, set construction **Logistical:** Scheduling Budgeting Contracting (crew and performers) Casting Location agreements Cast voice and dialect coaching

Phases	Operations
Pre-shoot-prep	**Logistical** Technical recees, risk assessing, unit access preparation, script read-throughs, costume fittings
Production	**Creative** Direction and performance Film recording Sound recording Stunt coordination **Creative/Logistical interstice** – unit publicity including stills photography, filmed interviews with key cast and crew, and documentary production (these elements go on to constitute the EPK – Electronic Press Kit) **Logistical** Scheduling Continuity reporting Production reporting Post-production scheduling
Post-production	**Creative** Visual effects generation Sound effect creation Graphics Image grading Automated Dialogue Replacement (ADR) Foley recording Sound mixing, music production Sound track editing
Delivery	**Creative** Production of deliverables: textless version, different frame rate versions, spotting version, audio description, subtitles, Digital Cinema Package (DCP) **Logistical** Clearances Chain of title Ratings certifications Unlocking tax credit Errors and omissions insurance policy
Marketing, Distribution and Reception	**Creative** Creation of marketing materials: online and social media, printed materials – posters, press book, flyers, cinema/TV trailer(s) Official international premiere
Archiving	**Logistical** Media and metadata management and organisation

Development

The film production process always starts with development; within this phase of any film, the scriptwriter or writers either generate a new idea or base it upon a prior text. In the latter case, if the script is to be an adaptation, a process of rights acquisition would be initiated, before moving to the writing of the script alongside the associated research. As Stephen Greenwald and Paula Landry suggest, invariably '[t]he development process is triggered by the acquisition of a *property* (a script, or story rights based on a literary property or other source)' (2009: 32). The producer(s) would normally oversee this process working alongside the production's legal team. In the case of *Ginger & Rosa*, the script was the Director/ writer Sally Potter's own original idea, so a process of rights acquisition was not necessary. With rights acquisition not a necessary initial component of development in this case, the main purpose of this phase from a logistical perspective was to secure funding for the film.

Ginger & Rosa was funded by numerous sources including financing from both the BFI and BBC's film fund, through co-production agreements (in this case Denmark and the Danish Film Institute – DFI), and pre-sales (including Germany). The Danish Co-Producer reflects on the collaboration:

> The reason why we got involved in *Ginger & Rosa* was they were in search of a Danish co-producer because Sally wanted to work with people from Denmark because she's exploring how it is to work with different countries, which I think is a great thing. It gives her new ways of looking at her films and also, I think we can bring things to the table that actually make films better [. . .] we managed to apply for support from the Danish Film Institute and we got the support based on the things that we should do here in Denmark.[10]

The DFI explain some of the monitoring processes that take place within a co-production arrangement:

> We like to see a cast list. We like to see a crew list, and definitely a co-production deal memo or agreement, depending on where they are, and then there needs to be a letter of intent or a contract by a Danish distributor concerning that they're going to release the film.[11]

From the creative perspective, it is during the scriptwriting and re-writing process that other creative planning also begins, which includes production designing and casting, these creative decisions then feed into the organisational and financial processes of budgeting and scheduling. As in all stages of the film's production, there needs to be a constant dialogue between creativity and logistical matters.

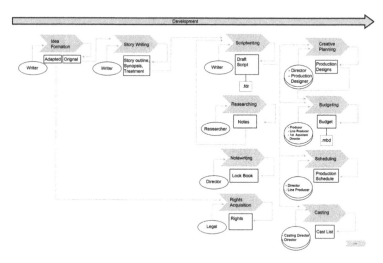

Figure 3.1 The initial development process as mapped by the DFAP.
(Lehmann, Atkinson and Evans, 2015)

These organisational and financial processes then feed into the overall financial planning and financing strategies of the project.

The first move away from traditional processes within the development stage of *Ginger & Rosa* was the casting process, in which the digital affordances of online technologies facilitated an alternative mechanism for the open casting process of the lead role of Ginger. As the Assistant Producer describes:

> We were looking for two 16-year-old British girls. We implemented this wider YouTube casting where 1,500 young girls auditioned via posting a scene from the film on YouTube on a private channel which we then viewed. I watched all of the videos, shortlisted them down to eventually a handful of about 30 who came in to meet Sally. A lot of good people came but we didnt find anybody who was really special.[12]

The process did not prove to be fruitful despite the high number of respondents and therefore the fact that the two lead roles required emotionally demanding performances turned out to be key to the financing of the film. One of the casting directors underlined the challenges of casting for these particular roles:

> You've read the script, haven't you? You know how difficult those parts are. It was just too difficult for most of them. Some of them were all right, but just that bit too young and it just didn't feel right.[13]

So the production reverted to the more traditional means of enlisting the expertise of UK-based Casting Director, Irene Lamb and US-based Casting Director, Heidi Levitt.

A further digital intervention became crucial for securing financing as a result of the casting decisions, and that was the Director's use of portable digital film and editing software. Joe Oppenheimer of the BBC, recounting an initial exchange with Potter, stated:

> she came in with an audition for Alice [Englert] and Elle [Fanning] which was incredibly compelling not the least she'd done a very clever thing, which was to film Alice in Australia and Elle in the States and yet had cut them together [. . .] although they were filmed in totally different places, it was a cut scene between Ginger & Rosa that worked.[14]

The Casting Director expressed the certitude behind the decision to cast Elle Fanning:

'She was amazing. The first test she did, the only test she did really, her English accent was perfect, it was just quite, quite, incredible. I mean you'd never have known she wasn't English.'[15]

The casting choices, as well as leading to complexities in production process down the line (see the following discussions concerning Automated Dialogue Replacement [ADR]), also presented challenges in contractual and logistical negotiations. As the Assistant Producer observed that this was a:

> . . . truly international cast for what is a British film. Elle Fanning, from America, and Alice Englert from Australia. Despite getting all this viable casting, which is really interesting and got us some good press [. . .] we had American actors on very tight schedules coming over for a few weeks, managing to fit all their schedules in to the same production period and British actors, like Timothy Spall. It was quite amazing that we've managed to negotiate all their deals on a scale that worked for the film, and get them all in to London at the same time. I think that was an exceptional element of production.[16]

After the principle casting led to key funding sources being agreed, the development phase officially concluded when an Inter-Party Agreement (IPA) has been signed between all of the financiers. One of the legal services team describes this highly complex process:

'We have one big inter-party agreement to which all of the financiers are a party, as is the sales agent, as is the producer and that's where everyone's rights and obligations get sorted out.'[17]

Pre-prep

The next step, pre-prep, then follows and further creative decisions are initiated – recees start to take place – a process in which Producers, the Director and the Production Designer attend various potential shooting locations. This is at a point where different countries and geographic locations are visited and assessed, not just for creative, artistic and aesthetic suitability but in order to maximise the potential of any available tax incentive or subsidy schemes. As Curtin and Sanson have observed:

> Producers have grown ever more fleet footed, playing off one place against another in a never-ending quest to secure the most favourable conditions for their bottom lines [. . .] Today's increasingly mobile and globally dispersed mode of production thrives (indeed depends) on interregional competition, driving down pay rates, benefits, and job satisfaction for media workers around the world. (Curtin and Sanson 2016: 2)

These financing strategies have led to what have been referred to as 'runaway productions'– where services are outsourced to regions where it is economically more attractive to budgets. It is a phenomena which has predominantly affected the American Film industry as Toby Miller has theorised: the 'New International Division of Cultural Labour' 'has had a devastating effect on unionized Hollywood craft and service workers, as well as technically sophisticated visual effects artists (VFX), and it results in a race-to-the-bottom competition between various cities such as Vancouver, London, and Hyderabad' (2011: 198).

Ginger & Rosa was shot entirely in the UK (and post-produced in Denmark). The UK is a very favourable location in terms of tax incentives for foreign productions, and has not been subject to the same damage or detriment implied in the term 'runaway'. However, this film used many of the practices that are alluded in this term – such as using the global talent network. According to the 2012 Oxford Economics report: 'Without the Film Tax Relief, we estimate that the core UK film industry would be around 70 per cent smaller, which would be equivalent to an average loss of total UK production of £600 million a year over 2012–15, of which at least £500 million would be inward investment' (2012: 50).

The report goes on to state that: 'Our updated analysis shows that in 2012 UK film costs were some 38 per cent lower than those in the US, and 15 per cent lower than those in South Africa' (2012: 55). The length of the working day in the UK is clearly a factor in the attraction of foreign co-productions, whilst also being subject to much controversy[18], the Co-Producer explains why the UK is a favourable context for film production:

> We work at the maximum ten hours a day here in Denmark, normally it's eight, but ten is probably the max. In UK you can easily work twelve hours a day, in which way makes it more effective to produce a film in the UK, because before you get the crew started up and before you have the lights preparation and stuff like that in place, it only takes one to two hours before we can start shooting, and if you have to do the preparation, then you have to wrap at the end of the day. The actual shooting time is very short here in Scandinavia. But in the UK, you get a very effective day when you work. (Co-Producer)[19]

During this period of location scouting, the crew is expanded, insurances are secured and a film production company is registered from which to administer all business related to the film. There is a 'script lock' at this stage which takes place before entering into pre-production. Of course, the script lock does not mean that the script will not change throughout the process, there are script additions and amendments made on a daily basis on-set, and within post-production the script is not necessarily followed at all. As Anders Refn, the Editor on *Ginger & Rosa* states:

> The editing is of course the last rewrite of the script. That's the last time you write the script before the film is put on the screen. [. . .] The script is just a step in the working process, and as soon as it has gotten on film or celluloid or whatever, then it's a new ball game and you have to find the film in all the material shot, then the script won't help you at all.[20]

Pre-production

The start of pre-production begins with the act of 'closing' – that is the moment at which all finances for the film are agreed and locked in place. One of the producers explains his experiences of this particular process:

> It's a mixture of a jigsaw puzzle and plate spinning. You're trying to put different elements in together in place and making sure none of the elements you think you've got in place fall out before you've got the final one. Until everybody comes together and says yes, basically, everyone has to say yes at one moment in time and they all sign a contract, like moving house. It's a chain. If one person drops out of the chain the whole thing falls apart.[21]

The budget – one of the key organisational and hierarchical production documents – is then established. Stratified into above-the-line and below-the-line roles, the budget document characterises and distinguishes the workers between the creative (above the line) and the technical (below the line).

The script, once a purely creative document[22] in the early stages of development, now becomes a purely logistical document. It is essentially treated as a digital database which is exported from one software (in this case *Final Draft* – an industry-standard scriptwriting and script-formatting software) and imported into another (*Movie Magic* – industry-standard software for Scheduling and Budgeting). The formatting, design and content of what were paper-only, typewritten versions of these documents have changed very little in their software versions. The software recreates facsimiles of the same format.[23] Scenes are broken down in order to produce a script breakdown – separating out character, location and prop details. The person undertaking the standby props role, explains how and why this information extraction functions:

> I do a script breakdown so when I get the script, I have to go through it and pull out and make a list of the props for the scenes and for continuity. Although a prop might be only scripted in one scene, although it's not mentioned in the scene either side of it, it might be needed for those scenes for continuity. I have to go through the script and break it down into a list and look at it in that respect.[24]

The beginning of the pre-production phase also triggers a number of other parallel activities (some of which began in the development phase) which feed from and inform one another. These include scheduling, the generation of an overall production schedule, a shooting schedule and a 'day-out-of-days' schedule – a document which specifies when each actor is needed to work during the course of the shooting schedule. This is a crucial document which enables the producer to negotiate favourable actor contracts. Scheduling and rescheduling occurs over the duration of the shoot to respond to changes: casting, creative planning, location scouting and sourcing, budgeting and cinematography. These processes all start to generate new documents and trigger other processes. For example, the creative cinematographic decisions generate a list of the equipment required to achieve the Director's and DoP's creative vision. Location negotiations also begin at this point, and the securing of permissions is imperative as the Production Manager explains:

> We have to licence anywhere we've got to get a permission to film because if we don't, we can't use the film that's shot on a particular location because you need the permission to hand it on to the distributors.[25]

In addition to resolving legal implications, logistical consideration is also key as the Location Assistant works to produce 'Movement orders' for every location – the purpose of which are to 'show people how to get to the different locations'.[26] The Unit Manager explains:

> We basically have a movement order telling everyone a mapped out route to the location. It gives you the directions to how we get to unit base and the location. It also gives all the kind of information you need in a day in terms of police, hospital, etc. so, it really helps out the crew when they kind of need that information about some location.[27]

The scope and depth of documentation is both vast and complex. As the Assistant Production Coordinator, both a wrangler and a conduit for much of the production documentation, describes its various forms:

> Contracts. We have to back up all insurance documents. We have to have proof of purchase of everything. So purchase orders, returns, notes, receipts, invoices. We do call sheets, and sides, and movement orders. Making sure everyone has all the details so if anything changes they have that info. We have risk assessments. We have logs for who's got what phone, logs for who has keys to the building, logs for couriers and cars. It's an endless list.[28]

As we can start to see, an established series of events and processes occurs on a working set, which generates a standardised and formulaic array of documentation that has remained relatively unchanged over the years. These enduring events and processes highlight the daily-ness[29] and the mechanised, routinised way that the crew's work is managed and crucially, monitored. As the Second Assistant Director (AD) explains:

> At the end of the day I also do an AD report, so the call sheets are kind of planned for the day, and an AD report at the end is kind of what actually happened on that day. That notes down the things that took place, what we achieved, what we didn't achieve and things like that.[30]

One of the key impacts of the new data flows of digital film pre-production planning emerges around the communication strategies which predominantly depend upon emails, telephone conversations, text messages and messaging apps. It is extremely difficult to map and capture these due to their velocity and volume, but it is fair to say that these new instantaneous communication mechanisms are a key contributor to the shift in production temporalities.

As the Director's Assistant explains: 'There's hundreds of emails going around every day. At first it was a bit wobbly how we were all going to communicate exactly and what everyone's role was exactly. I think we have that down to a T now.'[31]

The production phase for *Ginger & Rosa* took place over six weeks; as Figure 3.2 shows, the production period was very compressed. This invariably led to a number of behavioural imperatives both on- and off-set – impacting and influencing both communication strategies, operational initiatives and work patterns. In terms of off-set communication behaviours, the Post-production Coordinator based in Denmark observes:

> I think what surprises me most is that I've only been on *Ginger and Rosa* when it comes to British productions, but it's everything, everything is an email, and there's a lot of emails going back and forth. The communication is very email based, while I'm used to just picking up the phone and calling people. Everything is via email in this production at least. That's quite impressive because I think I've, during the months I've been on the production I probably have got a thousand emails just based on *Ginger & Rosa* communications back and forth. Some emails contain an 'okay' or a 'go ahead' or 'don't do that,' but there are many, many emails whereas when we work here it's very more man-to-man based or over the phone.[32]

There were certain moments in the production cycle, when the email volume intensified, as one of the co-producers in Denmark remarks: 'In the closing process, I think before we close the financing I had about a thousand emails from all the lawyers and producers and all the people involved in this process, which is quite a lot.'[33]

It is clear that instantaneous digital communication systems have led to pressures on the decision-making process, particularly in relation to production management.

A number of creative preparations in relation to the performance then begin to take place including: hair and make-up tests, wig-making, prosthetics and camera tests.

Set designing also begins at this point, and extras-casting processes also commence.

Given the time and cost constraints of on-set film production, rigorous preparation periods are essential for a successful shoot. As Potter notes of the production phase:

> By the time you get to set, you've already done a lot of your most important work. The key is all in the preparation [. . .] you can't shoot in five weeks in the way that we shot. That kind of speed is earned by slow and painstaking and very patient preparation, even if you do it fast, that's the feeling it has to have. No detail is trivial. Everything is worth getting right.[34]

Crew selection also continues apace during this period; this is generally now taken forwards by the HoDs. This then leads to the issuing and agreeing of crew contracts alongside actor contracting and child licensing for child performers which the producers oversee. These processes both then lead to work-permit generation for those performers and crew members from overseas.

Pre-shoot prep

Following the core pre-production phase, 'pre-shoot prep' takes place. During this short phase – the locations are 'recced' by representatives from all of the departments (Director/Writer, Camera, Sound, Production, Locations, Producers, Art, Assistant Directors, Construction, Continuity, Costume, Hair and Make-up, Property Security, Effects, Stunts) and a Health & Safety officer. The location department begin preparing access to the locations, and construction of sets on location takes place. Off location – rehearsals and read-throughs are taking place with the performers.

Production

Moving into the most frenetic, fraught, intensive and creative phase of production – the 'shooting', 'production' or 'principle photography' phase in which, as Figure 3.2 depicts – the full cast and crew participate.

Figure 3.2 depicts a circular timeline to illustrate the labour intensity across the different departments throughout the different phases of *Ginger & Rosa's* production cycle. Each coloured segment represents a day in the process using the raw production data taken from the production documentation (the schedule and the daily call sheets).

The key tenet of the organisation and management of film production assets in the film workflow is 'daily-ness' – that is, all of the resources that are generated are organised into systems that pertain to the day on which they were produced.

This 'daily' organisational rubric starts with the scheduling process within the pre-production phase, where daily call sheets are produced. Call sheets contain all of the necessary logistical information for the day's shoot, including actor and crew contact details, location information, scene and prop information, weather forecasts and sunrise and sunset times, and the length of the working day.

The call sheet is the one piece of documentation which all crew and cast members are given, and which unifies all of the necessary information and data that pertains to the day's activities. Sydney Lumet underlines the fundamental authority of this document: 'The call sheet is our bible. It's what we're going to shoot that day. If it's not on the call sheet, we don't need it'. (1995: 106).

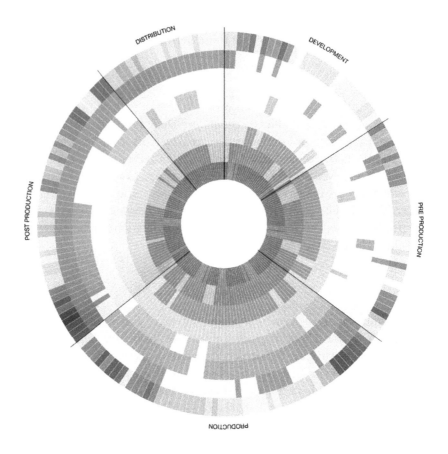

Figure 3.2 This infographic visualises the *Ginger & Rosa* production life cycle in its totality. (Produced by Bullet Creative, bulletcreative.com.)

"BOMB"

CALLSHEET 28

FRIDAY 23rd MARCH 2012

SCHEDULE: BLUE 09/03/12   CURRENT SCRIPT 01/0112;   GREENS 11/03/12; 01/01/12 PINKS 160212; BLUES 160212; YELLOWS 210212

PRODUCTION OFFICE / ACCOUNTS	ADVENTURE PICTURES	CONTACT MOBILES
291 Gallery 291 Hackney Road London E2 8NA	6, Blackbird Yard Ravenscroft Road London E2 7RP	Line Producer: Marshall Leviten 2nd Assistant Director: Andy Mannion 3rd Assistant Director: Darren Price Production Coordinator: Amelia Price Assistant Production Coordinator: Rachel Martin Location Manager: Jane Soans
Prod mobile	Tel +44 20 7	Assistant Location Manager: Georgette Turner Unit Manager: Ben Bailey

DIRECTOR: SALLY POTTER PRODUCER: CHRISTOPHER SHEPPARD PRODUCER: ANDREW LITVIN WRITER: SALLY POTTER	**ON SET: 1400** **N I G H T S H O O T** 1st ARTISTE CALL: 1115 (CROWD) 1300 (CAST) BRUNCH FROM : 1300 AT UNIT BASE DINNER: 1700 – 1800 AT UNIT BASE HOT HANDHELD MEAL: 2200 ON SET APPROX WRAP: 0100

Location 1: Gama Site, Brackenhurst Lane, Greenham Common, Newbury RG20 4HG	**Unit Base:** Gama Site, Brackenhurst Lane, Greenham Common, Newbury RG20 4HG

WEATHER: A dry and clear day / night. Max 15°C / Min 7°C	SUNRISE: 0553 SUNSET: 1819

UNIT NOTES:

PLEASE NOTE THAT TODAY IS NOW 11-HOUR DAY FROM 1400 – 0100 WITH A 1-HOUR DINNER BREAK AND 1 HOUR ALLOWED FOR TRAVEL. A LIGHT MEAL WILL BE PROVIDED ON ARRIVAL WITH AN EARLY DINNER FROM 1700 – 1800. A HOT HANDHELD SNACK WILL BE PROVIDED ON SET FROM 2200.
2. PLEASE RETURN YOUR SIGNED CONTRACTS TO THE PRODUCTION OFFICE. YOUR FINAL PAYMENT WILL BE WITHHELD UNTIL WE RECEIVE IT.

SC	SYNOPSIS	D/N	PG'S	CAST
62B	EXT MILITARY INSTALLATION Ginger joins Tony at the protest.	D29	3/8	1, 10*
73	EXT MILITARY INSTALLATION Ginger is arrested at the demonstration.	N29	2 5/8	1, 8*
	TOTAL PAGES: 3			

*PART COMPLETE

#	ARTISTE	CHARACTER		P/UP	ARR	B'FAST		M/UP	COST	TRAVEL	ON SET
1	Elle Fanning	Ginger	W	1200	1400	1400	T	1415	1400	-	1430
10	Andrew Hawley	Tony	WF	1115	1300	1300	S	1330	1300	-	1400
8	Annette Bening	Bella	WF	1230	1420	1420	F/T	1420	As req.	-	1500

STUNTS		SCENE	CALL	M/UP	COST	TRAVEL	ON SET
2 x Stunt Police Officers (Gary Arthurs, Martin Wilde) 3 x Stunt RAF (Aaron Topham, Derek Lea, Ray Nicholas) 3 x Stunt Protestors (Christian Knight, Sarah Franzl, Zarene Dallas)		73	1230	1230	1230	-	As req.
Total = 8							

S/A'S c/o Casting Collective, Casting Network, Ray Knight & Direct	SCENE	CALL	M/UP	COST	TRAVEL	ON SET
35 x Protestors	62B, 73	1115	1115	1115	-	1400
8 x Protestors SPAX 24 x Police Officers 5 x Police Officers SPAX 9 x RAF	73	1200	1200	1200	-	1400
41 x Protestors (Casting Collective)	73	1300	1300	1300	-	1530
33 x Protestors (Casting Network / Direct)	73	1330	1330	1330	-	1530
1 x Elle Double (Ray Knight)	73	1300	F 1330	1300	-	1400
Total = 152						

Figure 3.3 The call sheet from production day 28 of *Ginger & Rosa*.
(Adventure Pictures © Adventure Pictures Ltd)

Call sheets are produced and distributed by the Second Assistant Director from the Production Department, normally the evening before the shoot, via email and printed paper copies. These are accompanied by an additional piece of documentation, known as 'sides' which refer to the fraction of the script that are due to be shot that day. They are usually A5 booklets, covered by the call sheet.

This is imperative information as the Director's Assistant explains:

> Sally would sometimes make overnight script changes for the next day. They'd have to be typed up and redistributed to the whole crew. We have a process that we've developed where she will write the change then I'll type it up. She'll go through it again and see how it sounds. Say there was a new script, those changes would go to the production office who would then distribute to the whole crew and print out the new colour sheets for everyone. That was extremely important for someone like Penny Eyles who's the script supervisor who needed the exact script changes the night before. Sometimes that would be late at night.[35]

This illustrates the intensity of the work during the production phase in which there would be very few hours in the day when the film production system ceased to move forwards on its daily continuum. The intensity of this work fluctuates, the ebb and flow of work on-set is recounted most vividly by those inhabiting 'standby roles'. Their accounts exemplify the stark contrast:

> There just isn't a typical day on set, it varies so much. Taking this job as an example, we had the Rotherhithe Tunnel where once we'd put tax discs in their cars, that was really it for those scenes. There was nothing I could do as they went off and drove around . . . sit there literally just standing by getting cold. But then you've got the other day when you're in the pie and mash shop, and luckily I had another standby props helping me and we had to cook up pies, make mash, make the liquor, make cups of tea and we were as busy as you can be. We just didn't stop moving the whole time during those scenes. (Standby props)[36]

The Action Vehicle Department describes a similar experience of oscillating between contrasting moments of freneticism and inertia:

> It could be anything from panicking to get to the set because they want you early and they want the seats out and doors off, car turned on its roof. Anything to sit on the set and do nothing all day, not even get used really. Every day is completely different.[37]

As does the Standby Art Director:

> Every day is so different. Today is going to be lots of vehicles. So for me, there's not much I can do. I've just got to make sure everything looks pretty as possible.

Which is not much, because there's not much to do in a vehicle and outside of the vehicle maybe street signs move. But a day such as yesterday, where we were filming on the estate, there was so much to do. There was lots of set dressing around, so we constantly have to move to make it look right, to change the period from 1949 to 1962.[38]

The Gaffer similarly commented:

Today is starting off light because we're doing day exteriors, but we will end up doing a night exterior, which will get quite busy later on. So we're not so busy this morning, but different films need different things.[39]

These are microcosmic instances of what have been referred to as 'bulimic' patterns of work in creative portfolio careers (Pratt, 2000), endemic of the 'latent' nature of the organisation.

In addition to daily call sheets, many other aspects of the production period are characterised through the prevailing structure of daily-ness. It is a labour-driven model predicated upon an economics of production which is very often dictated by the availability and affordability of cast and crew members. In the case of *Ginger & Rosa*, as noted above, a number of the key cast were from overseas and only available for a limited period of time. Budgeting constraints were imposed by both actor and crew member daily rates.

The 'Creative Core Structure of Production' model (see Figure 3.4) takes forward the Personnel Structure and Working Relations depicted in Figure 2.2 in Chapter 2 to specifically illustrate the workflow and flows of communication between the different activities of production within the frenetic production phase. The layers are in a slightly different order to account for the activity that takes place during this period. This adapted version of the diagram illustrates process and the specific 'actions' and activities that take place.

In the 'Creative Core Structure of Production' – monitoring documentation is fed in an outward centrifugal flow, and work direction and the logistical framework is fed centripetally. As the Second AD describes:

We have different breakdowns from different departments. Stunt breakdowns, vehicle breakdowns, animals, things like that which I'm kind of . . . I take all those breakdowns of who has got what to do, and then all that information goes into the call sheet for the next day.

Many of the crew refer to 'dailies'– as quotidian practices specific to the day's work as specified in the call sheet. For example, the Costume

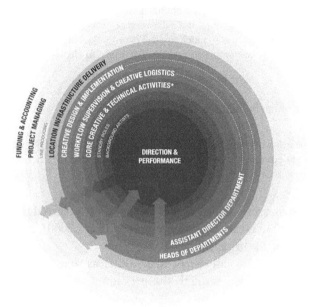

Figure 3.4 Creative Core diagram. (Author's own, graphic design by
Bullet Creative, bulletcreative.com)

Supervisor commented: 'I have to sort out my dailies, my petty cash, my
purchase orders for everything that's been made and hired out.'[40] The
Production Sound Mixer describes one of his daily routines:

> I prepare my day, so I have to open a new folder for the day. So it's day 16 so I
> prepare that and we decide which scene we are doing, we do that, so I prepare
> my sheet you can see here. So now we will do number, scene number, it's number
> 51. So I receive the sides and I put colour on them to know exactly which actor is
> speaking, and to open the good one, the good microphone every time.[41]

In each of the discussions with the Department Heads (HoDs), they
explain that during the production phase, they are always planning for the
next set, or next day. This is indicative of their position in the 'creative
core' within which they are at a distance from the on-set activity (with the
exception of the HoDs of both Camera and Sound for *Ginger & Rosa* who
were also the camera and sound operators respectively in this particular
production).

As well as daily-ness, other forms of fragmentation start to become evident in on-set processes and protocols. Prior to pressing the record button
on the camera, there is a strict ordering of events and terminology that is
followed verbatim as dictated by the Assistant Director Department. This
stems both from the historical need for a technical rehearsal appropriate to

analogue film (in order to save film, and to only film when necessary) and to maintain an ordering of technical processing checks.

These ritualistic on-set practices would also traditionally include blocking and coverage. Blocking is the process where a scene or shot is mapped out and walked through by the Director with the actors and crew members. A step-by-step process for action to be meticulously repeated – for the purposes of ensuring continuity. This is then physically marked out by taping markers to the surface of the floor to indicate positions where actors should stand for the purposes of pulling focus. Coverage is the filming process whereby the scene is repeatedly performed and captured from multiple-angles, to enable the editor and director different choices. The same scene is repeatedly shot from different angles to ensure this coverage – a wide-shot, mid-shot, close-up and so on enabling traditional narrative continuity editing. This manifests as an inherent dichotomy of fluid action and interruption, noted within the discourses of cinematic on-screen temporalities as the 'continuity and rupture' (Doane, 2002: 272) and the 'persistent impasse' of 'the apparent contradiction between film's static and discontinuous frames, and the continuous flux of reality to which they attest' (Pandian, 2011: 193).

The processes of 'blocking' and 'coverage' are critiqued by Geuens (2007), who states such practices 'contribute the most to the petrification of cinema' (2007: 412). Blocking, Geuens suggests, '. . . keeps cinema contained. With blocking, the old theatrical unity of time, space, and action reasserts itself' (2007: 417) and Coverage '. . . channels what could otherwise be a creative moment through a homogenizing grid; it forces the visualization through a neutral sieve' (2007: 418).

The Director Sydney Lumet is equally critical of these working conventions and posits the blame upon the editing department: '. . . certain rules, not only of editing but of shooting the picture, were established by the editing department. For example, every scene had to be 'covered.' This meant it was mandatory for a scene to be shot [. . .] the editor would often ignore a superior acting take because his job was much easier if he used a take where the cigarette action "matched"' (Lumet, 1995: 149–50). There are clearly conflicting imperatives between different agents within the film production process, which the Director must ultimately wrangle and prioritise. Reflections from the cast and crew of *Ginger & Rosa* revealed that a system of blocking and coverage was not imposed. Elle Fanning (*Ginger*) recalls:

> I felt like I could move around and do what I wanted. [. . .] It wasn't all about, oh, go and hit your mark there. We had no marks on the floor. It was just so very free. I loved that.[42]

Christina Hendricks (*Natalie*, *Ginger*'s mother) observes:

> People just don't shoot like this. [. . .] Normally you cover that person, and then
> you cover this person. This camera's roving and moving and catching moments,
> catching the end of a chair, and then this, then someone's moment they're having.
> It's really beautiful.[43]

Alessandro Nivola (*Roland*, *Ginger*'s father) describes how Robbie Ryan:

> . . . has a completely wild shooting style. Everything is handheld. They didn't
> really have a shot list coming into the scenes. We would stage the scenes based on
> what felt right, and then Robbie, the cinematographer, together they would spon-
> taneously decide what they wanted to shoot right then and there.[44]

Despite the pressured schedule, and the adherence to many traditional
location protocols, these testimonies reflect the on-set freedoms experienced by the crew and cast of *Ginger & Rosa* – wherein, within the
logistical structure of the film production, there was a central, focalised,
protected pocket which facilitated flexibility, experimentation, creativity
and innovation.

These observations inspired my development of the Creative Core
Structure of Production Model. This centralised structure is designed to
show the dynamics and production relations, and contours of organisation as an orbicular approach. It usefully helps to understand temporal
process – the direction of informational flows and communications, and
the inefficient representation of film production not just as a linear process. Instead it is an interactional and dynamic process, subject to shifts
and changes, as one decision leads to another and can take the production
in new and different directions. If this were an animated diagram, one
could think of it as constantly fluctuating, expanding and contracting at
different points in the process. For example, the level, types and complexities of financing dictate the breadth and scope of each of the rings,
some larger than others, and these are dynamic and can expand and con-
tract throughout the entire process.

The circinate structure captures what can sometimes be oblique interrelations and indirect communications flows, while acknowledging that
there is generally a strict and standard ordering to these. The rings also
show the various levels and oversight that all of the agents have in the
process, capturing the different levels of production agency. Diffusion
from the centre outwards, potency of agency reduces through each of the
circles. The Director and performers are most acutely focused upon the
fine-grained detail and minutia of production, working as they are upon

the smallest unit of the film production process – the individual frame and all that falls within its boundary. Here, the individual auteur is the nexus of all the decisions (which isn't always the case in other forms of film production), situated within a creative core – which preserves and retains creative autonomy, operating within an interactional model of reciprocal causations. The Boom Operator reflects on how his approach to communication is influenced by his proximity to the 'creative core' of the on-set action:

> You have to be discreet, you have to be sensitive, you have to be good at cooperating with everybody, because in the sound, you need the grip, the electrician, you need everybody to work with you. You are in the middle of the set, so you are next to the projectors, next to the camera. So you are in the middle of everything, so you have to be able to manage your psychological relations.[45]

This acknowledges his perception of the intensity of the creative core and the need to be mindful. As the Creative Core diagram (Figure 3.4) shows, technical operators are visitors within this space, entering when required, and able to nimbly navigate its creative contours through appropriate comportment.

Those in the outer rings – despite being the largest rings, are constituted by a limited number of crew that have the overall view of the entire process, with most only aware of their immediate role, department and work surroundings. The Producer talks about 'The ability to hold a big picture in your head because it really is about the big picture when you're a producer.'[46] The Second Assistant Director, speaking from the vantage point of an overview of all creative and technical activity, similarly observes: 'You've got to really be able to picture what needs to be done and the best way to achieve it.'[47]

'Background' artists form a textual ring around the Creative Core, they are marshalled and separated from the main action by the AD Department who are literally orbiting this space, and managing its flow and activity. This central pocket of experimentation is framed by the standard ritualistic practices enacted by the Assistant Director's department, parleyed by a series of familiar verbal cues that ensue, which instruct, shape and dictate the action of both cast and crew – 'Stand by,' 'Turn Over,' 'Speed' or 'Rolling,' 'Slate,' 'Action' and 'Cut'. These ritualistic processes of the AD Department were essential in previous film production practice for the use of large cumbersome cameras and grip equipment, which required intensive logistical planning. This is no longer a crucial activity in digital film production as the same economic imperative does not apply, but the legacy remains. Although this is not technically required for the purposes described above, it was perhaps for economic reasons and time pressures, as revealed by the Director herself:

> In the simplest way, shooting digitally meant that we could shoot a lot more, quantitatively, without worrying about stock running out, shooting ratio, that kind of anxiety. In a short shoot, in five weeks' shoot, that is very, very valuable because it means that you can overshoot a lot and just get it, get it, get it: give people the space to do it again, try again, try again, try this, try that, come closer, whatever [. . .] You still have the limit of time. There's still only, and in this instance, because we were working with young people who had limits in their hours, we were very limited with time.[48]

Procedural anachronism manifested in Potter's choice to frequently 'end board' shots – that is the instruction given to the Assistant Director to place the clapper/slate upside down in front of the camera in order to capture the information inscribed upon it, at the end of shooting. This instruction is used in instances where the camera has continued shooting, to capture action beyond what might have already been planned in response to performance and improvisation. From a co-producer's perspective, the economic implications of this shift are paramount:

> It makes it easier when you shoot because you're not depending on how many meters of film you use and also that the whole development process, etc. makes it a bit cheaper. On the other hand, if you have more material, you spend more time editing the film and the editing process might be longer because you have more material that you have to work with.[49]

Here we see the impact of the new technologies upon emergent production temporalities, where once, within celluloid film production, natural gaps for reflection, rest and rehearsal were afforded by the time that it took to change film magazines. These were changed every ten minutes (1,000-foot rolls of film were equivalent to 10 minutes of shooting time), in order to re-set cameras, positions and actions. Now that film has been replaced by data, where the camera can keep recording and where all key members of the crew can access a feed of the image, there are no 'natural' gaps left to reflect and prepare for the next shot as there once were. Christopher Nolan, Director of *Inception* (2010) and *Batman* (2005) and a proponent of preserving film as a medium has resisted these changes: 'The truth is the entire crew can only concentrate, the actors can only concentrate for so long, and then you need a two-to-three-minute break during which time you reload' (*Side by Side*, Dir. Chris Kenneally, 2012).

As Potter discusses in her book *Naked Cinema*, directors now choose to take other opportunities where 'natural breaks' arise – (which in the instance that she describes are created by production management imperatives):

> ... the strict rules concerning child actors' hours during a shoot (taking a break every hour, being chaperoned, continuing with school lessons with a tutor if shooting takes place during term-time) can benefit everyone. When filming *Ginger & Rosa*, Elle Fanning, who was thirteen at the time, regularly left the set to study maths, science, or literature. I used her breaks to prepare the next set-up, or rethink the scene, or take care of whatever was pressing. (Potter, 2014)

Although Mike Figgis has contended that:

> Does 'time to think' have to be the result of the inefficiency of a system? [. . .] It's really up to individuals to impose forms of discipline on the system that create space to think – because if you don't make that happen, the system itself will not throw up those kind of thinking breaks. (2007: 124–5)

It does not feel that the on-set time pressures are conducive to the luxury and freedom of choice that Figgis describes here, and it is suggested that there needs to be a reason or rationale to allow for these moments of 'creative' indulgence.

Similar gaps, governed by the industrial process of film production are afforded by the way that celluloid film needed to be processed to be viewed. Film reels were developed overnight and then printed to watch the following day – hence the industry terms 'dailies' and 'rushes' (so called because they were 'rushed' over to the film laboratory to be processed after the day's filming). The Director would normally view these in a film-viewing theatre – a calm space away from the hectic on-set action – which allowed time for careful consideration and contemplation. Martin Scorcese underlines the importance of the distancing of time and space in this process, between the Director and the set, 'the problem for me is that I still think you need to see rushes later, in order to concentrate with the performances, or just the movement, I still think you need to see them at a special time' (in *Side by Side,* Dir. Chris Kenneally, 2012).

Aside from a 'video-assist'[50] preview, the first screening of any footage would be via the dailies. Previously, in celluloid film production – the only chance to see the material being recorded would be by looking through the camera viewfinder – an opportunity afforded only to the camera department and the Director. In digital film production, there is now instantaneous access to the material that is being filmed at a high resolution, and ubiquitous access to the image, as one Digital Imaging Technician (DIT) described: 'on the last Marvel job I did, we had 16–20 monitors on set, some for the producers, some for the director, some for camera assistants, and then some for hair, make-up and wardrobe.'[51]

This new expectation of simultaneous access to the image by multiple agents, has a direct impact upon increasing the frenetic pace of on-set action, as the DIT goes on to describe:

> I'm regularly running 2-6 iPads on set and recording the live coloured signal out of the cameras. [. . .] Each iPad user then subscribes to an encrypted Podcast and is able to view the last take within 45 seconds after the cameras have cut, with sound and proper colour. [. . .] This is all happening in real time at the pace of production so everything must happen seamlessly.[52]

The portability of the digital camera recording equipment, has enabled more creative and artistic opportunities to advance filmmaking style and technique. The visual aesthetic of *Ginger & Rosa* was intentionally hand held – a responsive, dynamic and fluid approach was taken with frequent use of the close-up. Any shots which had utilized grip equipment during the shoot did not make it into the final cut of the film.[53] Robbie Ryan describes that the chosen style and approach with *Ginger & Rosa* was to:

> . . . shoot from a very point-of-view style [. . .] The way you do that is very simple, but it's a rule that you must follow in the way that you shoot it [..] It would always be from . . . over somebody's shoulder as in Ginger. It was all her point-of-view, the whole film. You have to follow the rules, very simple rules, but you can't go outside of her world [. . .] You can't be in a different room and Ginger's not in that room or you are always with that girl. It's very simple, but it's frustrating for some directors.[54]

And despite breaking the traditional rules of narrative film production, a new rule-set was put in place which governed his, and the Director's approach, which was incumbent upon a different set of limitations and restrictions:

> we did about maybe five or six top shots throughout the film and only the one that's in it is the one that it doesn't have Ginger in it. It's at the beginning of the film when the moms are having the babies and we did a top shot there, but the rest of them got took out because it breaks the rules.[55]

Logistics are clearly dictating the creative opportunities. But as Potter explains, creative restraint can be good, liberating even: 'You're always working within limits, whether they're self-imposed or imposed from outside. It's much better, to some degree, if you impose them yourself.

Not as limitation limits, but as a framework within which you can become more and more free.'[56] It is this framework that is enshrined within the Creative Core model. Despite the enduring daily-ness, the speeds and rhythms of film production practice – previously governed by the 'Fordism of filmic time and space' (Grieveson, 2012: 32) have now been opened up to fluidity and rupture, where digital technologies allow for fluid action to take place – such as continuous unbroken takes.[57] As Markos Hadjioannou has observed:

> In contrast, digital technology makes discontinuity a necessary process and also a favoured function. Whereas the relation between continuity and discontinuity is intricately complicated in analog and indexical media, the digital favors absolute discreteness and complete transformation. (Hadjioannou 2012: 31)

Whilst this may be true for the presentation and manipulation of digital images in capture and post-production, it is not the case in production workflows which favour discontinuity of shooting. The film is not shot in continuous order: where the classical narrative mode persists in a majority of output, scenes and shots remain fragmented, filmed in a way that is dictated by economic logics of efficiency (i.e. when actors and locations are available). Despite technical and aesthetic advances, production management remains a fragmented process, where the script is broken down, schedules produced, and so on; working in contradistinction and counter intuitively. This leads to a key question of this Chapter, and of digital film production more generally: how is a smooth and fluid workflow achieved and textual coherence ensured in what is essentially a highly-fractured workflow?

Workflow-warp is the name I have given to the emergent aesthetics of 'production time' which have manifested as a result of procedural anachronisms and shifting production temporalities. Workflow-warp is a manifestation specific to the digital film-to-data transitional moment, and its impact upon the patterns and pace of work.

Time compression + Role compression = workflow-warp.

'Workflows' in film industry parlance, is a term that originates in digital film production to describe the flow of digital data through the film production chain. It can also refer to the mechanised, serialised, reactive, cause-and-effect processes which occur within and across the various stages of film production, primarily to account for the movement of data through the production chain. An example is depicted in Figure 3.5. This particular workflow chart represents a workflow process that is routinely repeated within the camera department which involves keeping a record of the material being shot.

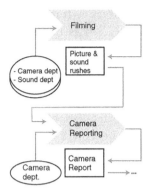

Figure 3.5 A simultaneous creative and logistical activity of data and metadata generation (one digital process, one analogue). (Lehmann, Atkinson and Evans, 2015)

As Figure 3.5 suggests, elements of the film production process run in a contiguous, linear fashion, with each of the main production processes sequentially ordered one after the other. The process of filming triggers the associated process of camera reporting, whereby the Assistant Camera Operator records information relating to the shots, such as the lens used, focus details, and so on, on a camera report form which accompanies the digital film files. The workflow chart in Figure 3.5 indicates a human agent in the process, and the actions taken in order for the next process to commence. The prior process would need to be completed and an output or instruction of some kind to be passed to the next agent within the production concatenation.

But with many instances in the workflow, it is no longer the case that one process has to be complete and locked down before the next one can commence. Instead processes can run simultaneously or anachronistically. Figure 3.5 highlights a case-in-point. These two activities of filming and reporting run separately, but with current technology can run simultaneously using the concurrent data-stream capabilities of the digital film camera.

These new possibilities, where enacted, have in turn generated a new phenomenon on-set and elsewhere in the production process. I refer to this phenomenon as 'workflow-warp'. By this, I refer to the affective impacts that the change in pace and speed at which people now work on-set, and in all other aspects of the production chain, cause. Workflow-warp specifically refers to the dynamically changing temporalities of the organisation of production *as a result of* digital technologies. To warp is to twist something out of shape, to distort; the term also works as an analogy to the Timewarp special effect in the Avid editing system – a digital tool which is used to dynamically manipulate the time of a clip, to speed it up, slow it down or reverse it.

To clarify – workflow is an organising principle of data ordering – the direction in which the on-set data flows – it is often referred to as the 'pipeline' – the production pipeline or the post-production pipeline (in some production credits there is a role attributed to this – referred to as a 'pipeline' consultant). Whereas workflow-warp is the impact that the velocity, with which data flows through these pipelines, imposes upon time and the rhythm of on-set behaviours. The prevailing characteristic of workflow-warp is a contradictory and sometimes simultaneous compressing and stretching of time which manifests in a number of ways. This can sometimes be experienced as an intensification as the rapid velocity at which data is generated expedites certain processes and the pace of work needs to increase to cope with this. At other points processes are slowed down and ruptured by ritualistic logistical procedures. It is rather like a symphony, which dynamically shifts from staccato to legato, and is very often a paradoxical experience as previously described by those inhabiting 'standby' roles (see page 78).

As I noted above, the Assistant Camera Operator used a paper-based system with which to record details relating to the materials being shot. I was interested to explore why the opportunity was not taken to automate and digitise some of these processes on-set. This was clearly an option whereby additional metadata could be automatically generated and recorded on camera, and additional contextual data could be manually entered and recorded into the digital film data stream, to be later made accessible concurrently as metadata. The Second Assistant Camera Operator explained that at the point of shooting *Ginger & Rosa*: 'we didn't have it engaged on the camera, that was relatively new technology back then, you can now.'[58] A shift in practice is highlighted here as these processes of metadata automation and manual metadata generation have become more common practice in digital film production workflow:

> I work on *Game of Thrones*, that uses the CODECS recorders just to edit metadata, to make the workflow streamlined, so on-set, I would keep the recorders with me and we'd cable the camera back to the recorders, on a trolley that's close to set, so we'd record down the cable. On the metadata, for every take, I would take the slate, the take, the date, the director, everything, so I control it right down to every detail. I can put any piece of information on there, if there's a problem with the take, if there's a boom in shot, or if there's a filter reflection, I'll put in a note on that. So when the drives go to editorial, later that evening, they have everything. They don't need to go through paperwork or anything.[59]

Fragmentation of shots and action have now given way to fluid, continual and responsive film production methods. It has been primarily camera and sound-recording technologies which have started to have an impact on and influence on-set protocol, but economic imperatives remain a significant factor, and have a direct impact on planning and organisational aspects of film production. As Elana Levine notes in relation to the logistical process of scheduling: 'the practices of writing and production scheduling [. . .] illustrate the way daily work routines negotiate textual meaning, at times fracturing it and at times fixing it' (2001: 73).

Continuity remains a key concern, and a defining principle of both film production aesthetics and workflow imperatives. It generates a significant amount of on-set activity and material, and also sustains a mechanised and routinised system of checks, as Levine noted in her 2001 study: 'Like the writing process, the production schedule requires continuity checks to secure the potentially errant meanings it might produce' (2001: 75).

Each of the main departments produce continuity reports on a scene-by-scene basis. The Costume Department, Hair and Make-up and the Continuity Supervisor all produce their own continuity documentation – which usually comprises handwritten forms with printed digital photographs. Departments evolve their own unique systems, as the Production Sound Mixer explains:

> I have a sound report from France. It was designed by an assistant I had before, and we did that because when I started to work a long time ago, 30 years ago, we used the NAGRA; not even stereo was out at the time, so it was a mono. After we went to stereo and then now we are multichannel, so we need a special sound report to be able to write on this what you put on each track.[60]

Post-production

As shown in Figure 3.2, on page 76, post-production was, and remains, the longest phase of any film's production life cycle. This phase can be broken down into a number of sub-phases, which in the past, were initiated in a strictly procedural fashion when key milestones had been met (for example, 'Picture Lock' at the end of the offline editing phase triggers the output of an 'Edit Decision List' which enabled 'either the original film negative, or the master videotapes, to be automatically conformed to produce a copy that matches the edited version' (Fairservice, 2001: 336)). However, post-production has become the most fluid and anachronistically malleable of all of the processes. Teams can access and work simultaneously on the film across all of the processes listed in Table 3.1.

This parallel set of activities is continuously managed by the Post-production Supervisor, a logistical role which: 'ensures that all areas of

Figure 3.6 A Hair & Make-up continuity record.
(Adventure Pictures © Adventure Pictures Ltd)

the post-production were all running together in a parallel form.[61] The Post-production Supervisor is a management rather than a creative role and one put in place for economic imperatives:

> The importance of doing this type of work early on was to ensure that delivery requirements are agreed before a contract is signed, on closing of finance, for a film, so that there are things we know that we can or cannot afford that are within the contract that is signed by all the financiers [. . .] working to the budget, making sure that we have enough money in the budget that we can use for our various processes in post, and also being involved in negotiating deals with the facilities.[62]

As this testimony illustrates, the post-production period and its constituent processes can start within the production phase. In the case of *Ginger & Rosa*, the dailies were being taken and transcoded into the Avid digital editing system[63], and organised into scene bins[64] by the editing assistant for both the editor and the Director to review. At the same time, the Edit Assistant was logging and transcribing all of the handwritten notes from both the camera reports and the continuity reports. The Assistant Editor explains:

> Then if there's any remarks and continuity comments and lens indication, this is all information for the editor. This would also be all the information that would have been on the continuity sheets. There's a continuity person on the set taking notes on what they actually did and where is it meant to go in the film. That [continuity sheets] comes with the rushes.[65]

The Assistant Editor is here referring to handwritten paperwork, which he transcribes into the online edit software, the camera reports which I referred to in my discussions above, and also the continuity reports which contain additional contextual information and notes from the Director (about the quality of the different 'takes', for example).

Daily-ness is once more evidenced through post-production nomenclature associated with celluloid technologies and techniques. See, for example, the organisation of the Avid bins. The bins are referred to as 'dailies' to indicate the storage of a day's worth of material. This is an example of the many instances of extant analogue terminology retention, the vestiges of photochemical workflow which will be discussed in more detail in Chapter 4.

The collapse of once temporally distinct processes was prolific in *Ginger & Rosa*, where all sound mixing, VFX, Graphics and Grading happened simultaneously across the two different post-production facilities in Copenhagen – *Short Cut* (for visual work) and *Mainstream* (for audio). The

Visual Effects Supervisor, who worked with a team of five compositors on the film to undertake approximately sixty visual effects shots explains the reasons for the extent of this work on what was a period, on-location film:

> Right from the moment that the offline is locked, we decide all of the shots that need work done. For this particular film, there was a mix of removal of modern-day objects from satellite dishes and everything thats not supposed to fit into the era of the 1960s in London. That's obviously quite a lot of work. Then aside from that, there's a lot of creative stuff that we might not have been able to shoot on set. For example, we have a scene which is set on the ocean, which they had to shoot pretty close to land, so we have land all the way in the background, which we completely erase so that it looks like they're out on open water instead. Also, previously, Sally had an idea about a trumpet playing a larger role, which she then later on decided for it not to be, so we actually had to take that out in a lot of sequences where it was placed in the recording.'[66]

At the same time that these visual effects processes were taking place, the colour grade was also underway, a process which was a blend of film and digital; there was both a 'grader' (working in a digital grading suite) and a 'timer' (working in the laboratory) of *Short Cut*.

In a return to the film production semantics of temporality, 'colour timing' is the name given to the photochemical film process undertaken in the film processing laboratory, which ensures that all shots are consistent and match in their colour and exposure. It is known as timing because of the manipulation of the exposure durations in the process.

Figure 3.7 The boat scene from *Ginger & Rosa* which required extensive visual effects 'correction', in order to remove the visible urban landscape on the horizon.
(*Ginger & Rosa*, 2012, Dir. Sally Potter)

'Colour correction' and 'grading' are the equivalent digital processes, although the digital versions of the process are still very often referred to as 'timing' in America. Colour grading is giving a look and a feel to the overall film, or scenes within the film. As the Digital Colour Grader for *Ginger & Rosa* explained:

> I think on this film [..] instead of creating a look that kind of represents the whole film – to squeeze the whole film into this kind of a look – for instance, *Oh Brother Where Art Thou* [Dir. Joel and Ethan Coen, 2000] is completely yellow.[67] You got the green in *Matrix*. Rather than doing that on this film I think we've gone with the feeling on each scene. How are the colors going to represent what this scene is about?[68]

At the time of the interview the grader was working on one particular evening scene where the main characters of *Ginger & Rosa* are sitting at a sea-front bus stop; the character of Ginger is lonely and left out of the situation, and the grader and the Director sought to exemplify and intensify this emotion by colouring the shot blue (see Figure 3.8). According to Barry Salt (2009: 47), as early as the period between 1900 and 1906 there were examples of night-times scenes being tinted blue. Then between 1907 and 1913, this convention became firmly established:

> In 1907 the use of blue tinting for night exteriors actually shot in full daylight, as they all were was fairly standard [. . .] By 1913 the other standard colour was orange or amber (yellow-brown) for candle-lit or lamp-lit scenes (Salt, 2009: 85).

The colour blue as a signifier of night time can be tracked throughout different aspects of the production process. For example there is a 'day for night' filter setting on the camera which imbues the image with a blue tone. The scheduling strip boards that will be discussed in Chapter 4 also use the colour blue to indicate a night-time scene. There are numerous studies in the theory of film colour which further expound these, and other such conventions (Bellantoni, 2005; Coates 2010; Misek, 2010; Peacock, 2010). The colour grading and/or timing are significant processes within the production of the film since they will ultimately provide the film with its final 'look' and its enduring visual style. As such, key directorial decisions are made at this stage, as the Digital Production Manager explained:

> Sally would come here and start by seeing tests that we had printed out into 35 mm, and then she would see different kind of stock material for the printing material to choose if she wants to go Vision or if she wants to go Fuji etc. [. . .] Then she would sit with the colour timer and do adjustments.[69]

The Colour Timer explained his process to me in more detail in relation to working on a digital film: '. . .you still need a colour timer to find the printer light when you make a print because it's going through the same process.'[70] The Colour Timer goes on to explain a pioneering technique of the laboratory which was implemented to save both time and costs on the process:

> When you cut the negative, there will always be a few frames from each cut that you don't use. Then the negative cutter, he or she would take 10 frames from each cut that were not to be used in the final film, but they represent the shot very well, so she would cut this together. Then you have a whole roll with only 10 frames from each cut in the movie. Then the colour timer started out timing those 10 frames, and you would look at them on the light table or you can invite the photographer to see it on the screen, and he will come with his comments [. . .] so instead of printing the whole feature, you will have just a small roll [. . .] We were actually a little famous here at this because we did it that way.[71]

Sadly, as the Colour Timer went on to state: 'I think actually that *Ginger & Rosa* will be the last film in Scandinavia that will have a colour timer.'[72] Indeed, according to his IMDb profile, it turned out to be the last film that he had worked on; *Shortcut's* film laboratory closed down shortly after the completion of *Ginger & Rosa*.

Further temporal shifts were manifested in instances of workflow-warp through the collapse of gaps in time zones imposed by geographic boundaries. One particular example arose in the Automated Dialogue

Figure 3.8 The scene described by the Digital Colour Grader, in which the colour blue was used to intensify Ginger's inner feelings of exclusion and loneliness.
(*Ginger & Rosa*, 2012, Dir. Sally Potter)

Replacement (ADR) process needed for *Ginger & Rosa*, given the extent of the extraneous levels of noise at each of the London locations. The various actors were dispersed across various locations but were also required for this process at the *Mainstream* post house in Copenhagen. Christina Hendricks was in LA, Alessandro Nivola and Annette Bening were in New York, Alice Englert was in Sydney and Elle Fanning was in London shooting another film at the time. The Re-recording Mixer describes the technology, which in 2012, had only just become available and workable:

> These days we have a system called *Source Connect* where we can actually sit here in Denmark and have a connection to for example Los Angeles, with the time lag of course. We are here very late in the evening and they are there in the morning and then we link up to a studio in LA where they put the actor and maybe the ADR supervisor which I then talk to. We set up a certain date and time then we link up. They're kind of controlling our system. When they press play, my computer rolls and I can press record and we could at the same time record the same line.[73]

As she goes on to explain – 'It's a kind of unnatural, artificial situation and some actors are not very happy about that. This system is a little bit sensitive. Sometimes it's better to be there with the actors but not to travel around the world.'[74]

Workflow-warp was present throughout the entire process, and therefore had a significant impact upon the work patterns of the crew. As the Director's Assistant commented: 'We're dealing with lots of time zones. Things have to be done at night or early in the morning.'[75]

Workload and work expectations were also affected by geographic distance, as the Post-production Coordinator describes her own challenges of having to generate and record 'Walla' for use in the sound edit. Walla is the term given to describe the unintelligible background crowd noise in public spaces.[76] The requirement for this only became apparent in the post-production process, and production logistics meant that it had to be quickly captured in Denmark.

> It's quite funny to sit in Denmark and try to find real native, British speaking people in the middle of the summer when people are actually on vacation. When I did that I basically stalked half of Facebook [. . .]] It was apparently too late, and they'd have to fly Sally in and Eddie the sound technician in, and it was a bigger process than I was hoping it to be. We found 5 British men and 1 British girl, and they did quite a good job so I think they were happy in the end, but it was a quite interesting experience.[77]

This collapse of time is indicative of the new global film industry technological infrastructure that has significantly advanced since the field work of this study was undertaken, as Michael Curtin & John Vanderhoef have subsequently observed: 'the development of internet and satellite technology has allowed real–time collaboration between geographically distant studios, further facilitating the transnational co-production of animation and special effects' (2014: 11).

This change in time management and in the compression of time has been seen as an inevitable corollary of digital film production:

> The electronic cinema envisaged a transformation of the traditional organizational structure of film production by enabling pre-production, production, and post-production to occur simultaneously. The script could change in response to the input of the actors, or the way a scene was edited. (Ganz and Khatib, 2006: 24)

Although the key production phases had points of overlap for *Ginger & Rosa*, their total simultaneity had yet to manifest at this point in 2012. Such temporal shifts lead to expectations of flexibility as examined in the previous Chapter, to be always 'on', and to work across geographic boundaries and time zones, collapsed in both time and space.

There is a distinct sense of the digital bringing a closeness and proximity to the process whereas celluloid retains a (very necessary – according to some directors) sense of being 'at a distance' which allows space for creative reflection, a moment for review and refinement, and a much needed break from the intensity of the experience.

Just as was the case in the production process, many post-production professionals have reflected upon these profound affective changes wrought by the transition from film to data: 'They don't always have the time to sit back and think about what they're doing, and I think if they work on film, they'd probably train their minds to do that a little bit more, so it's a different way of thinking' (Anne Coates, Editor of *Lawrence of Arabia* and *Erin Brockovich*, in *Side by Side*, Chris Kenneally, 2012). Similarly, Mike Figgis writes: 'A number of established filmmakers resisted digital editing initially because they used the time in which the editing assistant was hunting through the trims in order to think about what they were doing' (2007: 124). Furthermore, there is a conflict of opinion in terms of whether a higher volume of material for the editor to contend with leads to an increasing workload, or a more creative one:

> Now there could be instant replay, and changes and improvements made as a scene was assembled; the editing process was speeded up and a higher level of concentration maintained. More of the editing time could be used in decision-making and cutting, and less spent handling. It did not mean that one had *less* time to think, rather that one had more. (Fairservice 2001: 335)

Others continue to argue that the converse is true:

> For some editors, however, the sheer operational convenience and speed of com-
> puter-based editing undermines a cardinal virtue of working film the old way: the
> opportunity for 'thinking time'. The time taken to rewind film, to lace it up on
> a Steinbeck, to find extensions or file film off-cuts in a trim bin, allows the edi-
> tor a space to ponder and deliberate. These laborious mechanical processes often
> discouraged premature editing decisions, unlike the electronic process of laying
> shots down first and changing them afterwards. (Perkins and Stollery, 2004: 158)

Either way, it is clear that these new editing behaviours are at odds with slow and considered creative practice. The impact of the digital which has led to an 'always on', 'always online' society has been met for a call for slowness in other areas of the knowledge economy. For example, in higher education a shift towards slow scholarship has been proposed (Berg & Seeber, 2016), in news reporting – slow journalism (Boaden, 2016) and, more recently, an approach to slow filmmaking is suggested by Kim Knowles (2016).

Delivery

The delivery phase of the film, after post-production, is a highly digital process in which a number of video outputs, data files and metadata data files are delivered to meet contractual agreements. As the Theatrical Sales and Operations Executive *Artificial Eye,* the film's UK Distributor, explained:

> I am responsible for getting all deliverable materials from the sales agent or pro-
> ducer in this situation, *Ginger & Rosa* [. . .] out to different departments who
> then do their business [. . .] the marketing department creating images and the
> publicity department using different materials to promote the film. Also, for the
> home entertainment department to create DVDs and Blurays and also for the DCP
> [Digital Cinema Package], the digital print production.[78]

Time again becomes an increasingly significant factor and a recurring motif during this phase:

> These DCPs can only be accessed when you have a key, which is called a KBM
> which only gets sent out to the correct venue. I basically control that process as
> well. These keys for the DCP get sent out literally you have to validate the time.[79]

The film is also 'paper-delivered' at this stage which involves the preparation of a range of contractual paperwork and legal documentation

including clearances, the Chain of Title and Ratings Certifications. The Assistant Producer emphasises the importance of this process: 'paper delivery at this stage in the process which is quite an important factor and everything because it's dealing with the legal requirements of the people who are selling the films.'[80]

The deliverables are agreed during the contractual stages and include the detailed example of image size – distinctions between large-scale projection and small-screen television transmission and what affordances and limitations they imply. Creative decisions are never made in isolation from the logistical, and economic imperatives and constraints, as Bordwell and Thompson observe: 'A filmmaker's stylistic choices can be affected by distribution and exhibition' (2013: 44). Indeed, Potter herself was working with a new format:

> I did a lot of drawings, sort of storyboards. Partly because I wanted to explore the widescreen format, which I'd never worked with before. Partly because I knew in the end that I wanted the film to be shot handheld, [. . .] I did a lot of drawings within the format in order to understand it compositionally.[81]

The marketing of the film can begin at any point in the pre-production phase of a film, with varying intensity and emphasis; indeed in this case publicity and marketing ran hand-in-hand with the production of *Ginger & Rosa*, with the enlistment of a unit photographer to capture both film stills and behind-the-scenes imagery, as well as a 'making-of' and an Electronic Press Kit (EPK).[82] As one of the *Ginger & Rosa* Unit Publicists describes their specific remit: 'it means coordinating any media activity surrounding the launch of the film for distribution, its Internet launch for the festival or in this instance working on it during the production phase.'[83] In addition to sending press releases and images to the trade and industry press at the point of production, the work of the publicists can also directly impact upon the creative decisions going forwards and can influence and shape the final film. As mentioned in Chapter 1, *Ginger & Rosa*, originally known as *Bomb* was subject to a name change during the publicity period; the Unit Publicist explains:

> I read the script with very much the title *Bomb* in my mind, and it worked to me, I do understand it has connotations for example in America as you probably know the term bomb particularly in relation to a film means a disaster. [. . .] The Germans in particular I think had a serious issue with the title, based on their their feeling that the primary audience, which were women around the age of thirty five and upwards, we say would have grave exception to that particular title.[84]

Potter recounts the impact that this publicity reconnaissance had upon her own creative process:

> I got really fierce and agitated because I was very, very attached to the name. I thought it had so many layers of meaning in it, and it was so simple. It was so direct. It was so bold. And then got the same feedback from the English distributors. But I still was ready to fight for it, but meanwhile, we had one relatively small screening, somewhere along the way in London, and a young woman, very quietly, in the front row said that the title, she was very confused because she thought it was going to be a completely different kind of film. She kept waiting for it to be much more about bombs. I thought, 'All right, that's it. Done,' and decided to take a much simpler, modest approach to give the film, in effect, just a name, or two names, in this instance, so that we knew it was about a relationship. We knew it was about these two characters, and then let the audience find out for themselves what it was about, whereas *Bomb* as a title is, in a way, giving you the thematic pun right up front.[85]

The impact of other factors, beyond the digital, being brought to bear on the creative process, illustrates the ever permeable nature of the creative core boundary. What we can see, in the close examination of film production process is an infrastructure that is continually influenced by economics, efficiencies and expectations of flexibility.

Conclusion

Through a close examination of the production process of *Ginger & Rosa* we can surmise some of the key aesthetics of production to emerge within the film/data contemporaneous moment, which are: Daily-ness, Modularity and Workflow-warp (which refers to compressed and stretched production temporalities and procedural anachronism). The production aesthetics of daily-ness and fragmentation emerged within key stages of the film production workflow of *Ginger & Rosa*. Within the production phase, the principle of 'daily-ness' can be seen to persist within the vestiges of the Fordist studio model. Both Geuens and Caldwell have commented on the implicit system of checks and balances that are embedded within this mode of working: 'From film to film, the routine of repetitive gestures keeps the workers from straying' (Geuens, 2007: 418). In relation to standardised forms of production paperwork, Caldwell has conceptualised such documentation as 'Industry surveillance' which 'systematically disciplines workers through a series of long-sanctioned rituals' (2013: 161). Allen notes the long historical trajectory of these established 'monitoring' practices:

The surprisingly early development of guidelines for the writing of continu-ity scripts as they appeared in *Moving Picture World*,[86] and the use of such scripts to control production argue that standardisation made its way into film as a means of managing a production team if not as a structural element of narrative.[87]

Through this analysis of *Ginger & Rosa* we can observe an example of a pervading aesthetic of modularity in terms of both organisation and the incremental changes taking place within the wider film industry. As the DFAP ontology highlighted, despite the flexibilities of the new technolo-gies, film production remains an atomised and alienating process. Modu-larity endures in many aspects of the film production process, as David N. Rodowick has observed:

> Film editing is a logical consequence of the automatisms of analogical transcrip-tion, which lend themselves to producing discrete spatial wholes. But once con-verted to numerical form, the digital image, whether captured or synthesized, may vary in any of its parameters. Logically, it does not suggest or require the necessity of 'cuts' as discrete sections of space and duration. (2007: 171)

The film production workflow has been subject to incremental changes which have reacted to the impacts of digital and data; there has not been a holistic review or systematic overhaul of the film production process, rather gradational changes have been applied to a traditional system and it is these that have led to the distortive warps.

This Chapter has also demonstrated that technologies have radically increased the velocity at which film data and metadata is generated during the film production workflow, affecting the pace, structure and nature of the creative art of filmmaking. Celluloid filmmaking processes and prac-tices in place since the birth of cinema which provided natural gaps in the photochemical process allowing space for contemplation and consid-eration, have collapsed to be replaced by instantaneous access to the mate-rial which is being shot. In addition to playback and review, there is now immediate and simultaneous access to the footage that is being filmed. This has had both positive and negative impacts on the work of film pro-duction practitioners: either they are having to work harder (negative) or are able to work less (positive). The phenomena of workflow-warp has emerged and we could identify one of the responses to the impact of the digital on the film production process which is the emergence of the tran-sitional role of the DIT, which was discussed in the previous Chapter. The suture of the digital interstices and the intermediary process of Digital Imaging could be conceptualised as a form of workflow-weft through the weaving together of different departments of work and through the linking and unification of the disparate elements of the work process, thus creating a complex tapestry of material and digital practices.

Each of these three core aesthetics of production (daily-ness, modularity and workflow-warp) are all manifestations of film and data hybridised processes. Despite being shot on a digital format, film production iconography, symbolism and process, in both the creative and logistical dimensions, are retained in *Ginger & Rosa*, resulting in the emergence of film-legacy aesthetics. In the following Chapter, I explore the analogue/digital transitional aesthetics within both physical and material production spaces. I examine how film production people and process are combined in the various production documents, semantics, hardware and software, in order to establish more concretely, the pervading Production Aesthetic.

Notes

1. Location-based film production process and practice are in direct contradistinction to Computer Generated Imagery (CGI) and special-effect laden, sound-stage film production, where very different approaches exist.
2. As defined in Chapter 1 – I use the term craft-based to imply a film that uses traditional, physical and practical techniques wherever possible, in its creation of scenery, props, effects and so on. Craft-based films are always location-based where the use of digital VFX are kept to an absolute minimum. Craft-based film is normally that which pertains to realist drama conventions.
3. A 'production analysis' approach is described by Kawin as 'a matter of finding out just what happened, both on the set and in the front office, when a particular picture was being planned or made, and then applying that information when examining the finished product' (1987: 27).
4. As Alan McKinlay and Chris Smith state 'The strength of a labour process approach is that it reveals the dynamics of working in real situations and looks behind the hype and rhetorical claims that can surround new fields of work and employment' (2009: 10).
5. In an interview with the author, 30 April 2012.
6. 'Creative Accounting: British Producers, British Screens' was a conference convened by the University of the West of England (Bristol), UK, 19–20 April 2011, http://michaelklingerpapers.uwe.ac.uk/conference.htm
7. A full credit listing with associated filmographies are listed as an appendix to this book.
8. In an interview with the author, 14 May 2012.
9. In computer science terms an ontology is a representation vocabulary. Ontologies are designed to provide a semantic layer more sophisticated than a

semantic layer which uses metadata alone. Not to be confused with Robert Wood's proposition of an 'ontology of film' which is the development of a phenomenological approach (2001).
10. In an interview with the author, 9 August 2012.
11. In an interview with the author, 30 August 2012.
12. In an interview with the author, 16 July 2012.
13. In an interview with the author, 21 May 2012.
14. In an interview with the author, 14 May 2012.
15. Ibid.
16. Ibid.
17. In an interview with the author, 6 June 2012.
18. *Who Needs Sleep?* directed by Haskell Wexler, 2006, to be discussed in more detail in chapter 5.
19. In an interview with the author, 9 August 2012.
20. In an interview with the author, 30 April 2012.
21. In an interview with the author, 22 August 2012.
22. Although the formulaic nature of scriptwriting has been acknowledged by many studying the form including Julian Hoxter and Andrew Horton (2014) further discussions around script style and formatting will follow in chapter 4.
23. See the production materials from Sally Potter's *Orlando* accessible at www. sp-ark.org
24. In an interview with Kurban Kassam, March 2012.
25. In an interview with Kurban Kassam, March 2012.
26. In an interview with Kurban Kassam, March 2012.
27. In an interview with Kurban Kassam, March 2012.
28. In an interview with Kurban Kassam, March 2012.
29. In my article (Atkinson, 2016) I further explore the concept of daily-ness in relation to the feminisation of film production and film archival practices – which will be extended further in chapter 6.
30. In an interview with Kurban Kassam, March, 2012.
31. Ibid.
32. In an interview with the author, 9 August 2012.
33. Ibid.
34. In an interview with the author, 12 October 2012.
35. In an interview with the author, 23 July 2012.
36. In an interview with Kurban Kassam, February 2012.
37. In an interview with Kurban Kassam, February 2012.
38. In an interview with Kurban Kassam, February 2012.
39. In an interview with Kurban Kassam, February 2012.
40. In an interview with Kurban Kassam, February 2012.
41. In an interview with Kurban Kassam, February 2012.
42. *Ginger & Rosa* EPK interviews.
43. *Ginger & Rosa* EPK interviews.

44. *Ginger & Rosa* EPK interviews.
45. In an interview with Kurban Kassam, March 2012.
46. In an interview with Kurban Kassam, March 2012.
47. In an interview with Kurban Kassam, March 2012.
48. Ibid.
49. Ibid.
50. The video assist role that facilitated the previewing of a scene through a sepa-rate video output, became available in 1960 – which allowed Directors to view a substandard low quality video version of a take either during or imme-diately after it was filmed. For a critical exposition into the development, implementation and impacts of this technology, see Geuens, 1996.
51. In an interview with the author, 8 January, 2015 (male respondent M007).
52. Ibid.
53. There is only one 'top' shot used in the opening sequence of the film, which shows both Ginger and Rosa's mothers in labour alongside one another in adjacent hospital beds.
54. In an interview with the author, 26 October 2012.
55. Ibid.
56. Ibid.
57. Certain films have favoured a one-take aesthetic – the origins of which can be traced to Hitchcock's *Rope* (1948) which broke with narrative convention by disguising the cuts to give the illusion of being filmed in real time. Pioneered in the digital film domain by *Timecode* (Dir. Mike Figgis, 2000); *Russian Ark* (Dir. Aleksandr Sokurov, 2002); and *Victoria* (Sebastian Schipper, 2016). The critically acclaimed *Birdman* (Dir. Alejandro G. Iñárritu, 2014) was famously produced *as if* in one take – such is the appeal of this particular style – filmed by cinematographer Emmanuel 'Chivo' Lubezki famous for the awe-inspiring 13-minute uncut opening sequence of *Gravity* (Dir. Alfonso Cuarón, 2013) made possible by advances in photorealistic Computer Generated Imagery.
58. In an interview with the author, 15 October 2014.
59. Ibid.
60. Ibid.
61. In an interview with the author, 7 September 2012.
62. Ibid.
63. *Avid* is both the film and broadcasting industry's standard non-linear dig-ital editing software, within which the films 'rushes' are organised and 'cut'.
64. 'Bins' are the name given to the folders or directories which are created to organ-ise all of the clips into a meaningful order for the editor, i.e. into dailies (which is a US term), or scene numbers. The term 'bin' refers to the cloth sacks in which photochemical film was originally hung.
65. Ibid.
66. In an interview with the author, 21 August 2012.

67. *Oh Brother Where Art Thou?* was one the first films to be digitally colour graded.
68. In an interview with the author, 9 August 2012.
69. Ibid.
70. In an interview with the author, 9 August 2012.
71. Ibid.
72. Ibid.
73. In an interview with the author, 13 August 2012.
74. Ibid.
75. Ibid.
76. In larger productions, with bigger budgets, you will see this work being undertaken by a 'loop group' – a group of vocal artists who will be hired explicitly for the purpose of 'performing' background crowd noise.
77. Ibid.
78. In an interview with the author, 13 September 2012.
79. Ibid.
80. Ibid.
81. Ibid.
82. See chapter 5, page . . . for a full explanation of the contents and use of the Electronic Press Kit.
83. In an interview with the author, 6 June 2012.
84. Ibid.
85. Ibid.
86. Everett McNeil, 'Outline of how to write a photoplay', *The Moving Picture World* vol. 9 no. 1 (July 15, 1911), p. 27.
87. Janet Staiger, 'Dividing labour for production control', unpublished seminar paper, University of Wisconsin-Madison, 1977.

CHAPTER 4

Digital Film Production Space

Introduction

In this Chapter I move towards a deeper consideration of the symbolic manifestation of celluloid film production terminology and nomenclature in both the physical and digital *spaces* of film production. I attempt to synthesise the various 'aesthetics of production', a hybrid set of established conventions including daily-ness, modularisation, workflow-warp, identified in the preceding Chapter, into a pervading Production Aesthetic which is at once characterised by celluloid continuities and digital resistances. *Ginger & Rosa* is an emblematic case study in this regard precisely because of its many transitional facets but, particularly, in three different ways:

1. **in its blend of film and digital technologies**: it is filmed on a digital format, but uses celluloid processes as part of its distribution strategy – a release print was produced and distributed on film to certain venues. It also marks a significant historical moment as the last feature film to be processed before the closure of the film laboratory at *Shortcut*, Copenhagen.

2. **in its blend and diversity of practitioners** – crew members spanned both the film and born-digital domains: those who had previously worked in entirely celluloid ways and those practitioners who had only ever worked using digital formats, tools and technologies.

3. **in its context as a transnational co-production** (with Denmark), which worked across continents and time frames. As a result, it used new and emergent digital technologies to facilitate different aspects of the work including networked communication and post-production processes. The transnational dimension was further augmented by its international casting, with key cast members coming from America, UK and Australia.

I argue that it is these factors which led to a number of hybrid strategies which fused the pre-digital with the digital in the film production process and workflow. I locate and identify evidence of these transitionary practices, resistances and tensions, which at once can be considered *to both simultaneously celebrate whilst actively seeking to occlude* the digital in process and practice.

I aim to develop understandings about how fragments of the history of filmmaking and its practices come to be embedded within aesthetics of production through an exploration into the vestigial sign-system which manifest in production process, language, software and documentation. This exegesis of production materials is a similar approach to that one used by Sylvie Lindeperg in her configuration of 'Film Production as a Palimpsest' (2013).

In my explicit consideration of a very particular film production *space* germane to the film-to-digital transformative moment, I examine the physical and digital materiality of filmmaking tools – the hardware, software and 'the material, symbolic and representational practices of production workers' (Caldwell, 2009b: 202). In order to do this, I draw on film studies approaches such as apparatus theory (Baudry and Williams, 1974–5; De Lauretis and Heath, 1980) to examine production hardware, and film studies methodologies including close textual analysis to study the various production texts; as well as media archaeological approaches in order to examine the 'rhetorical tropes and discursive practices that constitute our richest source for excavating what the newness of technology entailed' (Gunning, 2004: 39). I also draw from new media studies in my consideration of production software.

Through processes of abstraction, I pay particular attention to the complexities that emerge in both the semantic and semiotic sign systems of filmmaking as a result of the continued imbrications of film and data in all aspects of the film production process. I draw out the presence of metaphor and analogy of celluloid in industry terminology and language inherited through industry lore, which remain extant and inscribed, and the etymology of a number of terms currently in use which reveal a perpetual use of film-based epithets to account for digital phenomena. Drawing on analysis of the materials, on-set observations and the interviews within *Ginger & Rosa*, and the interviews undertaken with film industry professionals, this Chapter reviews the filmmaking language both as it is embedded as common practice, and in the discourse that professionals engage in when describing and reflecting upon their work.

In Chapters 2 and 3, I proposed that digital filmmaking professionals operate under a combination of both formalised and tacit tenets of production, that originate from the histories of filmmaking. A deeper consideration of these, both the explicit and implicit cultural inferences, is key to explicating the oxymoronic nature of the term 'digital film.' Whereas Lisa Purse has argued that in cinema: '. . . digital technologies not only replace earlier technologies, they also replace the rituals and processes that clustered around earlier technologies' (2013: 2). I argue that many of the earlier filmmaking rituals and processes sustain and endure, preserved and repeated in every day on-set practice but also enshrined in the operational principles and iconography of software and hardware design.

First, I consider some different examples of procedural languages and nomenclature, evidenced in the production process. I move on to consider pre-production, production and post-production hardware and software, as processes move from the materiality of filmmaking craft to the digital immateriality and ephemeral nature of the digital filmmaking process. I then proceed to consider Celluloid Pedagogies which refer to the film-material-based educational experiences of filmmakers in learning their craft.

On-set interactions

Through my interrogation of spoken language on-set, I consider how it has been inscribed with analogies and metaphors of the analogue, in so-called 'new' digital practices. I do so through the consideration of the ritualistic procedure that takes place on-set before filming a shot. There are a number of terms which are spoken aloud, and in sequence, before action and filming commences. It is within this vocalised sequence that one can hear some of the vestiges of analogue language – a 'hybrid vernacular' – consisting of metonymic terms that refer to the materiality of film and the physicality of the film camera.

Once the set is prepared and performers and crew members are ready and in place, the first instructional call made by the Camera Assistant is to 'turn over' – this is the instruction given to the Camera Operator to start the camera – in this case, or on any digital camera, this means to press a button, which is usually red in colour and labelled REC (record). The origin of the 'turn over' expression refers to the Camera Operator literally and physically turning over the mechanical camera's motor. Immediately after this action, the term 'speed' (or 'rolling') is called by the Camera Operator to indicate that the camera is recording – its original meaning is that the celluloid film was running at full and stable 'speed' through the camera's gate: that the camera is effectively 'rolling' at 24 frames per second. This simulation is embedded both into the camera apparatus and the language used to describe it – 'frames per second'. This refers to the number of frames that need to be recorded and projected to give one 'real' second of running time. In film, this is 24. The length of 24 frames of 35mm celluloid film is approximately 18 inches – which is equal to

1.5 feet. The word 'footage' derives from the fact that film was traditionally measured in feet and frames. As Bruce Isaacs observes: 'Digital cinema looked like film. It moved with film's internal rhythms: 24 frames per second of film was perpetually equivalent to digital cinema's 25 frames per second' (Isaacs, 2013: 25). Within the Alexa camera, the project frames per second (fps) sets the time base of the time code and how many frames the time code counts per second.

'Speed' or 'Rolling' is usually followed by the instruction to 'slate,' or 'mark it' given by the Camera Operator to the Assistant Director: that is the instruction to hold the slate or clapper board in front of the camera. This enables the camera to record the necessary information marked on the slate/board at the beginning of the shot, so that the content of the footage that follows can be easily identified by the editor. Slate clearly refers to the *physical* medium of the board – this appellation persists despite these pieces of equipment now predominantly being made from acrylic material.

Details include the date, scene number, take number and other basic production details such as the title of the film and the name of the Director. Despite its redundant function as an analogue prompt – the creation of an audible and visible 'sync' point to enable the editor to link sound and vision together in post-production – the hinged clapper board, retains its key iconography and remains an important feature at the start of the digital film production process. The original 'clapper' was invented by F. W. Thring in the 1920s and consisted of two pieces of wood hinged at one end. This tool was evolved into the clap*board* by Leon M. Leon whereby the clapper was fixed to a slate on which key information could be marked with chalk as a visual on-film reference, marking the beginning of the shot with scene and take number, to be easily identified and located by the editor. This ritualistic process ensures that all shots can be matched and located via time code, the visible clapper board on the first (or last frame if 'end-boarded') serves as a reassuring visual signifier for the editor. It is redundant in the digital process, since this information can now be carried digitally on the camera and audio streams and, as was the case in *Ginger & Rosa*, the separate video and audio streams were 'jam-synced'[1]. However, Potter would very often 'end board' filmed sequences – which is the instruction to hold the board in an upside-down position at the end of the shot. The frequency of this instruction on the set of *Ginger & Rosa* is indicative of the fluidity and responsive approach to filming in this particular context, intuitively taking opportunities to capture unexpected moments of additional action and reaction. Although *Ginger & Rosa* used a traditional acrylic slate, in contemporary productions this is now very often replaced by a digital version, which can wirelessly receive and visually display time code from an audio recorder and further data entry methods to synchronise the auditory and visual elements after digitisation. The Arri Alexa – the camera used for filming *Ginger & Rosa* – had the ability to transmit the time code to the Clockit app or a TC Slate. Blain Brown explains this persistently common preference to retain the earlier non-digital versions:

> Although there are several software solutions available that can synchronize audio [. . .] nearly all professional productions use a time code slate and also use the clapper for sync. Some productions shot on film and even some digital productions still use only the traditional clapboard. (Brown, 2015: 264)

At the end of a scene, 'cut' is called, usually by the Director, and then, echoed by the Assistant Director, used to imply the cutting of the film, later reflected in the editing phase. The language used during the on-set process reveals a continuation of the discreet lexicon of terms centred around the use of a cine camera.

Production hardware

Within the production phase, the camera and sound hardware are the most visible, recognisable and iconographic aspects of the filmmaking process. They are also, as described above, the locus of the resultant workflow, languages and behaviours on-set. The Director of Photography described the moment when the choice to shoot on the Arri Alexa was made:

> We shot a test on film, 16mm, Alexa and Red Camera and the Cannon 5D and we looked at them all in the cinema and we all actually came out of it, me, Sally and the producers saying 'Yeah, film's the nicest' and then the producer said, 'No it's not'. I said, 'It isn't?' 'Yeah, but it's not really is it?' I'm going, 'Well – I knew I was on a losing battle and to be fair the Alexa was proven to be very up to the job.'[2]

This testimony illuminates one of the many 'transitional tensions' – the rub between film and digital – that occurred during the making of the film. In this particular instance, it appeared to manifest as a tension between the creative desires of the artistic team and the economic imperatives of the Producer. In addition to the Director of Photography, other members of the camera team expressed their preference to be working on the film format:

> I just prefer to work in film, but it's harder to get the opportunity these days, I think. A lot of the work I've done, a majority of the work I've done, has been

digital. Because I came into the industry around that time. Nowadays very rarely would I get called on anything that's shot in film. It would be mostly digital.[3]

Ginger & Rosa was one of the first UK feature films to be shot on the Alexa camera, which first launched in 2010. Bordwell and Thompson stated: 'The design *(of a professional digital motion picture camera)* reflects manufacturer's effort to make the new device feel familiar to cinematographers' (2013: 13). This is certainly the case in the Alexa's physical manifestation and expression: the camera emulates a film camera (see Figure 4.1) and as Arri themselves describe their camera:

> ALEXA is a 35 format film-style digital camera made by Arri, the world leader in professional cinematographic imaging. It combines leading edge digital technology with film camera features that have been refined over more than 90 years of Arri's history. The result is a camera that allows cinematographers with a film background to shoot digitally without the need for expensive training. (Arri, 2011: 12)

As pictured in Figure 4.1, the camera is encumbered with a number of analogue prostheses. The body of the camera unit is relatively small in dimension at 329mm long, 157.8mm wide and 152.9mm deep. To all intents and purposes it is a computer dedicated to recording and image processing, with software, firmware, IP address, a wireless network adapter to connect the camera to a network, and an Ethernet port for connecting and syncing the camera. The size of the camera unit is significantly increased through the addition of a large battery pack, a monitor, a lens and the additional rods and bridge to support its weight, an electronic viewfinder, a matte box, follow focus unit and shoulder pad. With the addition of all these elements, the handling of the camera remains the same as if it were a film camera. Celluloid operational activities are also mimicked: memory cards need to be loaded and attached to the camera in a similar mode to a film magazine being loaded. Indeed, when they are, the camera's internal menu includes a 'Next *Reel* Count' setting which incrementally increases in units of one every time a new memory card is inserted.

Through a delineation of key historical moments in cinema history, it is clear to see how the industrial proprietary nature of film technology and software have led to rigid film-based processes and protocols, which inhibit any deviation from established and accepted industry norms and conventions. Allen reflects on the historical dimensions of the proprietary nature of film equipment: 'An array of film gauges and variance in the number of perforations prevented interchangeability among different cameras until 1923' (1980: 31). Similarly, Decherney notes how: '. . . technical differences kept early movie companies from using each other's

Figure 4.1 Robbie Ryan, *Ginger & Rosa*'s hyphenate Director of Photography–Camera Operator, with the Arri Alexa Digital Cinema Camera. (Photographer – Nicola Dove © Adventure Pictures Ltd)

films and equipment. Film gauges and sprocket holes, in particular, varied widely from company to company' (2012: 203). With the Arri Alexa, along with other digital cinema cameras, we see history repeating itself in the adoption of specific proprietary compressions or 'codecs' which are dependent on the camera manufacturer and the relationships that they have with different software companies. For example, the Arri Alexa can *only* record onto Sony SxS PRO memory cards using the Apple Quick-Time ProRes codec (in the case of *Ginger & Rosa*, this was the Apple ProRes 4444 codec – this is the highest data rate possible and is suited to cinema applications.)[4] QuickTime Files are assigned the .mov[5] file extension; 'mov' is an abbreviation of movie, what Murray would refer to as a 'legacy media format' (2012: 5). These languages persist throughout film and cinema discourse, where chosen semantics reveal their reference to the past: going to the cinema is often referred to as a 'movie', short for 'moving picture', which is the descriptive noun given to account for the illusion of movement conveyed in early film technologies to the film strip. It is one of many references ported to the digital form as a reference to the industrial and technological inventions of cinema history. Other film metaphors and analogies embedded into the camera include reference to 'reel' and 'clip,' 'sound roll' or 'tape,' and 'scrubbing' which refers to the physical movement of tape reels to locate a specific point, so called because the activity felt as if the tape was being physically cleaned or 'scrubbed.'

In a further proprietary measure, the Alexa also has its own 'PL' ('Positive Lock') lens mount, upon which any modern PL lens mount can be used, but not older Arri lenses. The Alexa also has a number of additional proprietary 'licensed features' that can be accessed through the purchase and installation of additional license keys. These are linked to the camera via its unique serial number and cannot be ported to other cameras. These features include: 'High Speed mode' which extends the frame rate range of the camera up to 120 FPS, and 'anamorphic desqueeze.'[6]

In addition to the external controls and switches on the camera's body, there is an on-board menu system which enables access to various functions and settings. One such setting includes the 'Production Info Menu' screen, which is comprised of the following fields: Director, Cinematographer, Location, Production, User Info 1 and User Info 2. Given the memory capacity of the storage and the minimal space needed for text-based information, there is limited opportunity to add-in detailed information. The potential for the addition of detailed metadata pertaining to continuity information and other production notes has been discussed in Chapter 3, but this feature here highlights the proprietary limitations which were deliberately programmed into the camera at the time. These are all clearly market-driven features, designed and embedded to meet economic imperatives and commercial drivers.

In its output, the camera is also designed to emulate filmic qualities. *Ginger & Rosa* was shot in what is known as Log-C mode which exploits the full range of the camera chip's sensitivity in order to attain a 35mm 'cinema quality' image, which is the mode used to prepare images 'for output to film material or DI-like treatment'[7] (Arri, 2011: 63). It captures an image with the widest tonal range ensuring the greatest scope and flexibility for post-production manipulations, in other words, it will enable the 'film look' which as Sim describes is 'accepted parlance in digital acquisition work, technical manuals, and marketing material for digital cameras' (2012: 93). For its management, processing and reproduction of colour, the Alexa uses the 'Bayer Pattern Color Filter Array',[8] one of the DITs who I interviewed explains the significance of this:

> 'The chip, as it's designed, was invented by Kodak, and the chip was invented to simulate a LOG curve or a *Cineon* curve, which was invented to simulate the response of film in celluloid, so once we move away from having to emulate the chromatic response of silver halide in celluloid, we'll be able to get to a new technology epoch with digital cinema. Right now, I feel digital cameras are limited because they're holding onto film so much, the Bayer pattern sensor has inherent characteristics that try to emulate film, and once digital frees itself from film altogether, then we'll really have a new dimensionality to play with. [. . .] Within the next 5–10yrs, we'll probably see chips that are entirely new and don't rely on the Bayer pattern filter array.'[9]

As Chapter 3 highlighted in the long-abiding film-based colour grading conventions which persist in digital practice: 'In the rush to describe how digital technologies are changing film form, the case of colour grading reminds us to view them against a historical background that emphasises continuities, ancestry and the enduring sway of craft forms' (Higgins 2003: 75). We see these ancestral continuities enduring but also seemingly imprinting and imposing limitations on technologies that are not innate. Here we can apply what Hadjioannou has described as the 'digitographic' in an attempt to capture and frame this inherent dualism and transitional tension:

> . . .from a clearly technical basis, celluloid cinema *is a photochemical means of recording and projecting images that are both analogous to the material relations of the original source and are transcribed directly as material traces onto the filmstrip.* Digital cinema, on the other hand, *is a means of registering images as binary relations and algorithmic calculations, which are rendered in graphically visual images by a computer to be humanly perceptible.* It is in this sense that one can term digital images more accurately 'digitographic'. (Hadjioannou 2012: 29, original emphasis)

The digitographic is also invoked in Arri's description of the computational capabilities of the camera's sensor in terms of its data capacity,
whilst simultaneously expressing its filmic aesthetic capabilities: 'The
ALEV III sensor has a horizontal pixel count of 3.5K resulting in true
2K resolution. It covers the full Super-35 format and it provides a lati-
tude of 14 stops and a base sensitivity of 800 ASA' (Arri, 2011: 12). The
digitographic concept can be further extended to the *data*graphic, in order
to account for the capabilities and possibilities of simultaneous data and
metadata creation and output of the camera – the Alexa outputs an XML
file within which metadata can be recorded, but as noted, its capabilities
are not fully exploited by the camera and in this production.

In her observations of the differences between shooting on film and
shooting on digital, Potter expresses a medium-agnosticism:

> I think the differences are rather exaggerated. In fact, it's the moving image. We're
> recording live events with a medium that picks up sound and picture. It's digital
> instead of analog. I think one can fetishize it. It does have some individual quali-
> ties, but the other day I was in New York talking with Edward Lachman, one of the
> great DPs. We were talking about the look of the film, and after a while he said to
> me, 'It's so good you shot on film. You could never have got this.' So I said, 'This
> was the Alexa.' And he said, 'The Alexa? My god!'[10]

Here we can see the perceived aesthetic differences between film and digital diminishing, but to a point of reaching a hybrid status as opposed to
a pure-digital/pure-celluloid status, where it can neither be consigned to
one or the other. Potter expresses this:

> A lot of the distinctions, the visual qualities, are really very subtle now, and you
> can do a lot. Not to make it look like *fake film*, but to get from the digitally gener-
> ated image the velvety softness or the deep, velvety blacks or something that you
> *associate with film stock*. You can achieve this digitally if you work in the right way
> in post. It's like working in a darkroom or Photoshopping. It's a continuation of the
> process of the work on the image. (emphasis added)[11]

It is this notion of a nuanced distinction between a 'fake film' and an
'authentic' one, which is intriguing. Ryan explains how they attempted to
achieve the fidelity of celluloid film:

> When I was shooting on film I used Panavision cameras and Panavision lenses
> called Primos. That was a marriage made in heaven in my book because everything
> I shot [. . .] I always fell in love with so I thought, 'All right. Let's do this on this
> Alexa'. We will go with the same lenses and we will shoot it on a digital sensor
> instead of a film negative, but they just were unfortunately too sharp. The sensor

sees it differently than film did and they just jumped a bit, like they are too sharp so what you find out is a lot of camera companies are dusting off all their old lenses, as many as they can find and re-sort of housing them a bit and re-jigging them and calling them vintage because all the lenses aren't as high resolution lenses as the newer ones and they actually work better with the digital sensor [. . .] That's why the net came in because the net helps soften that.[12]

Here, Ryan refers to the use of alternate lenses but also to the netting that was applied to the lenses in order to soften the perceived hardness of the digital image produced by the Alexa in order to subdue the images digitality. This distinctive and discreet patina specific to *Ginger & Rosa* is evidenced in the softer, smokier, grainier look of the finished film. Here, both the film's aura, and the film camera's 'aesthetic imprint' (Sim 2012: 96) are visually cohered. As Flaxton describes 'to get a *look* from a clinically clean medium you have to distress the image and therefore lose data, and as we've established, DPs really do not want to distress an image that is already distressed by being compressed' (Original emphasis, 2011: 118). These claims are in spite of Arri's own assurance that: 'Arri imaging technology ensures the most organic, film-like image quality of any digital camera with natural color rendition and pleasing skin tones' (Arri, 2011: 13).

Achieving 'the look' is embedded into the functionality of the Arri Alexa. As the accompanying manual describes: 'Look files are a way for the user to influence the color appearance of the camera. A look file alters the way the sensor image is converted to video color space' (Arri, 2012: 62). These files are accessed through a 'SET LOOK' command, in which a number of presets can be accessed (and also programmed in). These include 'Day4Night', where a blue hue is applied to the image (see discussions in Chapter 3, page 14 for the historic precursor to this established colour convention).

As indicated at the start of the extensive discussions about the camera, the sound hardware is also very visible, recognisable and its presence is felt as a key aspect of the filmmaking process (see Figure 4.2 which shows Jean-Paul Mugel, the Production Sound Mixer, and his complex sound rig, coupled with the highly visible presence of a boom operator). The sound department used a ten-track recorder with a range of boom and radio microphones. The audio interface (analogue mixing desk, microphones) remain identical in their interface design, and all the practices remain the same. The only distinction is that, instead of the sound being output to tape, it is captured as a digital format. During the making of *Ginger & Rosa*, all location dialogue and sound was recorded on location, despite most of it being unusable in the edit due to a confluence of extraneous noise which infiltrated every scene – shot mostly on location

Figure 4.2 Jean Paul Mugel, Sound Department, on location with a multi-track mixer. (Photographer – Nicola Dove © Adventure Pictures Ltd)

in London, where the sounds of sirens, trains, planes and modern-day traffic were sonically inescapable. Sound-recording technologies have not yet become so advanced to be able to differentiate between and to eradicate very specific frequencies. The sound track was latterly built up through the use of ADR and Foley (as detailed in Chapter 3).

Post-production hardware

All Post-production processes in *Ginger & Rosa* were conducted on computers using specialist software packages including *Avid*, *ProTools* and *Flame* (with the exception of the film laboratory processes in preparation for distribution.)

In interviews, the Edit Assistant, the Editor and Post-production Supervisor all continually referred to the location of the offline editing as 'the cutting room'.

However, in addition to the software, there are a number of haptic interfaces – hardware that can be plugged in that interacts with midi-interfaces which enable the physical manipulation of these controls through a mate-rial interface. These enabled the software to be controlled in a more physi-cal way, augmenting the operator's experience beyond using a series of keyboard shortcuts and mouse clicks. These include the colour graders' interface, to manipulate both audio and visual levels. The physical inter-faces of the post-production tools are also emulated within the software using graphical representations of what were physical pieces of hardware. These are haptic in their design and include the visual representation of 'legacy conventions' (Murray, 2012: 5), such as nobs, buttons, switches, dials and faders (see Figures 4.3 and 4.4). As Caldwell comments, these are indicative of '. . . the profound ways that aesthetic convention and theoretical articulations had been *industrially* hard-wired into the inter-face designs of basic production machines that I had used or been around (video switchers, DFX workstations, nonlinear editing systems etc.)' (Caldwell quoted in Vonderau 2013: 19).

In the same way as Dan North has claimed, it is 'those very photochem-ical idiosyncrasies which gave the photographic image its claim to verity'

Figure 4.3 Audio Mixing Interface in Avid. (Avid Media Composer Software – Interplay Edition 7.0.3)

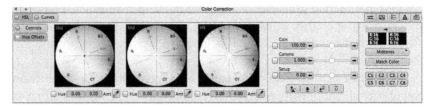

Figure 4.4 Colour correction controls in Avid. (Avid Media Composer Software – Interplay Edition 7.0.3)

(2008: 22), these 'legacy conventions' provide hardware and software with authenticity and eminence. I extend Murray's notion of 'legacy processes' (Murray, 2012: 299) to account for the resultant 'legacy aesthetics' and 'legacy emulations' which are enshrined and embedded into the software interface, to 'legacy behaviours' – the embodied and enacted responses by production personnel seen in the previous accounts of on-set protocols.

Through an examination of pre, production and post-production softwares – taking a 'Software Studies perspective' (Manovich 2013: 205, Wood: 2014), further understandings of the politics of production can be gleaned which had been hitherto overlooked or ignored.

Pre-production software

Within the pre-production phase of *Ginger & Rosa* a number of very established industry-standard softwares were used. These include the screenwriting and formatting software 'Final Draft', and the Scheduling and Budgeting software 'MovieMagic'. *Final Draft* is a specialist script-formatting software[13] and was used in all stages of the scriptwriting and redrafting processes. The script was regularly outputted on paper for distribution amongst the relevant Heads of Departments, reflecting the blended data/paper approach endemic to many aspects of the production process of *Ginger & Rosa*. The scripts were re-issued on different coloured papers to indicate the latest version numbers to those working on-set. *Final Draft* was first developed in 1991,[14] by Ben Cahan and Marc Madnick, in direct response to there being no 'word-processor capable of automatically formatting a script to Hollywood's stringent standards'.[15] *Final Draft* provides this formatting functionality governed by the codes and conventions of Hollywood's script formatting which have remained in place to the present day. According to The Black List's Script Standards Guide:

> All scripts should be written in Courier 12 pt. font. This standardized font size allows executives to estimate the length of the film based on the length of the script. It is no exaggeration to say that 99% of studio executives will NOT read a spec script that is written in a different font.[16]

Another scriptwriting industry source stated: 'If you ever want somebody in the film industry to read your story and seriously consider transforming it into a movie then there are a few rules you need to adhere to. Principally format'[17] – thus illuminating the dominance of Hollywood apparatus in the dictation of these expectations. Scriptwriting software programmes '. . . encouraged new writers to standardize format by learning the lessons taught by the software's default settings' (Hoxter, 2014: 123). Both the computer interface and the output paper format emulate the aesthetics of their analogue progenitors – Courier font emulates the native font of a typewriter. Millard explains the technologically deterministic reason behind this:

> One of the reasons that Courier was able to migrate successfully from the typewriter to the first personal computers in the 1980s was that it did not require much memory. This is because Courier is a fixed pitch font, in which every character has the same width, and therefore requires no kerning. Although perhaps even more important to note is that the packaging of Courier with the first PCs ensured that users would be able to replicate typewriter-looking documents, enabling a smooth transition to the new era of word processing and personal computing. (2010: 16)

And Hoxter accounts for the production-based reasoning:

> Final Draft even developed its own font, 'Courier Final Draft,' to resolve spacing problems with the digital version of Courier and with Courier New (released with Windows 3.1). This spacing fix helped to guarantee that the old Hollywood equation, in which one minute of screen time corresponds to a single screenplay page, would continue into the digital era. (2014: 123)

Here we see a return to the temporal invocations of filmmaking as examined in the preceding Chapter, and how the temporal imperatives of economics and planning are embedded into production apparatus and dictate work behaviours and workflow patterns.

Also notable is the integration of *Final Draft* into a standardised and universal film production workflow. The export functionality was introduced in 2002 when *Final Draft 6* was released, and enabled the file export of the script into the scheduling and budgeting software, *Movie Magic*.[18] An fdx file is exported, which can be imported into *Movie Magic* Scheduling and Budgeting, as long as the scenes in the script each start with a Scene Heading Element and scene numbers are included. Correct formatting is once again paramount, this time for functionality.

The scheduling process takes the script and 'breaks' it down (see Chapter 3, page 72 for a full explication). It is essentially a process of extraction where all elements and their requirements – cast, props, locations – are identified so that essential planning decisions can be made and enacted. The analogue tool for this process is pictured in Figure 4.5,

Figure 4.5 A production board, with moveable and interchangeable paper-based scheduling strips. In this example these are colour-coded to indicate the time-of-day. Blue indicates a night interior, white a day interior, green a night exterior and pink a sunrise exterior. (Author's own image)

referred to as a production board, strip board or production strip. These were originally physical artefacts that enabled the movement and reordering of scene information, as strips of paper, across the duration of a production shoot. The software emulates this in a graphical representation of the strips, and 'works the way schedulers think'.[19] The 'strips' that are seen in the software emulate the paper-based system of organising strips.

Figure 4.6 illustrates the proximity of visual style and functional convention to the original physical production boards, even though a grid calendar system could potentially be more efficient. These lead to the production of call sheets – the format and information of which has changed very little since they were first established in 1949.[20] Digital call sheets also similarly follow the same proforma designs as their typewritten progenitors.

WEEK 7

74	74	INT	POLICE CELL	NIGHT	3/8	pgs.	1, 24
			Ginger sits mute in small police cell.				
75	75	INT	POLICE CELL	DAY	7/8	pgs.	1, 15
			Police doctor tries to get Ginger to communicate but she remains mi				
76	76	INT	POLICE STATION	DAY	1 2/8	pgs.	1, 5, 6, 8, 15
			Marks and Bella collect Ginger from Police station. Police doctor sug				

--- END OF DAY 31 -- Monday, September 26, 2011 -- 2 4/8 pgs.

81	81	INT	HOSPITAL WAITING AREA	DAY	4/8	pgs.	1, 3
			Ginger and Roland wait for news.				
1	1	INT	HOSPITAL	DAY	4/8	pgs.	4, 7
			Natalie and Anoushka give birth.				
85	85	INT	REGISTRY OFFICE	DAY	2/8	pgs.	5, 6
			Back-views of Mark and Mark in front of the registrar.				

--- END OF DAY 32 -- Tuesday, September 27, 2011 -- 1 2/8 pgs.

47	47	INT	ROLAND'S ROOM	DAY	1 5/8	pgs.	1, 3
			Ginger asks Roland if she can live with him				
84	84	INT	NATALIE'S BEDROOM	DAY	6/8	pgs.	1, 3, 4
			Natalie and Ginger duet on the piano and 'start from the beginning.'				
78	78	INT	LANDING OUTSIDE NATALIE'S BEDROOM	DAY	2/8	pgs.	1, 5
			Ginger and Mark are trying to open the bedroom door. Natalie has lo				
80	80	INT	LANDING OUTSIDE NATALIE'S BEDROOM	DAY	4/8	pgs.	1, 2, 3, 4
			Roland smashes the door down as Natalie attempts to overdose.				

--- END OF DAY 33 -- Wednesday, September 28, 2011 -- 3 1/8 pgs.

77A	77A	INT	NATALIE'S KITCHEN	DAY	5	pgs.	1, 2, 3, 4, 5, 6, 7, 8
			Ginger breaks her silence and the truth about Roland, Rosa, and Na				

--- END OF DAY 34 -- Thursday, September 29, 2011 -- 5 pgs.

77B	77B	INT	NATALIE'S KITCHEN	DAY	5 3/8	pgs.	1, 2, 3, 4, 5, 6, 7, 8
			Ginger breaks her silence and the truth about Roland, Rosa, and Na				
79	79	INT	NATALIE'S KITCHEN	DAY	1/8	pgs.	1, 2, 3, 6, 7, 8
			Ginger rushes into the kitchen to get help				

--- END OF DAY 35 -- Friday, September 30, 2011 -- 5 4/8 pgs.

END OF SHOOT

2	2	EXT	ARCHIVE FOOTAGE	DAY	2/8	pgs.	
			Details of a nuclear explosions as buildings - inc hospital and house				
3	3	EXT	ARCHIVE FOOTAGE	DAY	2/8	pgs.	
			Images of the first Soviet nuclear test and public celebrations in Red				
9	9		FRONT TITLES			pgs.	
			Front Titles: Bomb etc.				
10A	10A	EXT	ARCHIVE FOOTAGE	DAY	1/8	pgs.	
			Kruschev watching a military parade in Moscow				

Figure 4.6 The digital version of scheduling strips output from the MovieMagic Scheduling Software. It adapts its own colour convention based on those established by the original production boards. (Adventure Pictures © Adventure Pictures Ltd)

Production software

There is no such software that is explicitly assigned or used in the production process, rather there is a continuation and crossover of software used in both pre-production and post-production within this phase. In addition, hybrid practices ran throughout the production of *Ginger & Rosa*, as my field work evidenced – paper, pens and clipboards have routinely been considered the most reliable tools across most of the departments to augment documents that are output by the software. More recently, a number of production management 'apps'[21] have been developed and released for use on-set via mobile devices. There has been a reluctance to use these previously, because of the limitations of the battery life of such devices. There were no such apps used within the production of *Ginger & Rosa* (aside from mobile phones which were used on-set for production office person-to-person communications, as well as iPads' camera function for filming stunt rehearsals, and by the art department for documentation purposes) – a hybrid digital/paper-based system was used throughout. Asked whether they would consider using a digital on-set production management system, they stated that they would not, because of the risk of not having enough battery power on locations where charging-up portable tablet or smartphone devices may not always be feasible. One crew member, the Set Decorator, expressed a frustration with the level and complexity of the paperwork:

> We have a thing called Order Pads, which I have to say in this digital age, if there's a budding entrepreneur out there this is the perfect thing to make your millions because we have something that's in triplicate, quadruplicate, and quintuplicate! [. . .] Every single item, whether it's a pencil or we've bought a load of furniture, has to have an order assigned to it or some petty cash receipts.[22]

Post-production software

Perhaps the most visible symbolic vestiges of photochemical workflow can be seen within the post-production phase, both within the software that is used to manipulate the data which has been shot, as well as in the terminology and phraseology of post-production parlance. Digital post-production processes are well established and have been in use for a long time, as Potter stated:

> I think the digital post-production process is something I've been used to now in quite a lot of films, even when they were shot on film. So that's not really new anymore, and I love it. I love the digital grading, the post-production work you can do, the transformations you can make, the corrections you can make in the image, so many things you can do with the image, and, of course, the [audio] mix is more flexible, working digitally, you're not doing a final, live mix that you have to erase and start again. That's a long time ago now, but that's how it was with *Orlando*, for example.[23]

In effect, these new affordances that Potter describes are not specific to the digital, as Janet Harbord observes, these phenomena are part of a continuum of cinematic practice:

> What we may consider a contemporary form of manipulation as digital production has developed out of prior forms of image play that extend as far back as Eisenstein – editing, montage and appropriation – traditions in which filmic images have been 'dressed', touched up and processed through practices that were not singled out as special effects but were part of the *craft* of film. (Harbord, 2002: 140, emphasis added)

The 'Digital Intermediary' is now a well-established transitionary process which bridges the film-to-data workflow: to take a digital copy of the film in order to work on and manipulate it, and then to place it back on the film for distribution and exhibition. As Julie Turnock explains:

> The digital intermediate (or DI), initially conceived in the late-1990s to replace photochemical color timing, has developed into a tool to smooth out differences among material generated in different platforms, such as different kinds of capture (digital or film) in the principal photography, the work submitted by various unaffiliated effects houses, digital matte paintings, the 3D conversion, and so forth. Artists digitally scan the final 'cut,' adjust the colors, attune the lighting effects, smooth the edges, and overall, homogenize the picture plane. [. . .] DI accounts for the velvety, almost airbrushed look in so many recent films. (2013: 46)

Ginger & Rosa, like many productions, was edited using the Non-Linear Editing (NLE) software package, Avid Media Composer[24] which is widely considered to be the industry-standard package. It enables the organisation of media (the name given to cover all formats of video, film, images, audio), editing, the application of basic effects via filters and transitions, grading, audio mixing and sound design. In 2012, the version in use was version 6, so all of the following observations are relevant to that particular version.

It is within this software package that many opportunities to inscribe, embed and imbue analogue mediality are afforded, from the visual grammar of the interface design to the manipulations that can be made to the footage. In the same way it has been noted that pure CGI productions can insert the mechanical qualities of the camera, and the lenticular effects of light on glass lenses, photorealistic effects, depth of field emulation manifest as visual 'skeumorphs'[25]. Analogue-filmic skeumorphs are present throughout both the physical and digital spaces of digital film post-production. In this instance, the software becomes a simulational space, in which the analogue apparatus and analogue conditions of production are emulated: these include virtual lenses, panning and zooming, adding filters that simulate the material texture of film, as Wendy Chun has contended: 'Our digital interfaces are an analogy to an analogy' (2011: 75).

William Brown has argued 'digital cinema deliberately looks like analogue cinema, in an inverse manner of certain strands of analogue cinema that tried to deny their analogue nature (as per the example of *Rope*). But where analogue cinema could never quite transcend its own limitations, digital cinema only *pretends* to have them' (2013: 10, emphasis added).

It has been proposed that these approaches and aesthetics have manifested due to an emotional resistance to new technology and an affective, romanticised attachment to the old. Stephen Prince anticipates the loss of particular viewing pleasures:

> On the shiny, silver DVD disk they are all that remain of cinema as a material medium, reminders of the mediums' physical state in its pre-millennial form. To those of us who loved the medium in this incarnation, let's celebrate the dirt, the scratches, the grain, greet them as old friends when we encounter them on DVD. In the clean, crystal-clear, and diamond-sharp world of digital video, they are the ghostly traces of former love, artefacts of the stuff that dreams once were made of. (2004: 33)

What is notable in many studies of digital film is that the infusion of analogue signifiers is becoming a preferred, and sought-after aesthetic through the visualisation of image artefacts denoting analogue presence. As Laura Marks observes '. . . artists are importing images of electronic drop-out and decay, "TV snow" and the random colors of unrecorded tape, in a sort of longing for analog physicality' (2002: 153). Nicholas Rombes has also noted: '*Planet Terror* and *Death Proof* reflect upon the physical *experience* of going to movies and the humanising elements of the 'mistakes' that characterised that experience' (original emphasis, Rombes, 2009: 4).

> Among digital video makers, one of the manifestations of the desire for indexicality is what I call analog nostalgia, a retrospective fondness for the 'problems' of decay and generational loss that analog video posed. (Marks, 2002: 152)

What is far less noted is any evidence of digital deterioration or digital glitches, which would normally manifest in frame 'drop-out', or 'dropped frames'. These can often be caused through a disparity in settings between the sensor frame rate and the record frame rate on the camera. These are hidden, not celebrated in the same way as analogue deterioration. The joins and ruptures in digital film material – these are all about gaps – the 'invisibility of the interstices' (Small and Levinson 1989) and loss ('Lossy compression' is the name given to the image deterioration and degradation caused by a lower grade compression process). This is in contrast to the naturally occurring faults of celluloid film which are considered to be additive and augmenting (the visibility of scratches, dirt and flicker).

An example of this visual 'value' can be seen in the 'Film Grain' effects filters that can be applied to digital footage in Avid, in order to render the image 'old', 'filmic' and authentic. In these cases the software is used to impose semiotics of substandard analogue quality. In the Avid interface itself, there are a core number of graphical representations which translate

Figure 4.7 The Effects Filters available in Avid include 'Film Grain'.
(Avid Media Composer Software – Interplay Edition 7.0.3)

prior analogue processes into digital representations, in a form of computational mimesis of a physical editing environment. In Avid, as noted in the section above, hardware is emulated in the software through the use of graphical and visual representation, in addition, the overall interface design simulates the physical workspace of an editor's workstation. The editor is faced with two adjacent screen monitors, one showing the source material through which to navigate and view footage, and to select clips, and the record monitor, through which the subsequent assembly of clips can be viewed. Non-linear editing is effectively non-destructive in the way that the original source material is not cut, changed or manipulated. Rather, the edit system makes reference to sections of this core footage and applies filters over it; these create new digital files, or new 'rendered' forms of digital files. But a language still persists which suggests the destruction or permanent changes to the materials, including 'overwrite.'

At the foot of the editing screen interface is a graphical depiction of a timeline and multitrack editor, where video and sound tracks are separated out into channels, and material is 'laid' and worked in independently using synching tools. The software makes use of terms such as 'Channels' and 'Tracks' to describe the different compositional layers, a nomenclature which clearly refers back to their analogue predecessors. Graphical representations of audio and video waveforms can be made visible on these tracks – a visual indicator of the shape and form of a signal.

The interface also includes a media organisation tool, with which media files can be organised and separated out into multiple 'bins'. Bins are the name given to the folders or directories which are created to

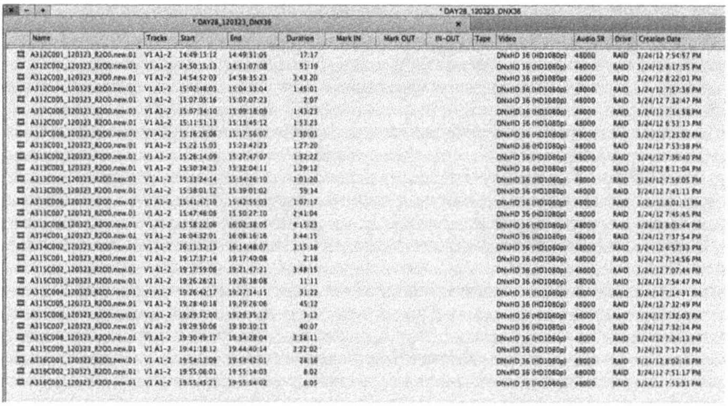

Figure 4.8 Inside an Avid 'bin', clips of footage are signified by a small pictogram of a single square frame of film strip. (Avid Media Composer Software – Interplay Edition 7.0.3)

organise all of the clips into a meaningful order for the editor, i.e. into dailies (to indicate the storage of a day's worth of material) and/or into scene numbers. The term 'bin,' a seeming misnomer, it refers to the cloth sacks in which photochemical film was once hung.

Avid facilitates hybrid digital/analogue approaches to work in its interface design. As the Assistant Editor highlights, when he talks through the manual process of inputting handwritten information and then subsequently linking it up to its digital source:

> I'll add information saying stuff like scene number, description of what is this actually happening. Then if there's any remarks and continuity comments and lens indication. This is all information for the editor. This would also be all the information that would have been on the continuity sheets. There's a continuity person on the set taking notes on what did they actually do and where is it meant to go in the film. The [continuity sheets] come with the rushes.[26]

The Assistant Editor here describes a hybrid process which amalgamates data production – i.e. the recording, capture and manipulation of purely digital data – with the analogue recording of metadata – the use of pen and paper to create handwritten notes, which are later transcribed and input into the Avid edit system.

In the Avid command palette (Figure 4.9), there are a number of buttons with icons which enact various different commands. These buttons can be assigned to different areas of the interface by the operator. Peppered with instances of extant analogue terminology, many of these commands denote analogue editing functions such as to 'splice' – the term given to

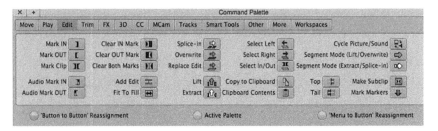

Figure 4.9 The Avid Command palette shows the different commands that can be triggered by pressing the appropriate button. (Avid Media Composer Software – Interplay Edition 7.0.3)

describe a physical join between two consecutive pieces of film. There was a tool known as a film splicer (or – mainly in Europe – film joiner),which was used precisely for this purpose. There are many other film-based ana-logue analogies and controls that are clearly not endogenous or germane to the digital software itself. These are deliberately written, and designed, into the software. 'Computers, like other media, are metaphor machines: they both depend on and perpetuate metaphors' (Chun, 2011: 55). These include 'Add Edit', 'Make subclip' and 'Freeze frame', commands that are all represented by the icon of a sprocketed piece of film. As Morgan Fisher proclaims: 'Film's material base is inseparable from our under-standing of it. That's why sprocket holes, even more than frames, are the universal emblem of film' (in Cullinan 2012: 70).

There are other micro tactical instances of celluloid iconography which may not be so obvious to the untrained eye. For example, placing an effect on one of the clips on the tracks creates a visual diamond shape. We can deduce from Mary Ann Doane's account below, the origins of this choice of visual indicator. She explains:

> In the editing of optical tracks, it was discovered that the overlapped lines of a splice caused a sharp noise in the playback. The technique of 'blooping' was devel-oped to conceal what could only act as an irritating reminder that syntagmatic relationships are not 'found' or 'natural' but manufactured. Blooping is the process of painting or punching an opaque triangle or diamond-shaped area over a splice and results in a fast fade-in, fade-out effect. In the editing of magnetic film, it is paralleled by the practice of cutting on a diagonal. (1980: 50)

These diamonds and diagonals persist in the visual iconography that can be seen on the Avid multitrack interface – both audio fades and video cross-fades are signified by a diagonal line which appears across the cut. Other transitional effects between cuts are depicted with a diamond/box shape. Another term is 'key frames' – these are used in Avid to denote a frame where an action will begin – the start of an effect, like a fade. 'East-man Kodak introduced edge numbering on its negative film stock in 1919. Called 'key numbers', these increased serially by one digit at sixteen-frame intervals' (Fairservice 2001: 332). Other commands include to Trim (referred to the frames of film cut away by the editor) and to Gang (these refer to the slots on a physical film synchroniser through which multiple strips of film could be threaded and synchronised). As Lev Manovich observes:

> The simulation of analog video includes a set of navigation commands: play for-ward, play in reverse, fast forward, loop, etc. In short: *to simulate a medium in software means to simulate its tools and interfaces, rather than its 'material'*. (2013: 199–200, original emphasis)

In the transport controls, further incongruous inferences to the physical manipulation of the media are made, for example: 'shuttle', 'jog', 'slip', 'ripple' and 'trim', all refer to the movement control of physical media through machinery. Again, making a 'semiotic connection' (Murray, 2012: 107) to previous practices and processes.

> The unfamiliar efficiency of the digital medium has led to the creation of vir-tual tools that precisely simulate the effects produced by the inefficiency of analog tools: the smudge tool in Photoshop, for example, does just that, allowing the user to partially eradicate and blend part of an image. It is iconized by a finger, and modified by setting the level of pressure with which the area is smudged. [. . .] Smudge tools and pressure-sensitive styluses are necessary because human beings crave analog effects produced by analog means. (Murray, 2012: 299–300)

These instances could be assigned to the realm of the 'homage' in the way that Lisa Purse has described:

> The prospect of end-to-end digital film production has prompted a nostalgic return to cinema's celluloid history, most explicitly through homage. Digital imag-ing technologies have been used to simulate earlier pre-digital cinema technologies and practices in various homages . . .' (2013: 3).

Furthermore, these examples embedded in the sign-system of Avid are all indicative of the past influencing present and future practices. Conversely, the impact and influence of digital editing software capabilities influencing contemporary film aesthetics has also been examined. Aylish Wood (2007:76) makes one such observation with regard to her analysis of the use of the split-screen function in Ang Lee's *Hulk*. She proposes that it is the use of *Avid* that is the key influence in the resultant aesthetics of the film. It is the possibilities that are afforded by the effects palette within the edit system, that enable a different stylistic to be applied – in this case –the multiple-split-screen. Similarly, Keith Griffiths has also noted the emergence of an 'Avid aesthetic':

> . . . the directors of *Pi* (Aronofsky, USA, 1998) and *Run Lola Run* (Tyker, Germany, 1998) seized upon the use of digital post-production technology to create a fast and frantic 'Avid aesthetic' that co-opts the old suits of the avant-garde merely to tailor more designer-wear mainstream narratives. (2003: 19)

It is this inherent reflexivity of the form around digital (in relation to Japanese film) – that Lee refers to as 'the visibility of the cinematic interstices in many contemporary Japanese films becomes a citation of cinema, laying bare the medium' (2013: 1).

These examples which illustrate the duality of Avid as a simultaneous carrier of established and traditional industry convention, whilst also providing a space to experiment and advance new aesthetics, exemplify Richard Grusin's observation of 'a digital cinema' as 'not [..] a distinctively new medium but as a hybrid network of media forms and practices, what I call a cinema of interactions' (2007: 210).

This conundrum is also captured in David Thorburn and Henry Jenkins' observation that:

> If emerging media are often experimental and self-reflexive, they are also inevitably and centrally imitative, rooted in the past, in the practices, formats, and deep assumptions of their predecessors. (2004: 7)

VFX Post-production

We have seen in both Ryan's and Potter's earlier accounts of concealing of the Alexa film camera's digitality, the paradoxical position in which the film both simultaneously celebrates whilst actively seeking to occlude the digital in process and practice. This paradoxical ethos is further extended through the use of practical techniques wherever possible in the film's production process. The Special Effects Supervisor explains the authenticity of these practical effects and the complex permissions process required to execute them:

> We had some practical cookers, gas cookers, and things like that to do. I'm actually just prepping to do a scene and we're just trying to find the right smoke fluid for health and safety for that area. Different areas, conservation areas, require different types of fluids.[27]

In *Ginger & Rosa*, there was a unique blend of practical craft-based and digital techniques. As examined in Chapter 3, in addition to practical effects, and 'real' locations, there were limited VFX, and these were all about 'fixing' issues and making corrections. The compositor, working on a 'Flame'[28] system, explains shots which required meticulous attention, and complex processes, in order to 'paint out' unwanted details which belied the time period of the filmic story world:

> It's this wire here – it's not supposed to be there because it's in the countryside house, so they wanted that taken away. As you take a good look at this, you'll notice that everything is moving in different parallax, so that's a lot of layers that has to be recreated in order to just remove the wire there. The film doesn't take place today, *I don't know when that's supposed to take place*, but I do know that when it did, you weren't supposed to have satellite dishes on your house. Again, you see all the cloth hanging out to dry that's so waving in the wind in front of it, you have light changes and things like that through the shot? Voilà, the dish is gone. Little stuff, little things like that all throughout the film.[29]

The VFX processes prioritised the erasure of any signs of digital life and culture in the desire for verisimilitude and authenticity, the eradication of evidence of the digital was made possible by digital means. These approaches all invoke Doane's claim that: 'All of these techniques are motivated by a desire to sever the film from its source, to hide the work of the production. They promote a sense of the effortlessness and ease of capturing the natural' (1980: 51), and Manovich's later assertion that: '. . . cinema works hard to erase any traces of its own production process, including any indication that the images that we see could have been constructed rather than simply recorded' (2010: 248).

Affective impacts

The design, architecture and possibilities of digital postproduction software clearly impacts upon the resultant aesthetics of the film, moreover it also results in the affective responses of the production personnel. There have been a number of accounts which express how the software impacts upon implicit behaviours and approaches to creative practice. In relation to Nonlinear editing software, Dylan Tichenor states: 'You just jump from point to point, and it changes the way your brain works a little bit. It's hard to teach rhythm and sensitivity' (in Chang, 2011: 65). Often, the use of software in editing is described within discourses of gameplay and the use of game analogies, including Babette Mangolte's observation: 'I see digital editing as checkers and film editing as chess. One needs a very long-term strategy before the first move while the other is reactive to one move' (2003: 267), and Mike Figgis' account of his own experiences of working with editors on digital systems: 'They're constantly moving their hand and trying things and dragging things out of bins and so on. And they get really good at it. It's like an addiction to computer games' (2007: 125).

Anders Refn talks through the differences between celluloid film editing and digital editing through a different metaphor:

> It's like riding the horse and carriage instead of driving a car. Just really, really very, very heavy and boring and long hours and this technique was so primitive was difficult to recut things also because it was expensive and you had to get new prints and so on. It was a lot of discussion before you did anything. Now you can just do a new version and then try it out what you want to do. I think it's a huge advantage. Of course to make a good film is basically the same problem hasn't changed at all. The only good thing about the analog way, working with it you have to have trained your visual memory because you had to really very carefully look through all the rushes and then know exactly where the good parts were, and of course that's so fundamental to my way of watching material.[30]

Refn's account captures the affective dichotomy implicit in so many of the accounts of those practitioners who were interviewed – the simultaneous appreciation of the efficiencies of digital processes whilst also harking back to the romanticisation of the original physical medium. The Unit Publicist captures the same affective paradox when discussing the production of promotional stills:

> What has changed hugely is the way we can get materials to press. When I started they still made slides, transparencies, for all the stills, which was a costly and time process because you have to make hundreds and hundreds of sets of them, and black and white photos, which I miss because it's those old-fashioned nice, glossy photos that you used to see in front of cinemas, and were brilliant for autograph hunters.[. . .] there is a romance of stills, it's a hell of a lot easier and cheaper because they just have one set online, usually on a downloadable website any journalist can just download a still if they want or I can email them. It's much, much easier; the same with the EPK things. You can email clips or links of clips, and that kind of thing instead of beta tapes, which until very recently were the standard.[31]

Celluloid pedagogies

The origins and antecedents of this romanticism were expressed in many of the practitioner's accounts of their own educational experiences. Through interviews with the practitioners, it became clear that Celluloid Pedagogies continue to persist across film-educational contexts – in universities, in film schools, in on-the-job training contexts and in knowledge-transfer activities. One doesn't need to look far to find evidence of these celluloid traces – it is clear from how the practitioners articulate their preferred approaches to learning using material and physical means. As Robbie Ryan explained:

> We learnt everything we could on film cameras. There were no digital cameras at the time. Video was beginning to be popular but we did our three hours on film and I think it's a very good learning curve because you just learn about exposure, you learn about film ... [. . .] The film basis of learning was great and we got to edit on Steenbecks which had a very, very tangible sort of feeling. You could feel the film as you put it into your camera. You knew that that lens was going to go onto that film. It was some kind of chemical magic would happen in the dark room.[32]

Such is the contemporary nature of many of these changes, current digital practitioners have not received digital training, instead they benefited from the accessible materiality of film methodologies. Editing is a particular discipline, seen as the locus of where film language is 'learned', developed and put into practice. Anders Refn reflects upon his experiences:

> I was educated from '67 to '69 in the Danish film school and then I studied editing because I was very fascinated by editing in the same place where we learn what film language is, that's in the editing process. You can see what works and what doesn't work and you can elevate the acting and you can train yourself in all those things.[33]

The importance of temporal awareness is also underscored through engaging with the 'material' film:

> Before the advent of digital non-linear editing systems, editors were taught to cut structure first, then rhythm [. . .] In the contemporary process, the shaping of rhythm is part of the shaping of structure. Throughout the cutting process, from the first cut forward, events are restructured and rhythms are refined simultaneously. (Pearlman 2009: 138)

The physicality and tangibility of time, is captured by the conjecture of Babette Mangolte:

> But increasingly, young editors are not trained in film, and the editing has no tempo. Is this because in the manipulation of a digital file for each shot is difficult to 'see'? Unlike the size of a film roll, the duration marked by the time code of a digital file can be displayed at various scales that you can change quickly and modify, but you also need to check to really know if what you are cutting is two seconds or twenty. In film, two seconds is three feet and twenty seconds is thirty feet. There is no way to ignore duration when you physically manipulate the piece of film. (2003: 267)

The 'workflow-warp' discussed in Chapter 3 which is endemic of on-set practices in the time of digital transition can also be ascribed to the editing and post-production processes – where there is an innate collapsing and expansion of time, where time itself is invisible, and ineffectual when intangible.

> My opinion regarding digital technology, thanks to my age and experience, is very conservative: I miss the subjective contact with the film material, I miss holding it, physically cutting in between specific marked frames, making a rough cut shot-by-shot. (Josef Valusiak, in Crittenden, 2006: 24)

These accounts all illuminate a pedagogical shift from the grounded episteme of film-based learning with the more experimental, intangible and uncertain 'doxa' of the digital. How will filmmaking pedagogic practice evolve as professionals increasingly engage with the 'immaterial materiality' of film (Lissitzky, 1925: 128) in forms of 'immaterial labour' (Lazzarato, 1996).

This crisis is made manifest into the pervasive physicality and physiological analogies of film which resonate throughout much discourse. Film is indeed a physical and organic medium, constructed from physical matter. These properties are celebrated – its gelatin emulsion base, the fact that it is light-sensitive, 'Film is like the body' Cullinan proclaims (2012: 84).

These accounts also illuminate the often-implied perceived superiority of the celluloid form, and its eminent position in the material classification, on the film–digital continuum. As Laura Kipnis observes: '. . . the language difficulties become a way of erecting an art-technology opposition, and that opposition is one of the most frequent ways that film figures its distinction from, and hierarchizes its relation to video' (2000: 215–16).

From an educational and professional development perspective, navigating, negotiating and evolving appropriate tools, mechanisms and approaches to learning digital film production are key to this particular transitional moment. The challenges imply that something is missing in the digital pedagogic process, through a lack of contact and connection that students have to the material. As technology cannot be maintained, and film processing becomes prohibitively expensive, and universities continue to invest in the digital, new challenges emerge. Students need to become attuned in the historical legacies embedded within the digital media for which an understanding of analogue referents and digital analogies is crucial. These histories and legacies are essential alongside encouraging students to go on to become innovators in new digital production methodologies, and the design and implementation of new tools.

Conclusion

The pervading discourse of this transitionary moment is one of loss, invisibility, disappearance and erasure. If we are to subscribe to the various testimonies expressing anxiety over the film-to-digital transition, we would perceive this to be a period characterised by uncertainty, reluctance, resistance and threat. Various accounts express the subordination of digital to analogue with many claiming that the digital somehow eviscerates the textual qualities of film (this we saw in the use of the camera netting). A range of responses from many of the different practitioners interviewed and other commentators and theorists demonstrate varying levels of response to the vicissitudes of the film-to-digital transition, from ambivalence to anathema. Tacita Dean in her 'FILM' exhibition of 2012 captures the latter:

> We must fight to keep a foothold on Mount Analogue, or risk a *colossal* depletion of irretrievable knowledge and skill, as well as the experience and history of over a hundred years of film and photographs made on film. If we do not, we are in danger of *losing* something of our humanity's heart. (2012: 2013, emphasis added)

A defining characteristic of digital film production processes is their ability to delete, overwrite and manipulate and this resonates in the pervasive language of death, crisis, uncertainty and loss in film industry trade publications as the digital revolution took hold:

> The indexical nature of traditional photo-realist images is often a topic of study, as it is the very principle of photography: passing through a lens, light leaves its trace, is preserved, and then restored. With digital encoding, this essential imprinting, this strong contiguity with captured reality, is lost. It is no longer a case of catching hold of and restoring a slice of profilmic reality, but rather of encoding the 'data' seized by the device. (Gaudreault and Marion 2015: 69)

This notion of invisibility is important for a number of reasons – to eradicate analogue OR the digital depending on the approach, and also the erasure of this transitional moment, when the transition is completed, reminds us of Žižek's comments quoted in Chapter 1, and is reflected in Berry et al.'s call to make visible the invisibility of the medium at a crucial time of transition:

As the digital increasingly structures the contemporary world, curiously, it also withdraws; it becomes harder and harder for us to focus upon, as it becomes embedded, hidden, off shored, or merely forgotten about. Part of the challenge for citizens of a regime of computation is to bring the digital (code/software) back into visibility for exploration, research and cultural critique. (2012: 44)

The gradual datafication of cinema at a time when cinematography was 'in the throes of a fraught historical juncture' (Sim 2012: 80), has evolved many associated conventions and aesthetics. The Production Aesthetic of *Ginger & Rosa* is a symbiosis of digital and film. Both an intermedial and converged moment – this oscillating bi-directional flow in which digital media and film were, and still are, constantly influenced and in dialogue with one another. In effect, what we have witnessed through the simulation of analogue in the various digital spaces of production that have been examined in this Chapter is the simulation of the digital and vice versa.

As I have shown, through the process by which film frames have become digital data, rather than solely an 'aesthetic of continuity' (Manovich, 2011: 138–142) such that is assigned to film-text-aesthetics (increasingly characterised by blending, smoothness and the continual take), I have shown evidence that there exists in film production, an *aesthetic of interruption*, punctuation and fragmentation, which is evocative of William Brown's notion of an '. . . irrational continuity: the impossible/digital exists alongside and interacts with the possible/analogue' (2013: 122).

Walter Benjamin stated that: 'In a film, perception in the form of shocks was established as a formal principle. That which determines the rhythm of production on a conveyer belt is the basis of the rhythm of reception in the film' (2007: 175). Benjamin's observations shed contemporary light on how the prevalent discontinuity embedded within filmmaking management – despite the fact that these are antonymic and antithetical to a conducive workflow – is carried forwards into the resulting aesthetics of the film. We see many instances where celluloid film practice has translated into digital remediations of these conventions, i.e. the modularisation of celluloid frames, cuts, beats, scenes is replicated in the modularisation of computational processes. This shift from analogue modularity to digital fragmentation is revealed in Tony Lawson's observation that: 'If I was working on a Moviola the film would be broken down into slates and takes. If I'm working on electronics it's the same, in a sense. They're broken down into individual sections' (in Perkins and Stollery, 2004: 156).

This atomisation of the production process is inflected in what Tara McPherson has referred to as a 'lenticular logic' (2012: 26), when writing about the UNIX computer operating system. She claims that it is 'a logic of the fragment or the chunk, a way of seeing the world as discrete modules or nodes, a mode that suppresses relation and context. As such, the lenticular also manages and controls complexity' (Ibid.).

We can draw some conclusions as to why the film analogy and metaphor has persisted and remained across and within the digital production spaces that I have examined for a number of reasons:

- On an industry level: the influence of the market on hardware and the influence of the Hollywood product is made manifest in the proprietary nature of film production software and hardware. These practices of restraint are demonstrated by soft surveillance techniques that are embedded into scriptwriting software and camera software. Filmmaking conventions and practices are limited by the design of these tools and the pace of digital media flows are stemmed.
- On a project level: the fact that there is a lack of opportunity for training and development outside of the film project cycle, has meant that film production practice and process has evolved in a piecemeal and iterative way; any hope of a radical intervention is impinged upon and stymied by the persistence of fragmented working practices. There has never been a full, independent review of the filmmaking process for example, although this could, of course, be true of many industries adjusting to the computational. Through the metaphor of 'workflow-warp' to account for the affective response to how these changes have been managed, and through 'workflow-weft' as the practical solution – through its suturing of the interstices wrought by new digital interventions. This 'material' analogy has emerged in related discourse, and resonates with my own conceptualisation of the warp and weft of woven tapestry:

> Today's communication networks are structured around 'patchwork' designs, software glitches are fixed with 'patches,' computer processors are being described as 'multi-threaded,' and over the past decade other 'material metaphors' have been embraced as a means of conceptualising and giving form to our new world of amorphous digital texts. (Arthur, 2008)

- On an individual and departmental level: there has been a habitual and formulaic reliance on the familiar, enacted and made visible by the anomalies and inefficiencies of celluloid practice and protocols. These practices are imposed by the working structures and preferential processes of the filmmaking craft to protect jobs, professions and livelihoods.

As an inevitable corollary, the Production Aesthetic of *Ginger &
Rosa* reveals that many practices and processes are obstinately preserved
beyond their actual relevance, there is an unnecessary retention of that
which would fall in to desuetude, if they were not so steeped in nostalgic
residue and the historical consciousness of film.

An enduring Production Aesthetic of 'digital film' is contingent upon
the intransigence of film as material and filmmaking as a material practice. These creative and technical choices become inextricably woven into
the fabric of the film object: analogue processes, protocols and language
remained throughout the film's making, and these analogue traces become
permanently imprinted upon and throughout the materials of the film's
production and remain as a record of the transformative moment, which
will remain a legacy of the film's history in its subsequent archiving (which
will be discussed further in Chapter 6).

I argue that this Production Aesthetic is characterised by a constant and
complex interplay between the enhancement and celebration of the digital
on the one hand, and the attempted eradication and masking of it on the
other. This neatly segues into the concerns of the following Chapter which
explores how the industry chooses to explicitly communicate its work, processes, people and innovation. Within these discourses, I examine how the
industry simultaneously inhabits the real, the imagined and the mediated,
and in doing so how they render their work both visible and simultaneously
invisible through their processes of representation. I will explore how the
film industry mobilises its Production Aesthetic(s) in a myriad of conflicting ways across forms of promotion and protest.

Notes

1. On set, this responsibility fell to the sound assistant/trainee who linked camera and sound time codes together at the start of every day.
2. In an interview with the author, 26 October 2012.
3. The Camera Assistant in an interview with Kurban Kassam, March 2012.
4. There are other codecs with lower data rates for television applications –
   ProRes 422 and 422 (HQ).
5. Apple launched the 'MOV' file format in 1998 as part of their Quicktime
   program using their own proprietary compression algorithm. MOV is an
   'MPEG 4 video container file format'.
6. An 'anamorphic desqueeze' refers to the process which corrects the aspect
   ratio of an image shot using an anamorphic lens – since these lenses do not
   maintain the original aspect ratio – instead they record the image horizontally
   onto the camera sensor so that it effectively becomes 'squeezed.' Arri have

actually produced a dedicated white paper to the subject (7 July 2011), such is the technical complexity of these processes.

7. 'LOG C is an intermediate color format and not designed as a display standard. Thus color grading becomes an obligatory post-production step and for proper previewing, creation of dalies or editing proxies it is necessary to use Look Up Tables' (ARRI, 2011: 64).

8. So named after its inventor, Bryce Bayer of Eastman Kodak.

9. In an interview with the author, 8 January 2015 (male respondent M007).

10. In an interview with the author, 12 October 2012.

11. Ibid.

12. In an interview with the author, 26 October 2012.

13. For a prior history of specialist software programmes for scriptwriting, see Hoxter and Horton 2014: 122.

14. In 2016, Final Draft was acquired by Cast & Crew Entertainment Services.

15. http://www.finaldraft.com/company

16. The Black List, Script Standards Guide #1, Accessed from: https://blcklst.com/help/script_standards.pdf, 7 April 2017.

17. http://www.movieoutline.com/articles/screenplay-format-a-guide-to-industry-standard-script-formatting.html

18. MovieMagic products were originally created by the Write Brothers, http://www.write-bros.com/; they were then sold to Creative Planet (no longer in existence), spun off to Movie Magic Technologies, then purchased by Entertainment Partners in 2002.

19. https://www.writersstore.com/movie-magic-scheduling-software/

20. According to http://www.merriam-webster.com/dictionary/call%20sheet

21. These include Yamdu: Film and TV Production Management Software (by ARRI); Cinecore: production management apps for film and TV, which claim to be 'Entertainment and media's only complete production management and collaboration tools for the entire cast and crew;' Cloud Film & Video Production Management Software Application, and FilmTouch™ : 'The Personal Callsheet Manager for Film Industry Crew Members.'

22. In an interview with Kurban Kassam, March 2012.

23. Ibid.

24. Avid Media Composer, based on an Apple Macintosh system was first publicly released at the NAB trade show in 1989. It was used on a number of feature films in the early 1990s, but the watershed moment came when Walter Murch used the software to edit *The English Patient* in 1996, for which he received an Academy Award. In 1994 Avid introduced Open Media Framework (OMF) as an open standard file format for sharing media and related metadata. The software has evolved and developed in line with other key film technological enhancements such as RED cameras (in 2008) and stereoscopic 3D capability introduced in 2009, 2k (and subsequently in 4k in 2014).

25. I have previously accounted for the presence of the skeumorph as 'indicative of a temporally and technologically displaced sign system' and that 'the use

of analogue semiotics still persists in many expressive digital forms (such as the sound of a shutter that emits from a smartphone when a picture is taken, the sonic emulation of a page turn of a paper-based book when clicking from page-to-page on an e-reader)' (Atkinson, 2014: 128). In my discussions of lens flare in the film *Gravity* I suggest this implies '. . . the presence of an actual camera lens whilst increasing the visual density of the scene. This optical simulation, the implication of the presence of an (absent) lens is a skeumorph' (Atkinson 2015b: 76).

26. Ibid.
27. In an interview with Kurban Kassam, March 2012.
28. Flame, made by AutoDesk is a software used for the design of 3D visual effects.
29. Ibid.
30. In an interview with the author, 30 April 2012.
31. In an interview with the author, 6 June 2012.
32. Ibid.
33. Ibid.

CHAPTER 5

Digital Film Production Representations

Introduction

This Chapter examines how the film industry has represented its work, processes, people and moments of change throughout the history of cinema, with an acute focus on the 2012 moment of transition. In this Chapter, I set forth how a film's 'Production Aesthetic' is mobilised and carried forwards within a ubiquity of representational modes that exist around a film's release to meet promotional ends and which are sometimes adopted in forms of resistance and protest.

As Michael Chanan earlier contended, film-industry professionals continue to occupy a unique and privileged position '. . . within the social formation as commentators *on or behind* the screen' (1980: 135, my emphasis). In contrast to other industries, the film industry can deploy its own core activity as its dominant tool of communication through which to create its own representations, to frame them, to communicate them and to control their flow and access by the wider public. This is happening in ever-more sophisticated and complex ways – whereby filmmakers inhabit constantly shifting subjectivities in their work as makers, creators, workers, commentators, rights owners, experts and audiences – and it is in the nexus of film-production representations that these multiple identities unify and coalesce. Indeed, John Caldwell contends that we are in a 'para-industrial' era where we see: 'a media industry that obsessively analyzes and continuously theorizes itself' (2014: 737).

Through an examination of the range of mechanisms that are employed to represent the labour of a film's production, this Chapter expounds that the discursive and political apparatus which frame film production are part of 'the *cinema machine,* a *dispositive,* an arrangement which give apparatus and techniques social status and function' (Comolli, 1980: 122).

Representational materials and their associated 'production metaphors' that are considered within this Chapter include title sequences, electronic press kits (EPK) and their constituent elements: photographic stills, production notes, filmed interviews with cast and crew, making-of documentaries and other supplementary special features. These materials also include representations of key production iconography and production apparatus (such as the clapper board and green screens) and which have been subjected to a reconfiguration as tools of protest on social media networking sites, and as physical props in demonstrations. My work is particularly focused upon the emergent digital methods that the industry uses now that they have a range of networked and social media tools at their disposal, and how this has impacted upon the flow, nature and temporal ordering of these representative materials within the film production and distribution cycle.

I examine the inherent dichotomy that the imperatives behind these mediations inhabit: on the one hand rendering certain workers and certain types of work highly visible, whilst on the other, simultaneously hiding people, processes and spaces of production. I argue that the representation, mediation and dramatisation of production work and the narrativisation of process, can very often occlude and obfuscate the 'true' economics of film production.

I then move to examine the shift towards the increasing recognition of the plurality of the film-production process, through the case study from *Ginger & Rosa* – the making of the *Anatomy of a Film* featurette from the *Ginger & Rosa* Blu-ray (Filmography: Atkinson and Holden, 2012). The Chapter concludes with an exploration into the subversion of materials of production for use in protest and resistance against the exploitation of certain production personnel and their labour.

Modes, Tools and Types of Representation

There are a number of formal industry-created representational 'paratexts' (Genette, 1987 and Gray, 2010), or 'production paratexts' (Caldwell, 2008a), that have already been noted throughout the book. These include the credit listing (as discussed in Chapter 3) which I propose as the primary and most visible representational text presented to the film's audience, topping and tailing the filmic text as an authorised and authoritative paratextual frame. Credits are the most explicit mechanism through which the industry communicates its hierarchies and chains-of-command. In the 1930s and 1940s, the main bulk of the credits appeared at the head of the film and along with the cast, only featured Heads of Department and core members of the crew. The full credits have since been left until the conclusion of the film, with only the producers and key members displayed as single titles at the start, and now includes a credit list so long that it appears to include every single person involved in the film however minor their role. This does not necessarily mean that every person who worked on the film receives a named credit, looking at profiles and roles on the Internet Movie Database (IMDb), many are 'uncredited'. The end credits are often the part of the film during which film audiences tend to leave the auditorium, and several productions have taken to embedding additional footage into the credit sequence such as bloopers and the like in order to retain the audience members' attention. More recently, as credits become more protracted, the strategy of including an end 'stinger' has emerged. Stingers include additional story and plot exposition, in the case of *The Twilight Saga: Breaking Dawn – Part 1* (2011) there was a widely publicised post-credit sequence which provided the set-up for what was to come in Part II of the franchise.

Since the beginning of film history, credit sequences have always been used to celebrate the scope and amount of labour which has gone into the making of a film as we can see from a very early Disney example, the voice-over explicitly celebrates and acknowledges the function of the credits: 'as its credit titles – longest in cinema history – flash across the nations screens – audiences for the first time realize the tremendous amount of man power required for the production of this epic making animated picture' (*How Walt Disney Cartoons Are Made*, 1939). More recently, we see these proclamations becoming more explicit with the final, end credit displaying statistics which quantify what I refer to as the 'labour metrics' of a film. Two recent examples include *The Peanuts Movie* (2015) in which the final post-credit screen stated: '12,000 jobs and a million work hours,' and the end slate of *Miss Peregrine's Home for Peculiar Children* (2016) stated: 'The making and authorized distribution of this film supported over 15,000 jobs and involved hundreds and thousands of work hours'.

The politics of credit sequences have previously been clearly underscored by Alan Lovell and Gianluca Sergi: 'Credits serve as a reminder of both the number of people involved in any Hollywood film project and the filmmaker's hierarchy that shapes them' (2005: 130). But this latest 'labour metric' strategy seeks to embed the politics and economics of the film-production process within the context of the new quantified data economy. In these two examples above, this is clearly made manifest as a result of the increase in the numbers of production personnel due to the extensive animation, CGI and VFX work involving large teams of digital labourers across the world.

Such is the complexity of film credits, the Directors Guild of America (DGA) has a dedicated department 'Credits Department' which deals with the specificity of credit formatting and the associated legal impediments. Its influence has been exercised and is made visible through a number of prevailing and universal credit conventions; take for example, their highly-specific guidance relating to the Directorial Credit:

> The Basic Agreement specifies placement, position, duration and size require-ments of the directorial screen credit. For feature films, the Director's screen credit must be accorded on a separate card, which shall be the last title card appear-ing prior to principal photography. This credit shall be no less than 50% of the size of the displayed title of the motion picture, or of the largest size in which credit is accorded to any other person, whichever is greater.

In addition, credit listings, in their production, function as a key site for contractual and financial negotiation, according to Stephen Greenwald and Paula Landry, credits are: '. . . often used as a bargaining tool in Hollywood, and can be a powerful incentive for talent to commit to a development project' (2009:42). See discussions in Chapter 2, page 27, where I discussed the complexity of credit list compilation and approval in relation to *Ginger & Rosa*.

The second and most commonplace set of industry-approved para-texts, which are produced in tandem with the film, is the Electronic Press Kit (EPK). This is a long-established and routinely produced set of mate-rials. In *Ginger & Rosa* the generation of EPK materials was set into the production schedule and budget, and a 'making-of' director, an on-set photographer and a small interview crew were hired by the unit publicists. One of the unit publicists on *Ginger & Rosa* describes the standard con-tents of the EPK:

> Stills is one thing. The second one is behind-the-scenes film footage, [. . .] inter-views with the cast and the main crew because these could be used by TV shows later on around the world [. . .] The third thing is what we call 'production notes,' and this is written material that will be given to press when there are screenings of the film. [. . .] The production notes will have the synopsis of the film. They'll have biographies, short paragraphs on each of the main cast and crew. In this particular case, we used a Q&A with Sally, which means journalists will have ready-made quotes from her about every element of the production. It's a really neat little pack.[1]

Another publicist describes their awareness of the reductionist nature of some of these materials which require pre-curation and editing before their circulation to the press:

> If you imagine that with all the work that Sally has put into this film in terms of the look of it, the script, the full look of it, the fact of the matter is probably people are going to make their minds up about the film from a still image. That's almost certainly the first thing that we'll see from the film so it's incredibly important that you get that right.[2]

Figure 5.1 shows the still image that the publicist refers to, that was chosen as the original press image which was circulated during the production of the film. This particular image was selected as it captured the essence of the on-screen relationship between the two female lead characters. The image was later flipped for use in the film's theatrical promotional poster to match the naming of the film, and to visually prioritise Ginger as the lead protagonist.

The Unit Publicist underscores the significance of the EPK materials as tools through which to promote both the fictional story of the film and also their importance in the story of the film's making. The Publicist explains that with the 'footage of Sally at work on the set, footage of her talking to the actors, we can emphasise the production value of the film'[3] thus invoking "the dual nature of an audience experience of a film; the feature itself and the story behind its making" (Atkinson 2014: 80).

These representational texts, the credit listing and the EPK, are traditional, long-standing industry-authorised mechanisms through which to promote the film during the theatrical distribution stage. Other representational texts that are created for DVD, Blu-ray and online distribution become more complex in their construction and communication.

Extended representations

As agents and owners of their own mediation, representations of film production have inevitably proliferated across various textual sites. Films about film production are as old as cinema itself – there have been numerous examples of narrative feature films which take film production or elements of the film industry as their subject matter, implying a continued fascination with the process, the 'magic' and also the *mundane* nature of behind-the-scenes film production. Perhaps the earliest known example of this form is *Behind the Screen* (1916), a short film directed by Charlie Chaplin, which has since been superseded by many others.[4] These offer fictionalised, dramatised and sometimes sensationalised insights into the film-production process, and some provide a more reflexive, meta-filmic account revealing the conditions, apparatus and politics of production, which can, on the one hand create, as Patricia Waugh states: 'A fiction that both creates an illusion and lays bare that illusion' (1984: 6) or as Thomas Elsaesser has noted: 'the production process can take on a textual form' (1998b: 143). Potter's own *Tango Lesson* (1997) is a reflexive take on the film-production process, and includes herself as the Director, reflecting on her own struggles with the scriptwriting process for her forthcoming film.

Figure 5.1 The original promotional image for *Ginger & Rosa* and the resultant poster promoting the film's cinema release.
(Photographer – Nicola Dove © Adventure Pictures Ltd)

The technological histories of cinema are also represented in films such as *The Artist* (2011), *Hugo* (2011), and *Oz The Great and Powerful* (2013). The story of the inception of sound into motion pictures is retold in *The Artist* (2011) through the film's content and storyline. The texture of silent filmmaking style is also imbued in its black and white presentation and the text-based intertitles. Both *Hugo* and *Oz The Great and Powerful* include early cinematic moving image inventions whereby old film technologies and mechanics of cinema are brought to life through digital technology. *Hugo* provides a history of the technological and artistic innovations of early cinema in its homage to Georges Méliès, which includes recreations of various different special-effects sequences from his films, and biographical details pertaining to Méliès. The film offers a meta-filmic rendering in its own spectacular showcase of the emergent storytelling capabilities of digital stereoscopic-3D (Atkinson, 2011), the advances in its use of the medium for storytelling are widely acknowledged and recognised. As Stephen Heath has noted: 'In the first moments of the history of cinema, it is the technology which provides the immediate interest: what is promoted and sold is the experience of the machine, the apparatus' (1980: 1). Furthermore, these three examples of *The Artist, Oz The Great and Powerful,* and *Hugo* illuminate a preoccupation with the *process* of filmmaking at this historical juncture.

Documentary texts about films and film production have also proliferated since the birth of film. Often seen as serving cinephilia, David Bordwell and Kristin Thompson (2013) start their tenth edition of Film Art 'by looking at the process of film production' (2013: 3) stating: 'We appreciate films more when we realize that in production, every film is a compromise made within constraints' (2013: 28). Similarly, Peter Lunenfield (1999) has contended that: 'The back- story – the information about how a narrative object comes into being – is fast becoming almost as important as that object itself. [and] For a vast percentage of new media titles, backstories are probably more interesting in fact, than the narratives themselves' (1999: 14).

An early example of the 'making-of' genre was created by Wallace Carlson, a pioneering animator working for Bray Studios responsible for films like *Dreamy Dud: He Resolves Not to Smoke* (1915). He also produced a making-of film called *How Animated Cartoons Are Made* (1919) which shows the animator working alongside Bray on the cartoon.

In Erich von Stroheim's 1923 film *Greed*, some of the first-known newsreel footage of its kind revealed the film crew making the trek to Death Valley (a Californian desert) to film the final sequence of the film. Reported in the newspapers, the Director stated 'the suffering of the men was intense. The air was stifling, and the sun beat down unmercifully. At one time I feared for the lives of the actors; I thought they were really dying' (in Denton 1925: 92). This typified the defining characteristic of this proto-making-of content invoking what Timothy Corrigan refers to as 'the commercial drama of a movie's source' (1991: 118).

In 1937, a film entitled *A trip through Walt Disney Studios*, which was originally only meant for RKO executives, eventually became *How Walt Disney Cartoons Are Made*[5] (1939) and screened as the trailer before the main feature film. It showcases the various stages of *Snow White and the Seven Dwarves* (1937) development – the writing of the first story lines, the drafting of the animation sequences and the hand-painting of 250,000 celluloid frames.

The complex blurring between the original text and its production (and the production of the production) is not a new characteristic and can be seen in many examples of the making-of form throughout cinematic history. Take for example Disney's *The Reluctant Dragon* (1941). The protagonist Robert Benchley, a famous Hollywood actor and comedian, playing a version of himself, visits Walt Disney Studios with the intention of selling the idea of the book of the same name, based on a story by Kenneth Graeme, to Walt Disney. He is given access to all areas and invited into different spaces to watch the film professionals at work, in various fictionalised encounters, including a life-drawing class, animation studios, music studios where he experiences the vocal scoring for the different characters including Donald Duck, the sound-effects studio, the cell-animation studio, the camera department, the 'Rainbow room' – the colour laboratory, the inking department, the modelling department, the story conference room, and the projection room. He is guided, by Humphrey, his officious chaperone who quotes various metrics about the studios (including the volume of celluloid that they get through each day) as they move from space to space across the 51-acre site. *Dumbo* (1941) appears to be the feature film in production at the time – suggested by the presence of the elephant in the life-drawing class and the train sequence from the film that we see being sonically treated in the sound-effects studio. The process of spot sound-effect and Foley[6] work is narrativised as if occurring in real time – various artists are seen enthusiastically creating the sounds of the locomotive train, as the famous sequence plays. The film is highly sophisticated in its levels and layers of storytelling which collectively combines the showcase of technologies: Benchley's arrival into the Rainbow room is marked by a move from black and white to colour film space, reminiscent of Dorothy's arrival into the Technicolor world of Oz; the revealing of detailed procedural and contractual limitations such as child chaperone limits; the showcasing of content – several excerpts from cartoons are included; and the politics of production are revealed in a final unconscious reference to Disney's aggressive approaches to copyrighting of adapted, unoriginal work. The film concludes with Disney beating Benchley to it as they sit down in the projection room to watch the already produced *Reluctant Dragon* film. The film is imbued with Disney's authorial signature throughout, songs from the soundtrack from *Snow White and the Seven Dwarves* (1937) including 'Heigh Ho' and 'Whistle While You Work' play across some of the scenes, underscoring the labour behind the film's making.

More recently, we have witnessed the flood of documentary ancillary materials that have accompanied film releases – from additional VHS tapes in special edition releases of films, to the DVD and Blu-ray extras. The inception of the DVD was a significant intervention which undoubtedly contributed to the advancement and complexity of these forms; as such the medium format has received much critical attention in its status as a new form of distribution (Knight, 2007) and its influence and impact upon a shifting film value chain (Bloore, 2009). There is much critical commentary around the consumption of DVD extras by audiences and how these function as new forms of digital cinephilia (Balcerzak and Sperb, 2009 and 2012, Tryon, 2009, Rosenbaum, 2010) and 'making-of' addiction (Arthur, 2004) enabling audiences to own, engage, interact and potentially play with the text (Klinger 2001; Bennett and Brown, 2008; Caldwell 2008b; Betz, 2010; Cobley and Haeffner, 2011; Atkinson 2014; Brereton 2015). These types of materials are generally engaged with at separate moments to the viewing of the main film itself, deploying different viewing registers which distinguish the fictional film from the behind-the-scenes factual content. The different modes of so-called 'factual' representational texts of film production span a range of subjectivities and intentionalities on the part of the makers behind them, depending on their imagined audiences. They can be used in pre–cinema-release promotional campaigns, political public-information campaigns and as artistic expressions in their own right.

The Discursive Constructions of Film Production

I will now proceed to a further detailed consideration of the different modes and types that these forms of factually-based ancillary content take on in their 'creative treatment of reality' (Grierson, 1996: 147) of film-production cultures and film labour. Although in this case, given the complexity of these representations and the increasing simulation of production practices, one could refer to this as the 'creative treatment of a simulation of reality'.

It is useful here to reflect upon Bill Nichols' (2002) six main modes of documentary production and to think about how they might most usefully be applied to documentaries that purport to document the film-production process. The modes, according to Nichols are: expository (which tend to be news-style, with formal interviews and direct address), poetic (exploring the 'inner truth' as opposed to objective reality), observational (otherwise known as 'Cinema Verite' or Direct Cinema), participatory (where there is direct engagement between filmmaker and subject(s) on-screen), performative (emphasises the subjective nature of the filmmaker as well as the subjective reading of the audience, and the impact and effect upon them), and reflexive, which acknowledges the construction of the events within the documentary.

We can see how limiting these may be in relation to film-industry-produced and self-documenting texts. Nichols' categories are based on assessing artistic merit and do not take into consideration the complexity of industrially framed texts.

Of course, these are not always mutually exclusive categoriesand one finds, when attempting to apply them to the contemporary making-of modes of film-industry-produced texts, that these draw on a *number* of techniques and take on a *number* of characteristics. Moreover, these categorisations are only intended to apply at a textual/content level and so are inadequate for the accounting of the context and framings, the perspectives from which they are told the economic and contractual imperatives in place. A far more complex, multi-modal system of categorisation and coding, and framework for analysis, is required to account for the different types of representational texts of film production.

Texts documenting film-industry practice can be characterised in at least five different ways: the **medium-channel** through which they are distributed; the **format** on which they are delivered; the **focus** of the object of study; their **authoritative framing** and their **style**.

Medium-channels include Cinema, Television, DVD/Blu-ray and, as a result of the dematerialisation of media consumption, also include second screen content, apps, web, online and social media channels. The **format** can span feature-length documentaries (for cinema or TV); shorter TV documentaries, which could be one-offs or a series; featurettes which accompany a DVD or Blu-ray release; to specialist museum installations; online videos and clips. The **focus** primarily tends to fall into six broad categories: Studio, Film, Director, Industry, Profession and Process. **Studio**-based examples are where the *site* of production is the focus concerned with the production output or context of one particular film studio, initiated by the example of the *20th Century Fox Studio Tour*[7] (1936). These also include: *Forever Ealing* (2002); *Shepperton Babylon* (2005); *London's Hollywood* (2006) and *From Borehamwood to Hollywood: The Rise and Fall and Rise of* Elstree (2014). **Film-**based examples are by far the most common focus of the form since they focus on one single film. Feature-length examples include *Lost in La Mancha* (2002) a film based on the failure to make Terry Gilliam's 'Don Quixote'; *Burden of Dreams* (1982) based on the making of Werner Herzog's 'Fitzcarraldo' and *Hearts of Darkness: A Filmmaker's Apocalypse* (1991) based on Francis Ford Coppola's Apocalypse Now (1979). **Director** are based on a sole director, for example *Stanley Kubrick's Boxes* (2008). **Industry** focus on the overall film industry or aspect of the film industry, for example *Side by Side* (2012). Based on one particular profession within the industry, **Profession** examples include *Cinematographer Style* (2006) and *The Cutting Edge: Magic of Editing* (2004). **Process-**based examples are illustrated by the animation models discussed earlier and are focused on a particular film-production process and its associated technological innovation, what Stephen Heath referred to as 'the experience of the machine, the apparatus' (1980: 1). A recent proliferating example are those sorts of films based on VFX processes, what I refer to as the emergent 'dynamically de-compositing composite.' The original film is subject to 'decortication', through the peeling-back of the finished film's cortex veneer, to dynamically reveal the filigree of the multiple CGI composited layers beneath, right back to the raw green-screen footage. These films dynamically imbricate process with product in the spectacle of the reverse-engineering of special-effects processes. These types of film proliferate in online spaces, in particular, YouTube channels belonging to post-production houses with which they showcase their work, including *Industrial Light & Magic*.

The **authoritative frame**, through which these materials present the narrative, includes: **Direct Industry**, whereby one or more members of the original crew, directly related to the production of the film, are behind its creation; **Indirect Industry**, produced by third-party film professionals, who are usually commissioned to do so (either as part of the EPK or to be included as a DVD, Blu-ray extra); **Counter Industry**, where members of the industry present an unsolicited counter-narrative such as *Who Needs Sleep?* (2006); **External expert**, a film critic, academic, or other non-media institution or individual such as in *From Borehamwood to Hollywood: The Rise and Fall and Rise of* Elstree (2014); and **Audience/Fan** examples, a recent phenomenon, such as *Room 237* (2012) which documents insights into fan and audience discourse around Kubrick's *The Shining* (1980) and

Back in Time (2015), a retrospective, historical *Back to the Future* (1985) documentary produced by fans of the film, through a crowdfunding campaign. To account for the different **styles** of content in these examples, I extend those proposed by Nichols above to include dramatised, fictionalised, archival, computational and interactive.

The contents of Table 5.1 debunk the idea that stylistic and narrative complexity has intensified throughout the years. As the early examples show, the ability of filmmakers to engage on different levels and in different registers has always been the case – in their highly-skilled ability to narrativise the production process in nuanced ways. There is however, the emergence of definite patterns relating to the shifts in **focus**. The focus upon the **procedural** and the new production apparatus appears to recur in moments of innovation, from the earlier films about animation, to those in 2012 focusing on the new possibilities and impacts of the digital, particularly in relation to CGI and VFX. In both eras, more sophisticated ways are deployed through which to communicate these – in the earlier examples through advanced meta-filmic narrative techniques and from 2012 through the harnessing of emergent interactive technologies. What is also notable is the latter involvement of external agents as the authoritative framing of these texts; only in the examples from 2012 onwards do we see different producers from external experts to audiences and fans. This shift arguably comes as a result of the new access to tools of production and the ability to harness the potential of networked and digital technologies.

I will now take some of those examples from Figure 5.2 for further consideration, in particular, those produced or based in the UK, focusing on their tendency, to varying degrees, to collapse the aesthetics of the film into the representations of their making, a trope first made manifest in the example of *Greed* (1923). This aesthetic is again made explicit in the example of *A Little Touch of Harry* (1989) – a televised making-of documentary of *Henry V* (1989), Kenneth Branagh's first feature film. The documentary is narrated by Judi Dench, who also starred in the film, whose words are as scripted (by Ian Johnstone) as the on-screen drama itself. The theatrical voice-over commentary is imbued with Shakespearean poesy, opening with the words of the chorus from *Henry V*:

> O! For a muse of fire that would ascend; The brightest heaven of invention. Shepperton Studios, England, November 1988. Kenneth Branagh is directing his first feature film. His chorus is Derek Jacobi. Truly a muse of fire.

Filmed at Shepperton Studios in 1988, *Henry V* starred a number of high-profile actors including Derek Jacobi, Christian Bale and Emma

Table 5.1 The evolution of the representational texts cited in this chapter, in chronological order. (By the author)

Illustrative Examples:	Channel	Format	Focus	Authoritative Frame	Style
How Animated Cartoons Are Made (1919)	Film	Featurette	Process	Direct Industry	Performative, reflexive, dramatised
Greed (1924) newsreel footage	Television	News-reel	Singular Film	Indirect Industry	Expository
How Walt Disney Cartoons Are Made (1939)	Film	Featurette	Process and Studio	Direct Industry	Expository and observational
The Reluctant Dragon (1941)	Film	Featurette	Process and Studio	Direct Industry	Performative, reflexive, dramatized
A Little Touch of Harry (1989)	Television	Feature-length	Singular Film	Direct Industry	Performative, expository and reflexive
The Cutting Edge: Magic of Editing (2004)	Television	Feature-length	Profession	Direct Industry	Expository
London's Hollywood (2006)	Television	Series	Studio	Indirect Industry	Observational and reflexive
Cinematographer Style (2006)	Film	Feature-length	Profession	Indirect Industry	Expository
Who Needs Sleep? (2006)	Film	Feature-length	Industry	Counter Industry and External Expert	Expository and observational
Prometheus second screen app (2012)	Second Screen App	Interactive	Process	Direct Industry	Archival, computational
Side by Side (2012)	Film	Feature-length	Industry and Process	Indirect Industry	Expository, participatory and reflexive
Room 237 (2012)	Film	Feature-length	Singular Film	Audience/ Fan	Expository, dramatised, archival
Ginger & Rosa making of (2012)	Extra features (DVD/ Blu-Ray)	Featurette	Singular Film, Process	Indirect Industry	Observational and poetic
Anatomy of a film (2012)	Extra features (DVD/ Blu-Ray)	Interactive Featurette	Professions, Process, Industry, Singular Film	Collaboration between Direct Industry and External Expert	Archival, computational, observational and expository
From Borehamwood to Hollywood: The Rise and Fall and Rise of Elstree (2014)	Film	Feature-length	Studio	External Expert	Expository
Gravity installation (2014)	Installation	Immersive Featurette	Process	Indirect Industry	Archival, computational
Inception installation (2014)	Installation	Interactive	Process	Indirect Industry	Archival, computational
Transformers: The Premake (2014)	Online	Featurette	Singular Film and Process	Audience/Fan	Observational, computational
Back in Time (2015)	DVD	Featurette	Film franchise	Audience/Fan	Expository, observational

Thompson, and Lord Snowdon worked as the on-set photographer. This particular example is chosen since it presents a clear example of the use of the film's story and style as a way to understand the film-production process; the documentary is not just dramatised but in effect it is re-theatricalised in a three-act structure. The narration, style and content very much reflect the high-art and quintessentially British origins of the film. The documentary focuses on the then 28-year-old Kenneth Branagh and the challenges he faced in making the film, working to a modest budget of £4.5 million. The film started to shoot before funding was in place; it had only secured a pre-sale to BBC for TV rights, as revealed in an interview with Branagh in which he talks of the complexities of the financial arrangements: 'The completion meeting was six bankers and twelve individual lawyers. In a way, it was a nightmare.' These off-set dramas are intercut with on-set action and formal interviews are undertaken with various crew members.

The glamour of Hollywood is eschewed for a more culturally superior mode of craft-based film production, as conveyed in the voice-over: 'There is an atmosphere in Silven Shepperton far removed from the brouhaha of Burbank. The odd 'darling' or 'marvellous' can be heard mingling in the air during what at times seems like a RADA reunion.' The documentary concludes with Branagh's King Henry V character walking through the battlefield to an orchestral score in the final scene of the film, which then cuts to Branagh as Director walking away from the film set invoking that he too is leaving a battlefield. The associative editing conflates the representation of the chaos of the battlefield with the chaos of the film-production process, exemplifying the pervading production metaphor of the film's drama. The documentary, which was screened on Channel 4, also illuminates the fluid interchange between cinematic and televisual registers, the remediation of the stage-play, to the cinema, to the television, an example of the convergence of theatre, cinema and broadcast.

Similarly, *London's Hollywood* (ITV1, 2006), took the work of the cinema as its focus and reframed it for consumption by a television audience. *London's Hollywood* was a six-part thirty-minute episodic documentary series, which took a behind-the-scenes look at Pinewood and Shepperton Studios. It is characterised by the televisual docu-soap-genre traditions of the late 1990s, early 2000s. It presented a serialised, televisual dramatisation of film production, with commercial breaks and cliffhangers, which is quite literally scripted, recast and performed as an entertainment in itself. The programmes mainly involve unknown films and productions that have never made it to screen, presumably because of commercial sensitivity and Non-Disclosure Agreements of the more well-known films that have been produced at the studios, who would have their own internally commissioned representations. The series is produced by an independent television production company. Broadcast on a UK-based commercial channel, it bears all the hallmarks of a television production. For example, prior to each commercial break, it presents a 'hook' to the next episode. It is 'live', depicting action as it unfolds. Visually bombastic, spectacular effects dominate – many sequences focus on the huge underwater pool at Pinewood, involving high-risk action, flaming water and young children, placing the audience at the heart of the drama of the film's making. The studios are conceptualised as a 'peculiar village', in a melodramatic rendering, complete with its idiosyncratic and archetypal characters. In *A Little Touch of Harry* we saw the drama of the film becoming the metaphor of production; in *London's Hollywood*, we see the reverse: since our understanding of the films being made is shaped by our insights into the production, it is, therefore, the production metaphor as drama.

Of particular note to the focus of this book, although not UK-based, but with a number of British contributors, is *Side by Side* (Kenneally, 2012), more importantly, it is a documentary concerned with the film-to-digital transition. The film explores the impact of digital upon every link of the image chain, from acquisition to exhibition, from the perspectives of industry professionals, crucially, at the pivotal moment of 2012. Presented by Keanu Reeves, who, along with the Director, interviews seventy practitioners including directors, cinematographers, producers, film festival producers, VFX artists and editors. Some are evangelical – Martin Scorsese professes the 'Reinvention of a new medium' – others reticent and some wholly resistant – 'I'm not gonna trade my oil paints for digital crayons,' stated Christopher Nolan. Through its inclusion of 'meta-production' techniques in which the constructed artifice of the film is revealed to the viewer, it exposes the making-of apparatus when an observational second camera pans to show the interviewer and the main camera in a simultaneous making/making-of aesthetic. The documentary also includes graphical visualisations which break down complex film and digital processes. The associated 2014 documentary, *Chris Kenneally: The Making of 'Side by Side' Documentary* (2014), reveals the labour and challenges of the endeavour in which 140 contributors were interviewed across the world.

Making of *Ginger & Rosa*

The Making of Ginger & Rosa (2012) is a craft-based film imbued with a gritty realism that exposes the authenticity of on-location filming, revealing different aspects of the on-set labour, the daily routines and mundane waiting, thereby mobilising the 'Production Aesthetic' of *Ginger & Rosa*.

Figure 5.2 The image of Robbie Ryan and the crew of *Ginger & Rosa* moving the camera equipment to one of the film's key locations exemplifies the dual narrative of a film's making, through its representation of the physical labour of film production. (Photographer – Nicola Dove ©Adventure Pictures Ltd)

John Matthews (the Director's) documentary is a combination of a fly-on-the wall observational style, intercut with interviews and his own reflective voice-over. Matthews reflects upon his intentions for the film:

> It's a first person film. It's my experience of the film set because it was my first film I've really worked on. So it's quite a different environment for me to be working in so it's kind of my journey but also reflecting what the film's about and showing people what a film set might look like, but if you've seen the feature film it's always interesting to see how they made that show; who's involved [. . .] it's about image making. I think that's what interests me. You know, that they're actually creating something for the screen and you're separate from that as opposed to filming ordinary life. This isn't ordinary life, this is a fantasy world, and there's something just interesting about that.[8]

The short film takes on the look and feel of *Ginger & Rosa* through a number of mechanisms and motifs; for example for the sound track, there is the use of the same familiar music track as was used in the film (*Li'l Darlin* by Count Basie). It is also textured in the same way through the colour, look and feel. The production metaphor in this particular example is the film's style – the stylistic continuity can in part be accounted for by the fact that the editor Michael Aaglund worked as the Assistant Editor on *Ginger & Rosa*.

The compression of the sites of production and reception manifests in a recurring reflexive aesthetic in which the content, style and presentation of the behind-the-scenes materials take on the representational characteristics of the film's diegesis. This process is a perpetual cycle in which the main event influences the look and feel of the promotional materials, and the promotional materials set the expectations for the aesthetics and mode of the main event, whereby 'the author is present in the text as a cinematic effect' (Andrew, 2000: 26).

The examples discussed above are all similar in the way they narrativise production and offer a production narrative, which tells a particular story, in a particular way. For example, in *Hearts of Darkness* (1991) Coppola likens the experience of the making of *Apocalypse Now* (1979) to the events of the war that it represents, a comparison augmented by the chaotic musical soundtrack of the documentary. Pat Brereton has alluded to this dichotomy between the artistic and commercial imperatives of these types of films, and his conceptualisation of them as 'smart films':

> Smart films posit a particularly complex dialogical engagement with cineastes as they often frame an ironic and playful exposition of the filmmaker's work, which in turn serves to sometimes contradict and subvert the normative semiotic exercise of the initial film-viewing experience. At all times, however, viewers ought to be made fully aware of the marketing strategy underpinning such apparently revealing exposés. (2012: 2)

Rather than contradict, I would suggest that the examples I have considered so far illuminate how these films become stylistically imbued with the films that they purport to document.

Representational temporalities

The impact of the digital was initiating other shifts in 2012 relating to the release and distribution strategies of behind-the-scenes content. Prior to 2012, there had been a clear temporal distinction made between the moment of a feature film's actual release, and the subsequent release of these behind-the-scenes materials referred to as 'second shift' (Caldwell, 2008a: 163). I have previously extended this notion to account for the emergent paradigm of the 'simultaneous shift' whereby all content is released and available simultaneously in developing experimental distribution strategies, exemplified by *A Field in England* (2013) in which *Film4* released a set of masterclass materials online on the same day as the film's release.

In *Beyond the Screen* (Atkinson, 2014), I started to consider how the temporal (and spatial) compression of both the film and the representations of its making start to manifest in new home-viewing modalities such as 'second screen' which deploy audio synchronisation in order to simultaneously deliver behind-the-scenes content to tablet and smart phone devices, to directly correlate with the main-screen fictional action. I draw on a case study of the *Prometheus* second screen app (2012), on account of the depth of access into the layers of the process that the app facilitates through its foregrounding of the deconstruction of various spectacular sequences (Atkinson, 2014: 83).

The production materials of *Prometheus* (2012) can be accessed synchronically and are interpolated within the film itself, via the Blu-ray player and the wireless network in order to trigger the content at the relevant temporal moments within the film's diegesis: on-screen action correlates to behind-the-scenes materials. The media is delivered within a corporatised interface that reflects and enshrines the fictional Weyland Industries brand identity. This viewing mode, which enables the audience to constantly switch between the registers of fictionality and their construction, reveals a production metaphor of process.

> Historically, unlike the 'all-at-onceness' of live news coverage, that is, fictional production necessarily referred to events in the past (On 'all-at-onceness', see McLuhan and Fiore 1967). With technological and para-industrial change, however, *the time of drama has increasingly collapsed into the time of the event being dramatized.* (Caldwell, 2014: 737, emphasis added)

More recent examples of this collapse of the film-production process into the reception of the film include two interactive museum installations that were designed to reveal and to facilitate access with the behind-the-scenes materials from *Inception* (2010) and *Gravity* (2013) in order to showcase the acclaimed, breakthrough visual effects (VFX) of each of the films (discussed in Atkinson, 2014).

These are both US productions, but are brought into this discussion since they were both post-produced in London, *Inception* at Double Negative and *Gravity* at Framestore, and the installations were both designed and created by UK-based 59 Productions in collaboration with the London post-houses. Both installations enabled the audience to physically step into and experience the spaces of production and the subjectivities of the makers (see Figures 5.3 and 5.4). This is another instance where the production metaphor of process is made manifest through the audience's interactional engagement with 'dynamically de-compositing composites.' This subjectivity illuminates the emergent phenomena that I have named *Simulacinema*. A portmanteau term combining the words simulation and cinema, which I am proposing should describe a new phenomenon in which an audience simultaneously experiences both the space of the filmic diegesis and/or the cinematic spectacle, and the attendant, but crucially, *simulated* space of its production. Simulacinematic spaces are characterised by the uncanny sense of inhabiting two conflicting ontological spaces, whilst also embodying two diametrically opposed subjectivities. *Simulacinematics* refers to the aesthetic and affective qualities of these spaces which merge film style and visual cinematic codes with production aesthetics.

It is a space that is routinely inhabited by performing artists, actors and film-production personnel, but it is the audience who are assimilated into a *simulacinema*tic space through their engagement with these two installations.

As we have seen in the traditional representative texts, the making and reception of a film tend to be chronologically displaced moments but within simulacinematic phenomena, by contrast, the two moments are folded together into simultaneous experiences in which the two temporalities converge in an experiential modality, all, at once, deliberately inhabiting, celebrating and performing 'the commercial drama of a movie's source' (Corrigan 1991: 118).

The intrinsic reflexive aesthetics of both the *Gravity* and *Inception* installations, in which their content, style and presentation took on the representational characteristics of the film's diegetic worlds, presents a conflation between the film and the processes of its making, just as we saw with the examples above.

The presentation of such processes, on the one hand disenfranchised the creators in their lack of presence, but on the other, elevated VFX work as a creative and innovative vocation. As such, I would contend that they are symptomatic of the social, political and cultural status of the troubled global VFX labour economy in which they were situated in 2012, in which VFX work is effectively hidden, and in some cases the voices of the practitioners are silenced (which will be discussed further, later in this Chapter). Such ancillary texts continue to reveal just as much about the certain processes that they have chosen to amplify as they do about what, and *who* they have chosen to hide. As both the masters and subjects behind these installations, the VFX artists have become victims of their own craft, which is at its best when they have completely erased and removed all traces of their own existence within the films and content that they have created. This discourse of the 'artistry of the invisible' work persists throughout a number of film-production professions and results in the paradoxical affective logic between what I have termed as the pseudo-visible and the hyper-invisible.

Figure 5.3 The 'fold-over' moment in *Inception*, which required the characters to crane their necks in order to watch the spectacle, is simulated in the installation whereby gallery visitors are required to adopt a similar pose in order to fully appreciate the visuality of the installation. (Image from *Inception*, 2010, Dir. Christopher Nolan)

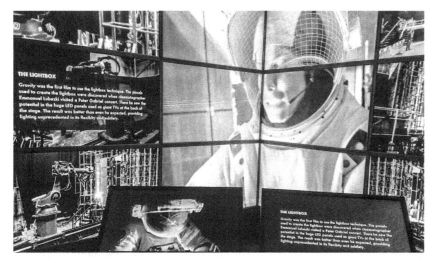

Figure 5.4 The design of the *Gravity* installation simulated the performative lightbox which was constructed as part of the making of the film. (Image from *Gravity*, 2013, Dir. Alfonso Cuarón and Framestore; Installation Design 59 Productions, Digital Revolution Exhibition, Barbican Centre, London, 2014)

Pseudo-visibility and Hyper-invisibility

I have coined the term *pseudo-visibility* to refer to the way in which film practitioners have an instant platform upon which to communicate their processes and working conditions, and to engage in what Kate Fortmueller would describe as a public 'performance' of their labour (2015). This performative and fictional dimension to these texts is captured in Cecelia Sayad's observation that 'performing authorship involves also the interplay between the fictional and documentary dimensions of the author's depictions both of their own selves and of their creative processes' (2013: 31).

Pseudo-visibility refers to the over-representation and saturation of certain roles and certain types of spectacular production work. *Hyper-invisibility* on the other hand, is the paradoxical corollary, where film-production professionals deny or render themselves invisible through their own production practices, as manifested in the VFX examples above. This aesthetic of erasure that the professionals perpetuate alludes to a similar type of paradox that Torsa Ghosal has identified as 'an "unprojection" – that is, the process by which films project a storyworld only to deny or erase it – in the context of media technology' (2015: 1).

Pseudo-visibility

Pseudo-visibility is one of the defining logics of the 'economy of film production' – the space in which revenue is generated around the commer-
cialisation of materials that relate to the making of films. In addition to the
materials discussed, there is an entire expansive ecosystem of goods and
experiences which enable consumers access to the materials of film and to
engage in experiences and simulations of their making.

Combined with this commercial access to the making of film, both in
mainstream cinema and in the independent film economy, there has been a
tendency towards a quasi-openness of practice – that is a controlled, selec-
tive and restricted insight, protected by the industry gate-keepers who
are the producers of this content. This is exemplified in many examples
including *Transformers 4: The Premake* (2014) where the film's producers oscillated between collaborationist and prohibitionist modes (Jenkins,
2006b) in their inconsistent issue of YouTube take-down notices. Certain
clips were permitted, whilst others were removed. Authorised narrative
insights, dressed in the rhetoric of being 'shown behind the scenes' and
revealing industry secrets, had been referred to by John Caldwell as 'modern media's classic double-bind: the accelerating trend towards greater
and greater self-disclosure and transparency alongside increasingly vigor-
ous attempts to legally shut down access to insider information as proprietary, and thus inaccessible to outsiders' (Caldwell, 2014: 732–3).

With the advent of digital technologies and networked communication,
there has been a proliferation of these types of material being circulated,
the flow and temporal reordering of the release and authorised access to
these materials has increased, and attitudes towards openness, particularly
in relation to independent film, are shifting. For example, in one instance,
the filmmaker released the full budget details of *Papadopoulos & Sons* (2013)
online before the film's release. *Colony*[9] is a platform for the distribution of
independent film and its related ancillary content. It enables the purchaser
to buy a 'bundle' of extra behind-the-scenes materials associated with the
film. Such strategies of circulating behind-the-scenes production matter,
which are, crucially, curated sets of materials, implies a deliberate obfusca-
tion according to Lisa Purse:

> Caught up in the paratextual 'real story' of a movie's technological sophistica-
> tion provided by promotional materials, which itself draws on a utopian cultural
> conception of digitally enabled technological empowerment, the spectator is much
> less likely to closely ponder the mechanics – and politics – of the film's represen-
> tational dynamics and visual narration. (2013: 26)

Purse's observation reflects the contradictory crux of this pseudo-visible logic – the seemingly relentless openness to process, conceals and occludes more than it reveals.

Hyper-invisibility

Many books and accounts in film production refer to the invisibility of those responsible for its making (Kozloff 1988) which echoes across other media industries (Bonini and Gandini, 2016). Instead, certain roles are foregrounded and subject to an over-representation, these include the Director, the Director of Photography, the Producer, the Camera Operator and more recently, the VFX Supervisor.

It is those below-the-line practitioners – those responsible for blending scenery and costume into a holistic, visual, imperceptible mise en scene, for hiding cuts, for overseeing production logistics and ensuring continuity, who are masters in the art of disguising and rendering imperceptible their presence and traces of their input. In addition to the VFX workers discussed above, these have been identified as including designers, scriptwriters, editors, continuity/script supervisors, casting directors and costume designers. Jane Barnwell observes a similar paradox to that which I have noted in relation to VFX workers, in the work of the designer:

> Possible reasons for the anonymity of the designer lie in the *invisible* nature of much of their work. The design is there to support the overall production, not necessarily upstage it. This is also in relation to the naturalistic codes employed in the vast majority of film and television. According to Allan Starski, the designer's responsibility is to make the audience believe the artifice they are watching is real (see Ettedgui 1999), therefore suggesting that the designer is *complicit in denying their own existence* in order to sustain this belief. (2004: 15, emphasis added)

Similarly, Julian Hoxter comments on the invisible labour of scriptwriting, which he states

> . . . is unique both in being at once present in the product of every other craft, as inspiration, as guide, and even as direction, yet (with the exception of instances of visual text such as intertitles) also simultaneously *absent* from the screen. (2014: 1, emphasis added)

Hoxter goes on to state that: 'Finished films reveal much of the screenwriter's world and craft, but they conceal more' (2014: 10).

Time and time again, the discourse of invisibility recurs in academic discussion, press, and industry:

> The central dilemma – and paradox – for costume designers is that their job is to visualize a character through a costume that should go unnoticed by the audience because it looks organic to the personality of the character. The invisibility of costume designers' labor on the screen, however, frequently means that they are marginalized on the set and in the press. (Banks 2009: 91)

Editing as a form of work is also considered to be a 'hidden' labour of filmmaking. In part, this is a result of representational texts favouring and foregrounding the spectacular aspects of on-set production and apparatus. In Chapter 4, I discussed how the camera was the central locus of activity in on-set film production: it is also the central piece of iconography in film-production representational texts and this is at the expense of other less visible processes. As Jean-Louis Comolli observes:

> To elect the camera as 'delegated' representative of the whole of cinematic equipment [. . .] the ideological representation that spectators have of work in cinema: (concentration on shooting and studio, occulation of laboratory and editing) between the *visible* part of the technology of cinema (camera, shooting, crew, lighting, screen) and its *'invisible'* part (black between frames, chemical processing, baths and laboratory work, negative film, cuts and joins of editing, sound track, projector, etc.), *the latter repressed by the former*, generally relegated to the realm of the unthought, the 'unconscious' of cinema. (1980: 125, emphasis added)

Editors also inhabit an interesting position since they exemplify the above- and below-the-line dichotomy – whereby the line is both an economic distinction in budgetary terms, and also a cultural distinction recognising what is deemed to be artistically valued. There is divided opinion as to the editors status in this regard. In an account of his role, Anders Refn, the Editor on *Ginger & Rosa*, suggests an elevated status, and one which aligns to the Director:

> You should have an awful lot of skills to be a good editor. You should have a sense of music. You should have a sense of literature, of drama, of painting, and a lot of psychology, and a lot of practical things, you should have technical skills, you should really, have almost as many disciplines as a director.[10]

The disagreement regarding editors as artists or cutters can be understood through the lens of 'art house' and 'commercial/studio' cinema. As Martin Stollery states, the definition of 'Commercial' unashamedly evokes the profit motive underlying the feature-film industry, and 'cutting' emphasises craft skill rather than the more artistic connotations of 'montage' or even 'editing' (2009: 377), going on to state that in this context 'Editing involves intellectual, creative and manual labour which cuts across class and occupational distinctions' (Ibid.)

There is, however, a clear consensus regarding the inevitable invisibility of the editor's work: 'Our work is by and large unnoticed and consequently misunderstood' (Tariq Anwar, editor, *The Madness of King George* and *American Beauty* in Perkins and Stollery, 2004: 4), and Kevin Brownlow goes further to state that: 'Editors are passed over by film historians because their work, when successful, is virtually unnoticeable' (1968: 286).

This characteristic invisibility of many aspects of the film-production process has inevitably meant that women's contributions have been further hidden from view, particularly since they inhabit those more hidden roles listed above. It is widely known females are significantly under-represented in feature-film crews internationally (Smith et al., 2013a and 2013b). More recently, there has been a flurry of mainstream media attention focused on the under-representation of women in the film industry, brought to the foreground by a number of high-profile A-list film celebrities. These have included Sadie Frost, who, to make her most recent film, *Buttercup Bill*, which she produced, employed a team that was up to 80 per cent female (2015) in order to raise awareness of the imbalance (Alberge, 2015). In April 2015, Meryl Streep established a Screen Writer's Lab for women over the age of 40, in order to increase the diversity of voices within the film industry (Lee, 2015).

One report (Follows, 2014a: 9) noted that the percentage of women on British films has barely changed in the past five years. One only has to look at the film releases of 2012 listed in Chapter 1, page 5, to reveal how few were directed by women. The camera department is particularly under-represented: 'of all the departments, the Camera and Electrical department is the most male, with only 5 per cent women' (a study undertaken between 1994 and 2013 of the 2,000 highest grossing films (Follows, 2014a: 3). There is a more promising picture in the UK whereby 11.2 per cent of camera/electrical departments are female. In the case of *Ginger & Rosa*, as is the case on many sets – the camera and electrical departments were wholly constituted by male crew members. Women accounted for 2 per cent of all cinematographers working on the top 250 films of 2012, and 98 per cent of the films had no female cinematographers (Lauzen 2012: 2). Women comprised 20 per cent of all editors working on the top 250 films of 2012, and 77 per cent of the films had no female editors (Lauzen 2012: 2). The female Re-recording Mixer on *Ginger & Rosa* echoes this lack of female representation in technical roles in relation to sound departments:

> There are a lot of female editors. Actually I think that's 50-50 male or female but in the sound department because there is a lot of buttons and technical stuff I think there are a lot of girls who think 'Oh, this is not for me'.[11]

By looking at the traditional problems of invisibility and occlusion within cultures of production, the conflict and tension between above-the-line and below-the-line work is brought into sharp focus. Historically, women have inhabited and been represented as inhabiting a particular set of roles related to the more mundane, more routinised form of production, including the 'in between', the emotional, and the logistical. As Sophie Mayer has noted, 'invisible labour in cinema' is often carried out by women. (2008: 140). There is an implicit and notable *feminisation* of certain roles in film production, which, as David Hesmondhalgh and Sarah Baker explain: '"feminisation" rarely refers to a predominantly male occupation becoming predominantly female. Instead it tends to denote an increase in the concentration of women within that occupation' (2015: 2). The gendered nature of film-production roles has historically been underlined through related representational texts. Take, for example, in *How Walt Disney Cartoons Are Made* (1939), the voice-over describes how:

> . . . the thousands of pencil drawings go to the inking department. Here hundreds of pretty girls, in a comfortable building all their own, well lighted, air conditioned throughout, colour the drawings with sheets of transparent celluloid [. . .] They next go to the painting department where more pretty girls apply the final colours on the back.

In *How the Fleischer Studios, Miami, Florida, made 'Aladdin and His Wonderful Lamp'* with Popeye (1939) – similar roles – the animation of the frames between key frames are referred to as 'in-betweeners', and it is predominantly women who are seen on-screen undertaking these roles. In an observation of earlier cinematic technique, in the 1910s, Fairservice noted how:

> . . . every distribution print was assembled individually from shots, scenes and titles printed and tinted appropriately by the laboratory and then cemented together by teams of young women employed expressly for the purpose. (2001: 332)

Women have continually been depicted as intermediaries in film-production work throughout history, and I have made a similar observation myself in Chapter 3 regarding the role of the Digital Imaging Technician. Their representation in more senior, creative roles is minimal. In the *Reluctant*

Dragon, one of the female Disney staff members exclaims incredulously when asked if she is responsible for operating the camera: 'The camera? Oh no I'm just in charge of the things they feed through it' (1940).

In her study of Costume Designers and the gendering of industry professionals, Miranda Banks asserts that: 'This necessity for diplomacy that is central to their labor defines costume designers' work as both a manual craft and emotional labor' (2009: 93). Erin Hill notes a similar emotional dimension of feminised work within the role of the Casting Director:

> Contemporary casting directors also attribute the field's female domination to emotional aspects of the work that, much like the feminized duties women's studio jobs acquired, are tied to notions of gender and require acts of feminine performance. (2014: 149)

In her study of the history of women's work in media production, Hill discovered that in the 1930s and 1940s: 'The women who produced and maintained the sea of paperwork on which each production floated formed the largest population of female workers and were arguably most important to the studio's daily workflow' (2016: 4). This feminisation of logistical roles has continued into the present day where there is a higher concentration of women working in production management, producing and continuity. One such role which maintains and marshals the 'sea of paperwork' that Hill describes is the Continuity or Script Supervisor. There has been a significant historical study into this role by Melanie Williams, and the notable feminisation of their identity as 'Continuity Girl' or 'Script Girl' (2013: 603). Freddie Young and Paul Petzold (1972) describe the role of the Continuity clerk as 'Throughout the production the continuity clerk, usually a girl, makes careful notes of all the furniture, clothes, and of the positions of props and details in the scene connected with them so that this visual side of the continuity is maintained' (1972: 32).

As Sue Harper points out, continuity's designation as a 'female prerogative' has resulted in an 'attendant lack of status' (2000: 4). Phyl Ross argued that continuity 'isn't a very suitable job for men, because of its very detailed nature' (1944: 14–19, 16). Sue Harper explored a number of roles within her 2000 study including Producers, Writers, Directors, Costume Designers, Art Directors and Editors. In these explorations, she concluded: 'It is clear that certain film professions can be more easily combined with childcare. Editing or scriptwriting fall into this category, while art direction does not' (2000: 234).

As Harper rightfully indicates, there have been a significant number of notable female editors (Wright, 2009), particularly working in

Hollywood.[12] There are, however, conflicting and changing histories as to the identity and the status of editors – see the article published in *American Picture Play* magazine in May 1916 (Cook), entitled 'The Film Surgeon,' it depicted the lone male individual editor as an 'important gentleman (Cook 1916:220), undertaking meticulous, artful, careful procedures. Then, when studio film production increased, the editing role evolved as a result of the introduction of the Moviola machine in 1924, which marked a turning point in the perception of this vocation. Driven by a variable-speed foot control, rather like a sewing machine, representations of editing work showed groups of women working en masse in factory-like conditions, and the role was presented within the context of a homogenised, routinised and mechanised workforce. 'In 1926, the Los Angeles Times informed readers that "one of the most important positions in the motion-picture industry is held almost entirely by women"' (Hatch 2013: para 1).

There are clearly cultural distinctions between Hollywood Film and European Film. For example, in earlier research, Siân Reynolds noted 'a significant number of editors of French films, even in the 1930s, and to a much greater extent thereafter, have been women' (1998: 66), thus supporting Jean-Luc Godard's gender distinction that: 'tourner est masculin, monter feminin' (shooting is masculine, editing is feminine) (1998: 94). Godard's view is reflected in the wider assignation of gendered suitability to the role which was initially characterised by the menial and mechanical labour of 'cutting', and predominantly undertaken by young working-class women.

Compounded by the invisibility of editing as a craft, women's presence in these roles is overlooked, and they are yet again rendered invisible by their own hand, in a similar way as Williams has observed: 'Continuity is a job that hinges on invisibility, noticed only if it is not done properly via continuity errors which render visible the processes of film-making that should ordinarily be invisible' (2013: 608).

This is the core characteristic of the hyper-invisible logic, film-production workers are complicit agents in their own erasure, their work and their identities remain hidden behind the veil of their own construction. This sustains and protects the exclusivity of precarious labour through hiding certain skills, whilst the pseudo-visible spectacle which over-represents key roles, ensures a high-demand for skilled workers through the perpetual celebration of certain types of work. Rather than working in contradistinction to one another, the double-edge logics of the pseudo-visible and hyper-invisible provide a form of checks and balances which buttress and sustain the economy of film production.

Collective Auteurship – Anatomy of a Film Featurette

Many have argued that the DVD provides a new platform which perpetuates a 'commerce of auteurism,' through the inclusion of obligatory 'extra features' including behind-the-scenes footage and the Director's voice-over, a discursive site which provides an opportunity to inflect further authorial insignia and singular unilateral intentionality to the text (Grant, 2008; Egan, 2015). Others have argued that DVDs opened up a channel for multi-vocal approaches and 'post digital notions of authorship' (Orgeron 2007: 60), through which to present and visualise the different aspects of film labour. Alan Lovell and Gianluca Sergi have underscored the significance of this channel to film-production professionals:

> We believe that in this (very human) desire to claim an individual stake within the larger hierarchy lies one of the keys to the understanding of the way Hollywood filmmakers operate. This negotiation is at the heart of how filmmakers understand their own contribution to filmmaking, both in terms of their own individual effort and how this impacts on the collective project. (2005: 59)

I here return to the concept of collective auteurship – a key facet of *Ginger & Rosa's* Production Aesthetic – which was mobilised in the production of the *Anatomy of a Film* featurette which featured on the UK release of the *Ginger & Rosa* Blu-ray and the US version of the DVD. During the research process for this book, I had the opportunity to curate some of the material for the production of this featurette through a model which I devised to propose a more holistic rendering of the industrial film-production process through the presentation of, and interaction with, the testimony, production, documentation, ephemera and observational footage.

The Anatomy of a Film was conceived as an antithesis to traditional making-of materials in its inclusion of a variety of above- and below-the-line production personnel – it included profiles of the Writer/Director, Producer, Director of Photography, Costume Designer, Production Designer, Hair & Make-Up Designer, Casting Director (UK), Location Manager, Editor, Production Sound Mixer, Stunt Coordinator, Art Department Assistant, Publicist, Special Effects Supervisor, Executive Producer (BBC Films), Re-Recording Mixer, Post-Production Supervisor (UK) and the Second Assistant Director. This inclusive approach captures Potter's ethos of openness within her production processes. The inclusion of the work of the publicist was a highly unusual strategy, as Bordwell and Thompson have noted through their extensive study of DVD extras:[13] 'The marketing of a film seldom gets described on DVD, apart from the fact that trailers and posters come with most discs' (2013: 48). It included

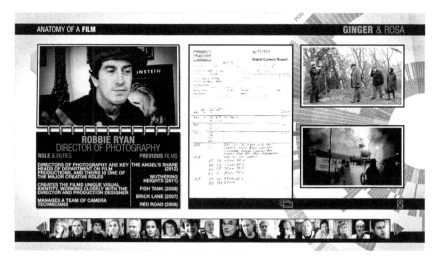

Figure 5.5 Anatomy of a film interface (Atkinson & Holden, 2012. Artificial Eye, UK, Blu-ray & Lionsgate, DVD, USA)

interview excerpts, from eighteen contributors in total – six women and twelve men. This is representative of the *actual* gender split on the film, and the associated production worker's metric, where men outnumbered women approximately 2:1.

In its design, the featurette aimed to present the possibilities of a contemporary visual archival interface (based on the proposed future designs of SP-ARK, Potter's own online production archive) enabling the simultaneous and synchronised access to many of the materials of production. As Figure 5.5 shows, the screen presentation was split into three windows where the viewer can see and hear excerpts from the interviews, above the outline CV and role profile of the interviewee. A further window showed behind-the-scenes footage (by Joseph Matthews) of that particular person within their natural work environment – on-set, in a production office or in a post-production facility. The third window cycled through production documentation either produced by, or associated with that particular person. In the interactive version of the DVD, the viewer could prioritise any of the screens to full screen viewing mode, and switch between the two audio streams (to be able to listen to the interview and of the behind-the-scenes footage). The presentation of the thumb nails timeline at the foot of the interface is flattened into a visual representation of the egalitarian chain analogy that one of the producers proposed in Chapter 2, page 71 (although if viewed in linear order do represent a production hierarchy of sorts).

From its conception, the featurette aimed to be as representative as possible in its presentation of a broad, diverse range of aspects of film-production work from as many different voices as possible across the production hierarchy, including both senior figures who were the Heads of Departments, and also junior members of the crew such as the Art Department Assistant and the Second Assistant Director. The interviews and the material also originate from different temporal locations across the entirety of the production chain – from on-set to post-production and from financing through to publicity. Through capturing moments in time across the production cycle, the sense of daily-ness and film labour was captured, thus the film's Production Aesthetic was mobilised particularly in relation to collective auteurism. The featurette was produced in direct collaboration with Potter and Adventure Pictures, who oversaw and signed off the content. Despite giving voice to a diverse and more representative range of the different agents within the film production, these are all shaped and framed from the perspective of the maker, the production company and the film's distributor who all took a view during the editing and curation process.

More sustained and acute responses to this pseudo-visible/hyper-invisible paradox can be located in forms of resistance and protest which I will now go on to discuss.

Resistance and protest

As predicted by Chanan, who believed that film-production professionals 'would become doubly aware of the ideological form of the media. From outside, as ordinary receivers, and from inside [. . .] as both subjects and senders' (1980: 118), the subversion of both the tools and aesthetics of production have started to emerge. This emergent ideological awareness is made manifest in the use of the film-production professionals' own voices and materials in more advanced and complex ways that go beyond mere promotion to instances of resistance and protest, in unofficial and unsanctioned media channels.

The same protocols, representational aesthetics and production iconography (as discussed in Chapter 2) have been mobilised in counter narratives and in campaigns of resistance, and which sometimes work in opposition to, rather than in support of industry promotional narratives. As I shall go on to examine, these fall on a spectrum which spans collective action to counter resistance.

There are also nuanced instances where the two oppositional subjectivities, of promotional discourse and resistance can coalesce. This is evidenced in the 'You make the movies' (2009–2010) anti-piracy campaign by the UK's Industry Trust. This campaign comprised a number of cinema and television advertisements depicting the general public in ordinary situations enacting iconographic scenes from films including *Jaws* (1975), *Sixth Sense* (1999), *Jerry Maguire* (1996), and *Reservoir Dogs* (1992).This campaign deliberately underlined the value of the audience through its 'You make. . .' maxim, whilst also simultaneously implicating them – whether intentionally or not, since all of the people featured in the adverts are seen 'copying' and 'mimicking' scenes from films. The 'authorised' resistance to the public by the industry came in the form of an accompanying 'making-of' video which included behind-the-scenes footage and interviews with production personnel. These were not about their processes, but about the impacts of piracy upon their own personal livelihoods and the threats to the sustainability of the industry. The campaign which centralised the audience as agents is 'corrected' by the producers in this ancillary content as they reinstate themselves as the creators and artists behind the films. The crew explicitly addresses the imagined audience and explain how their jobs are at threat through piracy. This has been a core trope within other anti-piracy propaganda as Roman Lobato has also observed: 'MPAA ad campaigns attempt to counter the belief that piracy is a victimless crime by featuring Hollywood technicians and tradespeople lamenting the threat that piracy poses to their livelihoods' (2012: 73).

In this example, we see an indirect critique, by the industry, of audience behaviours. The more direct critique of industry exploitation is communicated in counter-documentaries and films that show the darker side of industry practices, including *Who Needs Sleep?* (2006). Haskell Wexler's documentary, produced by the American Society of Cinematographers (ASC) and The Institute for Cinema Studies, USA, features interviews with Annete Bening and Julia Roberts. It is a documentary that highlights the deadly combination of sleep deprivation and long days of work for film-industry workers, focusing on the death of Wexler's co-worker. Brent Hershman, an Assistant Camera Operator died in 1997 in a car crash whilst working on *Pleasantville* (1998), after a 19-hour shift, preceded by 15-hour days. This led to a petition for 'Brent's rule' in 1998, to ensure a maximum 14-hour shooting day. It was signed by over 10,000, but has yet to be adopted.

In addition to overtly resistant texts such as those discussed above, production iconography and aesthetics of production have also been used as forms of symbolic protest. Take for example, the clapper board, the most dominant defining piece of production iconography and also the most visible in film production – its image is recorded at the beginning of every clip of footage that is captured on-set. This single icon which is used to represent and semiotically implicate the form is also a salient and habitual feature of visual promotional materials. The clapper board icon has also been used as a tool of protest – to raise awareness for Sarah Jones, the Camera Assistant who was killed on the set of *The Vampire Diaries* as a result of the director's and producer's negligence in February 2014. The 'Slates for Sarah' and 'Safety for Sarah' campaign was a below-the-line protest, through which to lobby to improve the working conditions for below-the-line technical workers, in which film crews routinely taped 'RIP Sarah Jones' to production slates (see Figure 5.6) and circulated images of these using the #setlife[14] and #slatesforsarah social media hash tags. Yellow film location street-signage was also used to display her name in streets around the SGA-AFTRA (Screen Actors Guild/Federation of Television and Radio Artists) headquarters. Such was the profile of this particular case that it was featured in the 86th Academy Award Ceremony's 2014 'memorial montage'.

As Caldwell had previously observed: 'Worker tools are far from inert. [. . .] they are cultural representations in their design and use. They are also instigators of subcultural craft expression among the workers who use, debate, and contend over them' (2009b: 203). As I have argued here and elsewhere production tools and materials are indeed apparatus with ideological implications.

Figure 5.6 One of the many 'Slates for Sarah' which drew attention to the campaign for increased safety and protection for film production workers, 2014.
(http://www.theblackandblue.com/2014/02/26/rip-sarah-jones/)

A similar use of production iconography prevailed in the VFX pro-tests[15] from 2012 onwards – brought to public attention through the high-profile bankruptcy and closure of Rhythm and Hues in the same year in which the film for which they were awarded an Oscar for best VFX was released (*Life of Pi*, 2012). These protests, predominantly occurring in the US, in response to a crippling system of global tax breaks, occurred both in physical on-street protests and in online social media campaigns. Green-screen iconography was repeatedly subverted to illustrate the invisibility and non-existence of special effect/computer generated imagery footage.

On the streets, VFX workers held up green screens for placards which stated 'Your movie without VFX' and wore entirely chroma-key-green body suits – the workers/protestors are embodying the pseudo/hyper paradoxical logic.

VFX practitioners changed their social media thumbnail profile pic-tures into chroma-key-green coloured squares, and circulated images of famous green-screen scenes from CGI films in which all the effects had been rendered invisible. In a context of a non-unionised section of the industry[16] the workers have resorted to the subterfuge of contemporary film production iconography through which to draw attention to their exploitative working conditions.

Figure 5.7 VFX worker protests, Los Angeles, 2014 (*The Hollywood Reporter* online, 2 March 2014, http://www.hollywoodreporter.com/behind-screen/oscars-visual-effects-rally-attracts-684493)

Figure 5.8 An example of one of the many protest images circulated on social media channels in response to deteriorating working conditions in the VFX sector. (Circulated across social media channels)

Conclusion

As I hope to have demonstrated within this Chapter, the industry is highly proficient and sophisticated in the creation of its own representation through its own medium, using its own self-referencing practices and mediated language. These have worked to meet a number of imperatives within film-industry production cultures – to showcase the work of professionals, and to protest against challenging and exploitative labour conditions. In their fetishisation of certain aspects of production – they meet a number of ends – they offer to the consumer the vicarious experience of production; they contribute to the marketisation of mediation within the context of the experience economy; and they ensure the constant over supply of entry-level production personnel, willing to work for free or to accept poor conditions such is the appeal of the 'magic' and excitement of the industry. As such these have further implications for the understanding and future study of the film industry. The circulation and mobilisation of these materials is proposed by Caldwell to form part of the 'para-industry' which he describes as:

> . . . an economic and cultural-industrial interface woven together by socio-professional media communities, through trade narratives, ritualised interactions and conventionalised self-representations that viewers and scholars must wade through before they can find a primary text or featured on-screen content. (2014: 721)

Within this context, we must question what will be reliable objects of study in the future, and how will these impact upon the integrity of the archiving, if para-industrial materials are to become authoritative historical records of film production, and thus a future source of film-production literacies? Indeed, many scholars already rely solely on industry-authorised, scripted and controlled disclosures, which, as I hope to have communicated are significantly compromised texts:

> Thus the historical variation of cinematic techniques, their appearance-disappearance, their phases of convergence, their periods of dominance and decline seem to me to depend not on a rational-linear order of technological perfectibility nor an autonomous instance of scientific 'progress', but much rather on the offsettings, adjustments, arrangements carried out by a social configuration *in order to represent itself, that is, at once to grasp itself, identify itself and itself produce itself in its representation.* (Comolli 1980:121, emphasis added)

How can the representational and simulated materials of film production that I have discussed in this Chapter support or hinder future retrospective historiographical production studies? And how do archival structures, principles and practice contribute to cultures of representations of film production in a moment of convergence? These questions feature as some of the concerns of the following Chapter.

Notes

1. In an interview with the author, 7 September 2012.
2. In an interview with the author, 6 June 2012.
3. Ibid.
4. Throughout the years, amongst others, these have included *Hellzapoppin'* (1941), *Singin' in the Rain* (1952), *Peeping Tom* (1960), *8 ½* (1963), *Le Mépris (Contempt)* (1963), *Day for Night* (1973), *Blow Out* (1981), *The Player* (1992), *New Nightmare* (1994), *Living in Oblivion* (1995), *State and Main* (2000), *Timecode* (2000), *Goodbye, Dragon Inn* (2003), *For Your Consideration* (2006), *Maps to the Stars* (2014) and *La La Land* (2016).
5. http://www.openculture.com/2011/04/how_walt_disney_cartoons_are_made_.html
6. Foley is the name given to the process through which sound effects are created and recorded in a studio after the film has been shot, in synchronisation with the action on the screen – such as footsteps, doors closing, etc. These techniques originated in 1914 – and are so called after their creator Jack Donovan Foley.
7. https://www.worldcat.org/title/20th-century-fox/oclc/423304663
8. In an interview with the author, 26 October, 2012.

9. https://www.wearecolony.com
10. In an interview with the author, 30 April 2012.
11. In an interview with the author, 13 August 2012.
12. A significant number of female editors with prolific careers including: Dorothy Spencer who edited over 70 Hollywood studio productions between 1929 and 1979 including *Stagecoach* (1939), Hitchcock's *Lifeboat* (1944), *Cleopatra* (1963) and *Earthquake* (1974); Margaret Booth, editor on over 40 films from the mid 1920s to the 1980s including supervising editor (uncredited) on *The Wizard of Oz* (1939) and *Annie* (1982) and editor on *Ben-Hur* (1959) (uncredited) and *Mutiny on the Bounty* (1935); Dede Allen who was active between the 1940s and 2000s and who edited films including *The Breakfast Club* (1985), *The Addams Family* (1991), *The Hustler* (1961); Anne Coates, a British editor, active from the 1940s until the present day and responsible for editing over 50 feature films including *Fifty Shades of Grey* (2015), *Erin Brockovich* (2000), *The Elephant Man* (1980) and *Lawrence of Arabia* (1962); Thelma Schoomaker, long-term collaborator of Martin Scorcese, working from the 1960s to present day, whose editing credits include *Raging Bull* (1980), *Goodfellas* (1990), *Hugo* (2011) and *The Wolf of Wall Street* (2013); and Sally Menke, active in 1980s to 2000s prior to her untimely death in 2010 – Menke was a long term collaborator of Quentin Tarantino, responsible for the editing of *Reservoir Dogs* (1992), *Pulp Fiction* (1994) *Kill Bill: Vol. 1* (2003) and *Kill Bill: Vol. 2* (2004).
13. See Bordwell and Thompson's detailed list of recommended DVD and Blu-Ray supplements (2013: 47–8), also augmented by their 'Beyond Praise: DVD supplements that really tell you something' series of blog entries.
14. The #setlife hashtag is used to share and circulate pictures and comments from film practitioners working on sets. This tends to be a positive and celebratory channel of communication – pictures depicting the latest equipment, picturesque locations and celebrity sightings.
15. http://www.fxguide.com/featured/coverage-from-the-oscar-subsidy-protest-live-updates/
16. In the absence of union support a number of counter, grass-roots organisations have emerged Including ADAPT and The Animation Cooperative.

CHAPTER 6

Digital Film Production
Preservation and Access

Introduction

This Chapter turns to the consideration of the processes of representation that are endemic in the historicisation of film production, through an investigation into the manifestation of 'representational attenuation' in emergent film archival paradigms at the 'pivotal point in historical research and the future interpretation of history' (Velios 2011: 257). Given that the film archive preserves, curates, presents and frames what are essentially representational texts, I propose a mode of exegesis that enables us to look beyond the obvious in our analysis and interpretation of film archival practices. Within this Chapter, I consider the notion of a film archive in its broadest sense to include physical, digital, online repositories, websites, platforms, and apps, essentially any curatorial entity which presents and enables access to the materials of film production.

I will take forward the questions identified in the conclusion of the previous Chapter: how can the representational and simulated materials of film production support or hinder future retrospective historiographical production studies? And how do archival structures, principles and practice contribute to cultures of representations of film production at a moment of convergence?

Just as the digital production apparatuses that were examined in Chapter 4 were imbued with the aesthetics of the celluloid film, I examine how film archives come to be characterised by the transitional aesthetics of the archival moment. I consider how the 'Production Aesthetic' of a particular film, author or canon, is transmogrified into a 'production legacy aesthetic'. I identify a production legacy aesthetic as that which (either authentically or erroneously) reveals the provenance of the archival asset (or the way in which it is framed) that enables it to be placed in its historical continuum.

In what follows, I underscore the significance of the archive as a *representational* object of study in and of itself through the demystification of 'archival legacy aesthetics' – which are the result of the rendering of organisational hierarchies and organisational principles as archival asset frames. I do so using the approach that I refer to as a 'structural archival analysis' – a media archaeological (Huhtamo and Parikka, 2011) approach which is focused upon the archival system itself, or to borrow Joel Katz' term - an 'archiveology' (Katz, 1991). As we shall see, the archival legacy aesthetics of the film-to-data transitional moment are rife with digital-to-film atavisms which implicitly communicate the structures, conditions of production and politics of digital film.

As well as explicitly retelling a story about the technical tools and technologies of the day, the approach to the organisation of knowledge can intrinsically expose approaches to working practices and labour conditions of the time, or a particular context and the politics of production. Online versions of physical archives and the nature of their digital design and their mechanisms of access and interaction can also be exceptionally revealing of structures and ideologies of access and control, since, as Michel Foucault proclaimed:

> it is from within these rules that we speak, since it is that which gives to what we can say – and to itself, the object of our discourse – its modes of appearance, its forms of existence and coexistence, its system of accumulation, historicity, disappearance. (2002: 146)

In this Chapter, I will first consider the notion of 'the Digital Dilemma' – one of the most pervasive discourses cutting across archiving and accessing of cinema in 2012. I then expound the different archival modes through a number of case studies, including the national BFI archive, Stanley Kubrick's archive, and draw upon my own involvement in both the SP-ARK[1] archive and the Deep Film Access Project[2]. These latter two are research projects born from collaborations between film researchers, computer scientists, archival institutions and film-production professionals. Both projects sought to innovate film studies approaches and archival methodologies, in the first instance by presenting materials generated from the film production process in order to facilitate and further academic study within the field, and in the second, through the proposition of an alternative archival model for a hybrid data set which challenges and advances current film archival practice.

Digital dilemma

The impact of the digital has been subject to much conjecture relating to the potential lacuna in the history of cinema in an era of 'present-mind-edness' (Pietrzyk, 2012), compounded by the ominous threat of a 'digital dark age'. My research was set against the back drop of the 'Digital dilemma' (Science and Technology Council, 2007 and 2012), poised at the bleeding edge of obsolescence, in which both Hollywood (2007) and the independent film sector (2012) grappled with the storage and preservation issues of digital film. Indeed, the perpetual state of a film-to-data transition is often attributed to the lack of satisfactory storage and preservation capabilities of digital technologies. In Chapter 4, it was suggested by many professionals and commentators, that celluloid film is a far more vulnerable medium than its digital counterpart due to its susceptibility to physical damage and degradation over time, in alignment with Adam Ganz and Lina Khatib's previous claim that 'Film is a comparatively unstable fragile medium. It needs to be protected from light and extremes of temperature. [. . .] The digital images that replace it have no physical existence, can be copied for nothing and are more or less indestructible' (2006: 24). However, as digital film production has evolved, and the pace of technological change has increased, it is actually the reverse that is true – the digital has proved itself to be a fragile and unstable medium due to rapid changes in compression standards and the accelerated obsolescence of storage data. As long as appropriate physical conditions are ensured – a stable temperature, with the correct humidity and light levels, film can be preserved for a very long time and, in terms of accessing physical film, all that a viewer needs, to be able to see the celluloid record, is a source of light with which to shine through and project the image. Motion-picture film is, therefore, described as a 'direct-access medium' (Academy of Motion Picture Arts and Sciences, Science and Technology Council 2012: 12) in contrast to motion-picture data, which is an 'indirect access medium' (2012: 13). Its futurity is still fraught with challenges. As Laura Marks comments in her discussion of 'digital mortality': 'Digital media are as fragile as analog, if not more. Digital video's vulnerability is more evident in low and obsolete technologies' (2002:157).

Within the discourse of the Digital Dilemma, the film industry is considered to be in crisis in terms of attempting to secure a robust, affordable and realistic archiving strategy for digital film, due to its size and data complexity. These concerns tend to be focused on the preservation of the digital film object itself (Fossati, 2011; Thompson, 2011) and are not necessarily considered with the multitude of accompanying materials, data and metadata that are generated through a film's production, which are my own key areas of concern and of fundamental importance. As Martin Hand has stated: 'Metadata produces an audit trail for an archaeology of the future where dead objects can be rediscovered and their previous lives understood' (2008: 151). If this issue is ignored or sidelined, the notion of 'rescuing fragments' as the new task for cinephilia (Toles, 2010) will become a reality.

The importance and significance of film archival efficacy for the future of film and media studies cannot be understated. The exposure to previously hidden women's histories and representations has been reliant upon archival materials (Harper, 2000, Hill, 2016). Significantly, Emily Carman (2016) was able to map the trajectories of professional freelance women, which had been, up until then, omitted from mainstream Hollywood histories through the retrospective archival studies of documents, contracts and other legal documentation from the period. As Adrienne Rich states: 'Re-vision – the act of looking back, of seeing with fresh eyes, of entering an old text from a new critical direction – is for women far more than a chapter in cultural history; it is an act of survival' (1979: 35). Within the context of the Digital Dilemma, there are further key challenges at stake relating to the archiving of digital film, which I have identified as: Reliability, Vulnerability, Volume and Data Complexity.

In relation to digital film **reliability**, as *Ginger & Rosa's* UK film distributor noted, the use of digital files in cinema exhibition has not been without its challenges:

> I've experienced films that have run completely normally on the screen for three weeks at a time, and then after being ingested (which is the process of the feature film being moved from the external hard drive onto the server at a particular venue), just like that they sometimes disappear and there's no real explanation why that happened. I think that's just one of the downsides of the digital revolution, there are just things that are not easily explainable.[3]

As the Academy of Motion Picture Arts and Sciences also acknowledges, digital data is subject to 'invisible failure mechanisms' (2012: 13), and can be just as susceptible to 'visible' damage as its celluloid predecessor. Digital media can suffer from a range of irremediable manifestations including bit rot, digital artefacting, frame drop-out, format and system decay, file entropy, and lossy compression[4].

But as David Berry et al. claim, these 'glitches' may come to serve as an element of a significant medium legacy aesthetic which is key to latterly positioning the origin of a piece of digital film, video or moving image in its historical period or process. They refer to 8-bit retro as: 'a 'down-sampled' representation of a kind of digital past, or perhaps digital passing, given that the kinds of digital glitches, modes, and forms that are chosen are very much historically located' (Berry et al. 2012: 42). This reflects Paolo Usai's prior assertion that 'there would be no history of the image if it were not subject to decay' (2001: 41). The signs of time passing are frequently romanticised for film – 'Its materiality gives it humanity. It has a physical lifespan' (Iles, in Cullinan 2012: 84), the same is absolutely not yet true of the digital format although these very well may be subject to the same re-evaluation in due course. The visual manifestation in digital film damage may come to play an important role in its provenance in future digital histories.

Another issue which is of great concern within the context of the Digital Dilemma, and the archiving of born-digital materials is the **volume** and velocity of digital file propagation, made manifest by rapidly increasing storage capabilities. The *Ginger & Rosa* data set was over 20 TB. This was relatively small in size in comparison to CGI films, those with extensive VFX, and stereoscopic 3D production, which automatically doubles the size of the data set and the complexity of on-set data-wrangling processes. As we saw in Chapter 3, shooting ratios are now much higher, and endemic of digital film production which can be characterised by its distended 'over production,' where vast amounts of digital film can now be shot without the economic cost implications which had previously inhibited film production. Excessive digital file production is characteristic of the digital film-production chain which is subject to relentless processes of back up, copying and cloning, such is the concern about the medium's unreliability. The Camera Assistant explained this process for the production of *Ginger & Rosa*:

> We make three backups a day. One stays in the truck here with us, one goes to the editor, and one goes to production, so there's three drives, three copies of the footage in three separate places, so it's quite a safe system.[5]

Digital film files are also repeatedly cloned and copied later in the post-production process to enable different workers to access them simultaneously to undertake various procedures. These activities then generate numerous other media, data and metadata files. For example, the sound editing and mixing process involves the creation of additional music, sound effects and Foley files. Visual special effects processes also generate all manner of digital files, which exist in complex metadata structures and multi-layered visual composites, which can exponentially increase the overall 'film data' package.

This leads to considerations of **data complexity** in terms of all of the different file types and formats, and multiple versions of the film and its constituent elements. This complexity was compounded in the context of *Ginger & Rosa*, since it generated a hybrid data set which blended born-digital materials, with film-based and analogue media and documentation, a majority of which is dispersed and unlinked across various physical and digital sites of storage. Herein lies the innate problem of film-production data complexity, that is that the links between the media data, are only made meaningful by the logic of the film-production process itself. That logic is one of market imperatives, where files are chronologically linked in a workflow that is in a continual state of forward motion. During the making of any independent or commercial feature film, the dominant imperative of all those involved, is to move efficiently through the film-production workflow, on schedule and on budget. As such, files are changed, overwritten and deleted as part of the efficiency methods employed throughout the process in order to facilitate smooth data-flow and to keep processes running smoothly on-set. The inevitable data-loss is compounded by the fact that there is generally no established archival strategy factored into the film-production process: materials become quickly separated across geographic and physical locations, dispersed across hard drives and servers, making the collation of the data at the end of the production fraught with challenges. The established film production chain is one where elements of the film are passed from one department to the next, rather like handing on a baton in a relay, from production agent to agent. There is no imperative to archive, save or preserve the data or the film in these preliminary stages. Data is changed, overwritten or deleted. Likewise, at the point of delivery, data is not stored or maintained as a matter of course. This is even further compounded by the rapid obsolescence of different file types and compressions associated with digital film, and the inability to open and read files without access to appropriate storage and playback media, and the associated compression/decoding software, which in turn leads to the **vulnerability** of its preservation and future access.

Film archival modes

There are three main organisational principles within film archives that I would argue are key to understanding how they manifest 'production legacy aesthetics' and 'archival legacy aesthetics'. They are the upper-most hierarchical level (known as the fonds), the dominant organisational principle and the Accession & Cataloguing Principles. Of course, there are also numerous sector, national and international film archival standards and metadata schema under which these principles operate, which I will detail in a moment. Similarly, the film industry is subject to the requirement to implement technical standards for formatting audio visual output in terms of resolution, compression, frame rates, etc.[6], but there are no such technical requirements for the formatting of production metadata and associated digital film metadata in textual terms. As I have noted, within the film-production process, there is no future archival orientation of the materials, it is not about ensuring these files or the associated data are legible for a future public, rather the sole imperative is to impel the film-production process forwards.

I will now comparatively analyse a number of film archive initiatives and their operational principles in and around 2012, examining the axiomatic assumption that archives are indexically neutral and objective spaces, which bring to bear a particular (institutional, organisational or individualistic) view as to the nature of film production, and labour organisation.

The BFI features as the national institutional example: it is the most significant in terms of its size and influence. In 2011, the BFI went through a process of amalgamating a number of their archives and databases into one system[7] – Adlib[8] (de Esteban 2013). Adlib works in conjunction with the BFI's Collections Information Database (CID) which was made publicly available from April 2013[9] and is compliant with Spectrum.[10] It further conformed to a number of international archival standards and protocols. These include ISAD-G,[11] the Open Archival Information System Standards (OAIS, ISO 14721: 2003) and the European Committee for Standardisations (CEN) [EN 15907] (BFI, 2011: 18). EN 15907 provides a set of technological approaches 'for the purpose of exchanging metadata about cinematographic works' (BSI Standards Limited (2012: 4). The standard was established to ensure interoperability between archives which sought to 'provide a bridge between the data that exists and the new emerging technologies chosen to represent this data' (BSI 2010:4). The BFI embedded this model into their own database, adapting it to televisual works (which constituted the majority of BFI holdings at the time). The BFI's upper-most hierarchical level is dictated by the fonds, which is defined by the Society of American Archivists as: 'The entire body of records of an organization, family, or individual that have been created and accumulated as the result of an organic process reflecting the functions of the creator.'[12] As Figure 6.1 shows, the fonds can be the work of an individual creator/director or a previous owner of a collection.

At the top level of the hierarchical structure is the Director/owner of the work, followed by the work itself (the film – referred to here as the 'series'), the item classification (here referred to as the 'sub-series' and then the individual item with its associated description and technical specifications).

Table **6.1** Comparative table listing the different archives that are discussed within this chapter, and their defining features. (By the author)

Archive/ Feature	Upper-most level (Fonds)	Medium base*	Predomi-nant mode of access	Dominant organisa-tional principle	Catalogue navigational mode (interface)
BFI (2013)	Director/ Film/ Collection	film/ analogue/ digital	Physical	Object	Filing cabinet
Stanley Kubrick Archive (2007)	Director	film/ analogue	Physical	Film and Object	Filing cabinet
SP-ARK (2012)	Film (*Orlando*)	film/ analogue	Online	Process	Film production process and GVI**
Deep Film Access Project (2014)	Film (*Ginger & Rosa*)	digital/ analogue/ film	Online	Process	Film production process and GVI
David Cronenberg: Virtual Exhibition (2014)	Director	film/ analogue/ digital	Online	Film	Themes and GVI
A Field in England Masterclass Materials (2013)	Film (*A Field in England*)	digital/ film/ analogue	Online	Process	Film production process and GVI

* the dominant/primary media is listed first
** Graphical Visual Interface

In an interview with BFI library and collection specialists,[13] they described how the archival principle is like going into separate filing cabinets of the various different collections: the interface itself visually represents this analogy as a traditional folder and file system. The accession and cataloguing processes undertaken via digital and online catalogue and record systems, appear to replicate and emulate the traditional physical organisation of an archive. They went on to explain how a proficiency in

Hierarchy browser

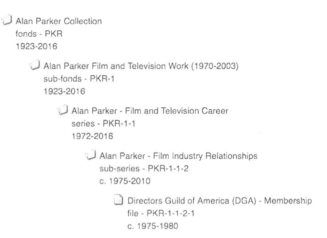

Hierarchy browser

Hierarchy browser

Figure 6.1 Three different structures from the online interface of the BFI CID database. Each example reveals how the fonds is dependent on the source of acquisition. (BFI)

archival searching is a prerequisite to the successful location of items. As the BFI's collection policy states:

> Information architecture – all datasets shall have a variety of access points. To avoid search inefficiencies, ambiguity and duplication, all access points shall be standardised and derive from a single authoritative list for each category, such as film titles or people. (BFI 2011: 18)

Since this is a catalogue which brings together all of the physical and digital collections of the BFI, some of the items are available to view digitally on line, whilst a majority are only accessible by a visit to one of the four physical locations.[14]

The BFI also work under the FIAF Cataloguing Rules (1991) which amongst other directives instruct the archivist to 'write a concise, objective, non-critical summary of the content of the work.' This illuminates the authoritative, regimented approach to archiving which suggests an adherence to consistency and objectivity.

The BFI database presents a remediation of the physical archive into the digital space. Both the filing-cabinet system, and its associated

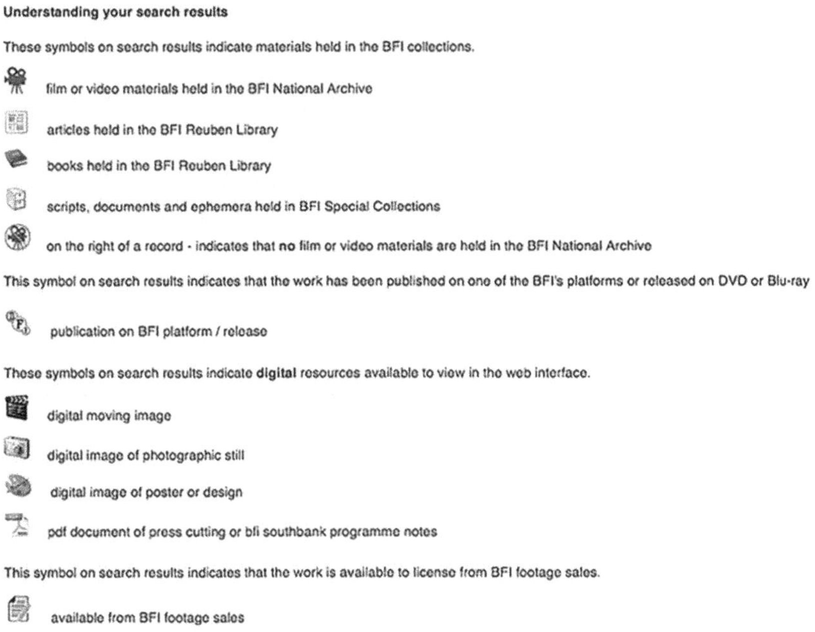

Understanding your search results

These symbols on search results indicate materials held in the BFI collections.

film or video materials held in the BFI National Archive

articles held in the BFI Reuben Library

books held in the BFI Reuben Library

scripts, documents and ephemera held in BFI Special Collections

on the right of a record - indicates that no film or video materials are held in the BFI National Archive

This symbol on search results indicates that the work has been published on one of the BFI's platforms or released on DVD or Blu-ray

publication on BFI platform / release

These symbols on search results indicate digital resources available to view in the web interface.

digital moving image

digital image of photographic still

digital image of poster or design

pdf document of press cutting or bfi southbank programme notes

This symbol on search results indicates that the work is available to license from BFI footage sales.

available from BFI footage sales

Figure 6.2 A key depicting the different symbols used within the online BFI database. (BFI)

icons depicted in Figure 6.2, replicate analogue process and practice. As we saw in Chapter 4 this is a characteristic also inherent and embedded within film-industry process and practice, whereby analogue process and practice are enshrined in emergent digital working procedures and terminology, as a transitional measure, which in that case served as a means to support film-analogue-practitioners forwards through a period of digital transformation. Within this context, inflecting the film-to-digital transformation upon the digital manifestation of the archive, it marshals analogue archivists and archive users into the digital domain.

There are a number of independent archives that have been created to preserve and showcase the canon of an individual film director. In these cases, the director becomes both the key organising principle (the fonds) and the defining aesthetic of the archive. These examples include the archives of Stanley Kubrick, David Cronenberg and Japanese Director Akira Kurosawa[15]. As Michele Hilmes has stated in relation to this approach:

> The 'individual author approach' has many advantages, following recognizable and well-worn paths of understanding creative production – still valid and important, even within a wider industries approach – and all of the historiographical conveniences that come with that: a limited field of focus, an automatic periodicity, a bounded narrative, and a congruence with the way that source materials tend to be produced (e.g. collected papers of individuals in archives, search terms in indexes, biographical works, journalistic coverage, etc.). (2009: 23)

Hilmes here describes the cultural familiarity with this format, it is one that is immediately recognisable, accessible and intuitive to navigate. Stanley Kubrick's archive provides an example of this form, which has been housed by the University of Arts London, since its donation by the Kubrick estate in 2007. It is a physical archive, covering 853 linear metres, and first arrived in 977 boxes (Mahurter, 2007). Its online catalogue is subsumed into the institution's library catalogue. There are no digital versions of the assets available online, which is in part due to the complex rights issues that are associated with the archive[16]. Access to the items is via personal visit only. The archivists attempted to retain as much of the original ordering of the extensive personal production archive as possible – which was through the organising principle of the films. Where there was no original filing system, the archivists defaulted to organising the materials into the key film-production phases. The extensive archive includes production paperwork, production photographs, magazines and press cuttings, fan letters, correspondence, memos, equipment, props,

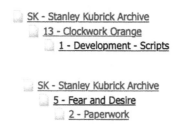

Figure 6.3 The cataloguing structure of Stanley Kubrick's Film Archive.
(University of the Arts London)

costumes, business documents, personal papers for all of Kubrick's films including unfinished projects (such as *Aryan Papers*, *Napoleon* and *AI Artificial Intelligence*), items and film stock relating to the two making-of documentaries produced by Vivian Kubrick for *The Shining* (1980) (released) and *Full Metal Jacket* (1987) (never released). As Figure 6.3 shows, the materials are organised in a flattened structure compared to that of the BFI, but in common with the BFI, the fonds is the director, followed by the film.

Kubrick's meticulous attention to detail in the collection, preservation and organisation of his production materials (depicted in the television documentary *Stanley Kubrick's Boxes* (2008)), is carried forth into the digital version of his archive, through the archivist's adherence to Kubrick's own idiosyncratic archiving principles. During my own visit to the archive, I was able to look through Kubrick's fan letters, which were neatly filed in their original state in three separate files marked - 'good' 'bad' and 'cranks.' In the associated book that curated and showcased some of the archival materials (Castle 2008), the same archival aesthetic resonates in which the main organising principle is again the film and the stability of the collection of assets is anchored to the text of the film.

Jacques Derrida highlights the role that these structures play in *constructing* the history and truth of the past they are recording:

> The technical structure of the archiving archive also determines the structure of the archivable content even in its very coming into existence and in its relationship to the future. The archivization produces as much as it records the event. (Derrida and Prenowitz, 1995: 17)

The accession and cataloguing principles can be distinguished in two key ways: the **structural** – film and object criteria in the case of the BFI, and the **temporal** – process criterion which I will go on to discuss.

Within the structural approach, the organisation of the archival assets are not temporally ordered: there is no indication as to their origin or provenance within the temporal workflow of the film's production. This is as a result of, and then leads to further voids in the capture and perseverance of the procedural aspects of film production and the conditions and politics of production, and what Rachel Moseley and Helen Wheatley referred to in their observation of televisual archives' lack of inclusion of feminist programming, as 'archiving the ordinary' (2008: 153). Jacqueline Wernimont underscores the fundamental issue of archives in this regard:

> Digital archives unite two historically gendered fields – computer and archival sciences. Literary scholars who depend on archival or rare book materials still confront, whether they acknowledge it or not, the legacy of an institutional form through which patriarchal power exercised the authority to determine value, classification, and access. (2013)

Vicky Ball and Melanie Bell make a similar observation:

> This invisibility has been compounded by implicitly gendered archiving and cataloguing practices which have obscured or marginalised women's contribution to the production of film and television. (2013: 551)

The dominant organisational principle of the object is inherent in both the BFI and also in the archive of the National Media Museum[17] which includes physical film and media equipment and technologies. They use the MIMSY XG object database for cataloguing. Within the collection catalogues, these are anachronistically organised through categories, such as *Document: Production: Daily progress report*. Its generic material status, 'document', is prioritised as the top level in this model, followed by its type. The 'material' object type takes priority in this system, other object categories include Design, Document, Ephemera, Photograph, Poster, Script.

This is as opposed to assigning the task or the person behind it as the top level. These design approaches tend to exclude anyone else in the narrative of the film's creation. This object-led approach to archiving is dictated by institutional acquisition processes and the use of proprietary archives, libraries and museum software as was the case with BFI's use of Adlib.

The organising principles and strategies described above are imposed upon the collections after the filmic event, that is the asset collection is disassembled, if indeed it ever existed as an assembled version. In most film productions, particularly independent ones, the assets that are generated are all saved in different locations, to different devices and are the responsibility of different departments and individuals. CID enables relationships to be identified.

As I contended in the previous Chapter, invisibility is a recurring motif in film production in which practitioners perfect the invisibility of their process by the nature of their work; the film industry is a heavily guarded industry, with gate-keepers at all levels. As discussed in Chapter 2, the film industry is also a very difficult domain to enter professionally – so the film archive is also at risk of emulating a system of closure, through a closed system of restricted access and one in which the self-representations of their process become subsumed into future archival strategy. As was revealed in Chapter 5, this is an industry that lacks representation of women in certain areas, and so the archive risks following the logical continuum or perpetuation of an aesthetic of omission. Thus the politics of archival strategies and archival aesthetics, have led to certain tendencies which have rendered invisible the contributions of many. These at best occlude, and at worst render invisible women's contribution to the film-production process. As Griselda Pollock has contended: 'Vast areas of social life and huge numbers of people hardly exist, according to the archive' (2007: 12).

Feminist archive studies (Moseley and Wheatley 2008; Callahan, 2010), have highlighted issues around the occlusion of female film practitioners. As Ball and Bell have commented:

> Many of the roles in which women have been employed leave little or no archival trace. Much film and television production practice goes unrecorded anyway, but this is particularly acute around auxiliary or 'supplementary' roles where a disproportionate number of women have made their contribution to production. (2013: 551)

The invisibility of both process and personnel as previously described in Chapter 5, is inscribed in such a strategy in which the final film is prioritised as the core archival object under which all associated archival assets are organised.

There are a number of exceptional female archiving projects, underrepresented female histories of production. These include 'The Women Film Pioneers Project'(WFPP)[18] which is a freely accessible, collaborative online database that showcases the hundreds of women who worked behind-the-scenes in the silent film industry as directors, producers, editors and more. There is also a website created by three British-based women script supervisors which aims to promote greater understanding of the craft,[19] as well as a site set up by costume designer, Jane Petrie[20] which reveals and documents some of her working practices.

SP-ARK

Sally Potter provides a unique insight into the potential for the archiving of film production (Atkinson 2012b) through her subjectivity as a creative collaborator. Her own online archive SP-ARK which presents, in interactive form, the film/analogue production materials from Potter's 1992 film *Orlando*. SP-ARK is based on a purely film-asset base, it is a digitised version of a physical film archive, with no born-digital materials, all footage shot on film, some video assets and all typewritten or handwritten production documentation. Its dominant organisational principle is based on the ordering of the traditional film-production workflow cycle, from Development, Pre-Production, Production, Post-Production, The Finished Film to Distribution (see Figure 6.4).

Archival items are arranged into further taxonomical sub-categories of the different elements of production process, in the temporal order in which they were generated, based on the long-embedded history of film-production workflow. This is to be expected given that the archival organisational structure derives from the film-production company responsible for the production and generation of the materials which are housed within it.

Figure 6.4 The SP-ARK archival interface and its constituent search and navigational mechanisms. (Adventure Pictures © Adventure Pictures Ltd)

In this sense, the archival infrastructure itself provides insights into the nature of film production for the period in which it was designed, or in this case, for the film for which it was designed – *Orlando*. It is also a structure that reveals the associated Production Aesthetic. The SP-ARK infrastructure itself was defined and designed some twenty years later taking the structuring of the materials as its lead and as a result, within its content, we can already start to see a number of 'production legacy aesthetics,' for example the creation of 'video assist' was a function of a particular pre-digital era. Production legacy aesthetics are also implicitly embedded into its structure, in the strictly linear production process. As was discussed in Chapter 3, the key tenet of the organisation and management of film-production assets is the film workflow: that is, all of the resources that are generated are organised into systems that pertain to the day on which they were generated. Within the digital environment of SP-ARK and through the application of the known and established synonyms of film production, the primacy of the daily-ness is made manifest.

Sophie Mayer has described SP-ARK as making 'visible the unvalued, and thus feminized, activity of Filmmaking [. . .] It reflects the daily-ness of labour involved in filmmaking as opposed to the heroic narrative portrayed in mainstream films' (2008: 201). The key organising principle of the archival resources was based on the film-production workflow and the interaction between the different processes of that workflow, thus representing the process as a collaborative, procedural, labour-intensive and inclusive endeavour, the 'production legacy aesthetic' of collaborative auteurism. This stands in stark contrast to the BFI and Stanley Kubrick archives which prioritise the Director. As Yvonne Tasker has noted:

> Auteurism privileges the authored text over the complexities of context. At the same time, the work of feminist film historians in documenting the contribution of women to the film industry represents not only an important attempt to write women's history but a rejection of the claims made by, or more typically on behalf of, one person – the male director – to have priority over the text (2010: 213).

Aside from the production taxonomy, archival navigation is facilitated by multiple search mechanisms, free text search, tags, related linked items, and the unique 'pathways' feature which enables users to engage in interpretation, conversation and dialogue around the different archival assets. An 'archival legacy aesthetic' emerges in the pathways' 'blogging' functionality, which was a specific digital engagement mechanism of this particular moment in time.

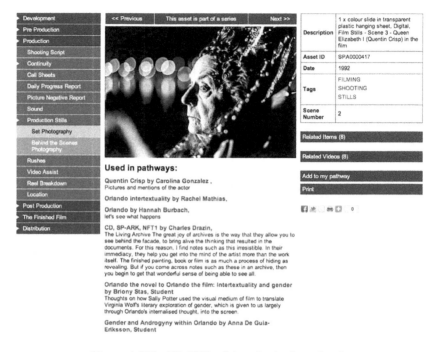

Figure 6.5 The SP-ARK collaborative 'pathways' tool.
(Adventure Pictures © Adventure Pictures Ltd)

The Deep Film Access Project

The Deep Film Access Project (DFAP), which was based on a hybrid data set, produced an archival model proof of concept. I draw on the research process of this project in order to tease out the key considerations and challenges of reliability, vulnerability, velocity and complexity, through my own subjectivity: as a researcher working towards an archival ontology, working atemporally; as the collator of the production materials; as witness to their creation, to archive curator and then as creator of the DVD featurette *Producer*. Each of these roles brought into sharp focus the challenges of digital archiving practices.

DFAP was undertaken in collaboration with film-production practitioners and archive-curation specialists, aiming to support a new framework of standards for recording and linking data during the production of feature films. In addition to Adventure Pictures, project partners included the BBC Archive Development, the BFI, the National Media Museum and Screen Archive South East who all advised on standards, accession and cataloguing principles and software.

The DFAP was based on the entire corpus of materials generated by *Ginger & Rosa* which, as I have already extensively examined in this volume, was digitally shot but retained many craft processes and as such resulted in the creation of a hybrid data set. The subsequent archiving of *Ginger & Rosa* involved the extensive scanning of a significant amount of analogue material, including handwritten continuity notes from the script supervisor, costume and hair and make-up continuity, Potter's own 'Look Book', a key piece of development documentation which was central to her creative process. The archival process also included collating innumerable digital documents, many of which had physical manifestations with additional handwritten notes, including script updates. The video recorded interviews, which were undertaken with every single film production worker,[21] were a further crucial facet of the DFAP ontology through which to understand and contextualise the archival materials.

The hybrid archive aesthetics manifested in three key ways: first, separate, distinct film and digital assets that exist side by side (pure-digital or pure-analogue assets), second, assets that have properties of one another (printed documents with handwritten notes), and third, entirely *mutated* assets (digital film data).

The hybridised archive was and is the most dominant contemporaneous archival paradigm, which I would argue is indicative of the 'digital film' transitional moment in which film and data, analogue and digital, are imbricated within the same system of preservation, access and interactivity.

It is important to comprehend the sheer volume of the data that is produced and replicated and the highly repetitive nature of this (for example, the multiple 'takes' that might be shot of the same scene), the many different versions of the script that might be created throughout the process (every time one amendment is made, a new version of the script is recreated), and the vast amount of frames that are created during a minor VFX manipulation. My own affective response to increasing digital data levels was one of workflow-warp – information fatigue caused by data volume.

Another critical aspect is the reliability and vulnerability of the data. This is not about the reliance upon the digital medium itself, but the production process – in which in post-production – files are overwritten, deleted or missing. For example, in the case of *Ginger & Rosa*, as I found out to my detriment, before the film's distribution, all FX files were deleted (post-delivery) at the point of archiving.

Independent films that [. . .] secure some form of distribution do so after a much longer time period than movies produced by the major studios. This time period

quite likely exceeds the 'shelf life' of any digital work; that is, by the time distribution is secured, the digital data may become inaccessible. (Academy of Motion
Picture Arts and Sciences. Science and Technology Council 2012: 4)

The SP-ARK archival infrastructure was taken as the reference point
from which to develop a set of organising principles for the DFAP ontology, given that it had already been developed in collaboration with film
professionals and academics.[22]

The data set was highly complex in nature due to the relationships
and interconnections between a diversity of data types, from scripts and
emails between directors and producers, to budget information, shooting
schedules, digital film and sound files, and Polaroid photographs taken for
continuity. This was further complicated by the chains of communication
within contemporary film production process – what was once a series
of letters, and typewritten documentation, now takes the form of endless
strings of email communication, copied, blind copied, etc. (as examined in
Chapter 2 in the manifestation of workflow-warp).

These factors – reliability, vulnerability, volume and complexity, made
it an exceptionally challenging task to bring together the data set in its
entirety in order to begin the modelling and ontological design. An incomplete archive, it involved the recreation of many production documents
and files by the film's production team in order to resolve any recesses and
discrepancies in the workflow. All data, files and materials that were generated were implicitly interlinked, but with connections both unrecorded
and lost throughout the production process, making the archival process a
sometimes circuitous one, where interstitial chasms, caused by the inherent processes of erasure, required retrospective fixing and suture.

Links between items were broken, and the assets had to be re-organ-
ised and re-assembled in accordance with the archive's organisational
structure. The film production process is myopic, in that the key objective
is to get from one stage in the production process to the next in order to
sustain the pace and velocity of the workflow. There is an issue of implicit
digital communication systems (phone calls, text messages, emails and so
on) which surfaced when I attempted to build an ontology for film production – these implicit and inferred communication networks are problematic for archival purposes and for the structuring of film-production
data, these many caesuras disrupted the cause-and-effect flows of digital
data production.

The approach taken to the ontological and archival modelling was a
use-case scenario, where all of the materials relating to one scene undertaken on one shooting day were chosen. The particular scene selected was

one of the most complex in the film and involved all of the production departments in its execution. Taken from one scene (73), on one shooting day (28: 23 March 2012), at one location (Greenham Common), the materials that were gathered cut across all the departments involved in the production, and across all the processes, development, pre-production, production and post-production. Files included script pages (printed and then handwritten), casting contracts, child licences, digital film rushes, sound files, schedules, budgets, location agreements, call sheets, graphics, filmed interviews with practitioners, iPad preview footage, archive video for research on Aldermaston, Avid editing files, and all behind-the-scenes content (see Figure 6.6).

A file-naming system had to be established to make consistent sense to the computer scientists in order to effectively organise these files for the ontological design process.

Figure 6.7 illustrates the development of the ontology[23] which is based on the workflow processes, broken down into flexible and modularised activities (known as 'operations'). This is so that they are 'moveable' and can run simultaneously or anachronistically, as the digital film production process evolves. Each operation is undertaken by one or a number of production personnel or 'agents', and results in the production of a 'product' – which could generally be considered as one archivable unit, such as contracts, work permits, reports, call sheets or video files (file extensions are also added, since there is a level of complexity around the diverse range of digital file types that can be generated – often the output of bespoke, proprietary software platforms that are only readable on those platforms, such as Final Draft (.fdr) and Movie Magic (.mdb). In contrast to SP-ARK and other archives, this process ensures the assignation of a process and a document to a particular crew member – the provenance and legacy are indelibly linked to the person who created it.

The concatenation of processes reflects the daily-ness and modularity of the production workflow, thus laying bare the conditions of production. By working closely with the film production professionals who were responsible for generating the assets, the archival structure could take shape, based on the temporal ordering of workflow throughout the production. The DFAP provides a system that facilitates complex and multi-perspective interrogations of archival materials from multivalent perspectives and users.

Figure 6.8 illustrates the application of the 'use-case' and how the materials can be accessed in multiple ways, based on the interactive capabilities of an HTML 5 framework. The DFAP ontology facilitates multiple chronologies: the finished film timeline chronology (scenes 1–89), the

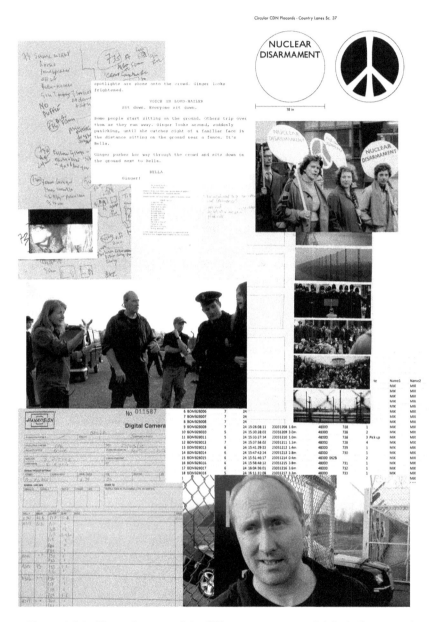

Figure 6.6 An illustrative array of the different use-case materials including research materials, the script, pages from Potter's 'Look book', graphics from the Art Department, continuity notes, camera report, sound report, crew interviews and behind-the-scenes footage. (Adventure Pictures © Adventure Pictures Ltd)

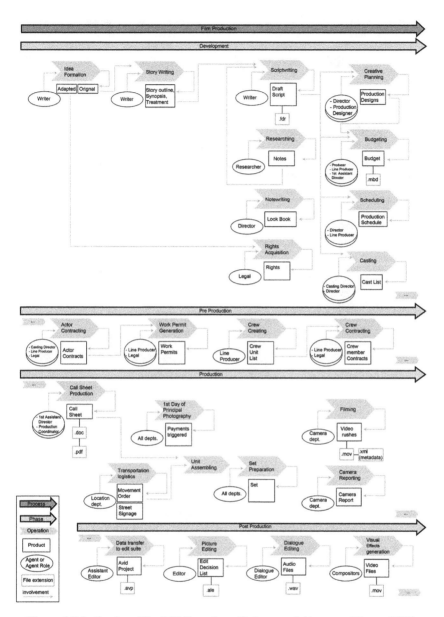

Figure 6.7 A slice from The DFAP ontology. (Lehmann, Atkinson and Evans, 2015)

Figure 6.8 Visual design of DFAP archival interface, populated by materials from the 'use case'. (Produced by Bullet Creative. bulletcreative.com)

production process chronology (days 1–871)[24] which is accessed via the navigable visual timeline at the top of the screen; production role ontology which can be accessed via the various crew interviews (depicted in the middle-centre of the screen), or event or story ontology. This facilitates the tracking of a particular 'production narrative' through the archive (examples in relation to *Ginger & Rosa* could relate to the name change of film from *BOMB* to *Ginger & Rosa* or the innovative casting process which involved a YouTube casting call). A number of R&D projects have explored this potentiality – for example the BBC storyline ontology or stories[25]. Produced in 2013, this example again highlights the latent fascination with *process* that was noted in the previous Chapter – a characteristic concern of a transitional moment, prevalent within an industry undergoing technological change. This predilection towards process also manifested in other online archives of the time. Take David Cronenberg's online virtual exhibition[26] that adopts an interactive timeline approach, allowing the fluid navigation of the archive which is stylistically designed and imbued with the authorial imprint of Cronenberg through the application of a number of dominant authorial aesthetics.

Similarly, in the example of the online masterclass materials of *A Field in England* (2013), we are invited to 'Follow the Process' to access the various testimonies and stories from different crew members. In this instance, the archive takes the form of a narrativisation. Within narratological studies, archival structures are often aligned to the logics of the database and their associated organisational aesthetics (Hallam and Roberts, 2011), whilst links are frequently made between emergent narrative structures and the database (Hayles, 2007). The idea that the archive can take on a textual form or a performative one, as proposed by Simone Osthoff in the conceptualisation of a performing archive, transforming it from a 'repository' to a 'medium' (2009), is illustrated through Athanasios Velios' proposition of 'creative archiving' in his creation and analysis of the online archive of author and artist John Latham.[27] The archive is designed in such a way that the shapes the users experience are from the point of view of one of Latham's fictional characters. The user's subjectivity is shaped as the casual, the informed and the intuitive. Depending on the point-of-view access, each user will experience different archival search and access modalities. The casual user will be able to undertake a basic database query, the informed user can engage in an archival search based on the Archival Thesauras, and the intuitive user will be able to access a sophisticated classification system based on John Latham's time-bases.

These experiential, thematic and textured experiences, of born-digital archives where 'process' appears to be germane to digital structures, where both the production process and the viewer are implicated in the process of searching, engenders a closeness to the archive that is in stark contrast to the distancing aesthetics of the authoritative and patriarchal hierarchical structures of the BFI. This is one possibility amongst a myriad of digital and open archival affordances and futures. (Further have been identified in Atkinson and Whatley, 2015.)

Conclusion

These opportunities of course face pragmatic challenges, where audience and user expectations exceed what is currently possible technically and institutionally for a number of reasons. The BFI, for example, is limited by funding, resources and national cuts to support for the arts. And as Martin Hand contends: 'The dilemma is whether it is possible to make things accessible in this way while preserving an archival ontology' (2008: 32). But, aside from audience access, there are many untapped archival potentialities from the perspective of the film industry, particularly through the use and reuse of production materials which are repeatedly created in production processes; currently, this represents a significant amount of *wasted*[28] effort. Take for example the notion of an economic archive – the opportunity to cut money from a production budget through the ability to source, access and use the archival assets, which are regularly repeated across all location-productions.

When I visited the Stanley Kubrick archives, I was struck by the amount of collated production-planning materials which could be used for other productions. There was one bulging folder, marked 'gateways' in which there were what seemed like hundreds of photographs, depicting stately home gates throughout the UK, for potential use in the film *Eyes Wide Shut* (1999). If these images were linked to geographic information, a location scout with a similar brief could make use of such a rich resource without having to replicate the work. These could create efficiencies and opportunities in both the creative and logistic processes, where the director is able to look for the most artistically appropriate opportunity and the producer will be taking into consideration location logistics, accessibility and costs. There are also opportunities for access which can be afforded to disciplinary areas outside of film: location stills, for example, provide unique historical records of the changes to a location over time. Using the innate opportunities of digital technologies (GPS in digital cameras) would further augment these possibilities since the image metadata could be used in conjunction with other tools and sources of online information such as Google maps, heritage-listing databases, photo archives and zoning regulations. Putting issues of IP and copyright aside[29], repurposing born-digital assets such as 3D environments for CGI and VFX films, could be used in the converged economy, across film, broadcast, game and architecture.

If links between data can be preserved at the point of acquisition ensuring contiguous data-stream access for future users to locate and cross-reference materials, and if a pipeline could be created that could export digital film-production data and metadata into preservation and archiving software this would offer innumerable opportunities for researchers, film fans and future audiences. In 2012, there were new technological developments, but as we saw in *Ginger & Rosa*, practice was yet to catch up. At the time, an 'mxf' – open file format[30], enabled the packaging of video and audio essence files with their associated metadata and, since the development of a 'master archive package'[31] in 2014, illuminate the technological advances which provide the opportunity for more effective linking of data and metadata.

Despite these opportunities, existing and emergent challenges relating to the digital persist and stymie innovation. If digital film preservation and storage was the focus of the Digital Dilemma in the 2010s, then metadata preservation and restoration will be the challenge of the 2020s. This involves the effective re-linking and rebuilding of metadata sets and the interrelations between the objects when part of the film-production flow, in order to ensure its integrity and representational accuracy. There can no longer be the reliance upon object quiescence in physical archives – that is when an item is archived and it remains in a state of unchanged stasis – in the case of the digital, objects can and will be dynamically altered, augmented and enhanced where 'the archival object is not an object at all but a *dynamic configuration*' (Hand, 2008: 153).

This Chapter captures the digital archival dichotomy of excess and loss. The paradox of the Digital Dilemma is that on the one hand, there is the irrepressible metastasisation of digital film data, and on the other, there is its recalcitrance to complete disappearance. The overwhelming sense of its presence (through the physical infrastructures of data storage and management and movement of data) is countered by the threat of its total absence and disappearance as an immaterial medium. Discourses of loss and endangerment (Cullinan, 2012: 8) persist in the archival discourse of 2012, just as they did in the industrial discourse: from Mike Gubbins' lost demographics (2011), to Jan-Christopher Horak's omissions (2007), to the impacts upon the lack of a visible history (Knight, 2012). This dualism persists in other parallels that this Chapter has illuminated – between distance and closeness, objectivity and subjectivity, archival inclusion and omission.

The presence of an archival aesthetics has been revealed which inevitably shapes any and all future engagements and archival excavations. The attenuation and cognisance of the various production, archival and medium legacy aesthetics, should become the lenses through which future scholars, students and cinephiles will form historicised understandings of film production, practice, process and politics.

Notes

1. SP-ARK is freely accessible online at: www.sp-ark.org.uk (Accessed May 2017).
2. This was an AHRC-funded Big Data project – http://arts.brighton.ac.uk/projects/deep-film-access-project-dfap (Accessed May 2017).

3. The Theatrical sales and operations executive, Artificial Eye, in an interview with the author, 13 September 2012.
4. Lossy compression is the name given to the image deterioration and degradation caused by a lower grade compression process as opposed to loss*less*, which is an uncompressed format.
5. In an interview with Kurban Kassam, March 2012.
6. These standards are predominantly set by the Society of Motion Picture & Television Engineers, SMPTE, and the MPEG Industry Forum (MPEGIF).
7. This included 1.4 million items from TecRec (Technical Records), Technical data from 56k film items from DDE (Direct Data Entry), filmographic records of approximately 800,000 film and television titles from BID (BFI integrated database), 50,000 subject headings from SIDX (Subject index), and 120,000 barcoded records (de Esteban, 2013: 110).
8. Adlib is a collection management system which is used across Europe by many institutions including the Imperial War Museum, London and the EYE Filmmuseum, Amsterdam.
9. http://collections-search.bfi.org.uk/web (Accessed May 2017).
10. Spectrum is the UK Collection Management Standard.
11. ISAD-G: General International Standard Archival Description
12. http://www2.archivists.org/glossary/terms/f/fonds (Accessed May 2017).
13. Peter Todd, BFI Librarian – Research and Enquiries, MariJose de Esteban, BFI Information Specialist – Collections and Information, at an interview with the author, 10 April 2014.
14. The BFI estate is spread across three locations – the Conservation Centre in Berkhamsted, Hertfordshire, the Master Film Store in Gaydon, Warwickshire, and two locations in London (South Bank and Stephen Street).
15. Access to the archive which contains over twenty thousand pages of Kurosawa's screenplays, photos, storyboards, drawings, personal notes, and newspaper clippings is via this link: http://www.afc.ryukoku.ac.jp/Komon/kurosawa/index.html (accessed May 2017). Since the entire archive is in the Japanese language, there is an English guide available here: http://akira-kurosawa.info/guide-to-the-akira-kurosawa-digital-archive/ (Accessed May 2017).
16. Rights owners include the Stanley Kubrick Estate; Universal International; Metro-Goldwyn-Mayer, and Warner Bros. Entertainment.
17. Renamed as National Science and Media Museum in March 2017.
18. https://wfpp.cdrs.columbia.edu/about/ (Accessed May 2017).
19. http://www.scriptsupervisors.co.uk (Accessed May 2017).
20. http://costumedetail.blogspot.co.uk (Accessed May 2017).
21. By myself and Kurban Kassam from Adventure Pictures.
22. The current online version of SP-ARK (accessed May 2017) was first developed as a knowledge-exchange activity between the University of Essex and the University of Surrey in 2010, supported by the Technology Strategy Board. The partnership involved the development of an image-browsing interface which allows users to visually analyse clips from the film, from single frames to complete shots.

23. This is a simplified version of the actual ontology which was created in 'OWL' by DFAP researcher Jos Lehmann. OWL is a set of languages used for knowledge representation in the form of ontology authoring. OWL is the prevalent language of ontology implementation in web semantics and is the standard for the Semantic Web (Lehmann, Atkinson and Evans, 2015). The OWL ontology will work as the 'back end' of any archival interface development in the future.

24. The Development phase commenced in June 2010 and concluded in December 2011, Pre-production ran from January–February 2012, the Production phase started on 17 February and completed on 27 March 2012, Post-production started during the production phase and finished on 5 September 2012. The distribution process started at this point with the film's eventual UK theatrical release on 19 October 2012.

25. http://www.bbc.co.uk/ontologies/storyline (Accessed May 2017).

26. http://cronenbergmuseum.tiff.net/accueil-home-eng.html (Accessed May 2017).

27. http://www.ligatus.org.uk/aae/ (Accessed May 2017).

28. The politics of excess and waste within feature-film production have been keenly discussed by many academics. Bennett (2015) undertook the examination of the aesthetics of excess revealed through a study of on-screen content.

29. Which were the focus of my AHRC-funded TRI-PACT project – Tracking Intellectual Property Across the Creative Technologies (2014–15), AHRC project reference AH/M010481/1.

30. Developed by the ProMPEG forum, and recognised as the industry standard by the SMPTE, and also as an archival standard by the EN 15907.

31. The Master Archive Package (MAP) is a JPEG2000 archival element created in the Fraunhofer JPEG2000 software suite, developed by the Presto4U project in 2014 https://www.prestocentre.org/resources/creation-master-archive-package-map (Accessed May 2017).

CHAPTER 7

Epilogue

Writing this book, five years on from the temporal origin of its focus of study, the film industry and film production has continued to be impacted by digital interventions in innumerable ways. Since 2012, new creative and logistical responses to technological innovations have proliferated, resulting in new types of film production and new exhibition practices. Subsequent watershed moments include the artistic and technological achievements of *Gravity* (2013) in its pure-digital aestheticism and technical accomplishments; and the live distribution and 'live' production aesthetics of *Lost in London LIVE* (2017). Both examples exemplify the total convergence of both the *spaces* of and *times* of production in the context of a *pure* digital film-production economy and ecology. However, as Figure 7.1 illustrates, a clapper board from *Lost in London LIVE* (2017) features in the associated making-of film, and is emblematic of the film-to-digital moment which we still inhabit. It is truly a redundant piece of production iconography in this instance, since the film was shot in one take, with one camera, and was broadcast live. Yet the clapper board still persists as the key visual signifier as to the ontology of the feature film. Nonetheless, these two examples each demonstrate how the continued convergences of industries, software and working practices have directed the research agenda across a number of academic fields to these emergent phenomena, fuelling debates concerning issues such as emerging models of labour organisation and new forms of production.

The vantage point of 2017 has enabled me to retrospectively position the film, *Ginger & Rosa*, its study, and the Production Aesthetic, in their respective lineages of film history and film analysis. From this critical distance, it is possible to appreciate how and why 2012 was a key defining moment for film in the UK, liminally poised at this celluloid/digital impasse, at which the two mediums co-existed and converged most vividly through the envisioning of its Production Aesthetic. This Production Aesthetic, now redolent with and evocative of that particular moment which retained, preserved and enshrined the celluloid, the film, in the digital, emerged in a specific independent craft-based[1] mode of

Figure 7.1 The image of the clapper board from *Lost in London LIVE* (2017) which is taken from the associated making-of film. (*Lost in London*, 2017, Dir. Woody Harrelson)

production. As such it was able to illuminate the film-to-data transitional moment most acutely as the final locus of resistance in the film-industry ecology. This independent craft-based production practice is of course just one trajectory amongst a number of modes of film production in the wider global film-production ecology. There is pure CGI production, animation, special effects, each with their own nuances, characteristics and idiosyncrasies. The balance between art, commerce and technology, also weighs differently in each of these different film-production modes. What binds these different modes together, however, is their commonalities in relation to labour organisation, and their constituent production personnel who are drawn from the same pool of human resource. As members of the wider project network examined in Chapter 2 – film professionals work across a range of film projects – and as such provide continuities and standardisations in practice as implementers of new tools and processes, agents for knowledge transfer, enactors of change, and interlocutors within and across processes, and as such they are justifiably the focus of study in this book, as the key source of experiential knowledge.

To summarise the characteristics of the Production Aesthetic that emerged as a result of this study:

- **Collaborative auteurism and transitional auteurship**: This emerged as a result of Sally Potter's own working practice and ethos, and resulted in the conceptualisation of the ' "Creative Core" Structure of

Production' model. There are two distinct subjectivities here, both inhabited by Potter; on the one hand a collaborator par excellence, harnessing, adopting and adapting to the ideas and talents of her creative team, and on the other, Potter as a transitional auteur, taking on the role of a digital ambassador of sorts, who deftly traversed these two domains and successfully managed collaborations across the material domains and practices. A role in which we have seen her frequently inhabit through her other ground-breaking digital engagements and digital interventions in her practice, *Yes* (2000), *Rage* (2009) and, of course, SP-ARK.

- **Workflow-warp** – the impact of the incremental inception of digital interventions into a film workflow which led to the shifting and morphing of workflow temporalities. A further corollary emerged – **workflow-weft** – the process through which fragmented, modular, and atomised processes and departments required suturing together – through the intervention of new production roles, resulting in an anamorphosis of processes and practices. Although this has manifested as a complex tapestry, my analysis of this truly transitional production process has elicited this series of key insights. In the analysis I have laid bare the contradictory meshing of tensions, insecurities and reluctances that reside uneasily along with possibilities, opportunities and innovations and I have illuminated the innate distortion lying behind the apparent coherence.
- I have shown how a film's **Production Aesthetic** is mobilised for multiple ends by the film industry – in a process of commodification and in instances of resistance to more pressurised and unfavourable working conditions.

Situating the notion of the Production Aesthetic within a wider field of film-industry studies, I have also located this as part of a globalised ecosystem of film practices, within which certain qualities can be identified:

- **Transitional** temporality is evidenced most keenly through the intermedial, converged and symbiotic aesthetics, which combine to create an aesthetic of invisibility and erasure – and the representational paradoxical logics of 'pseudo-visibility' and 'hyper-invisibility'. These are logics which continue to exclude marginal voices but conversely also give access to new voices and audiences. These elements have also exposed a self-perpetuating preoccupation with cinematic process, manifested in the phenomena which I have described as the *simulacinematic*.
- Our future history of, and comprehension of this recent past is threatened by the Digital Dilemma archival excess and loss dichotomy, whilst also being increasingly shaped by the various production, archival and

medium legacy aesthetics, which construct historicised understandings of film production, practice, process and politics.

These paradoxically polarising practices (collaboration/auteurism; distortion/coherence; pseudo-visibility/hyper-invisibility; commodification/resistance; and excess/loss) which form the Production Aesthetic of *Ginger & Rosa* are interwoven at their moment of metamorphosis and are characteristic of the 2012 period of transition. Although, Stuart Comer would contend that this is a persistent condition, not specific to any particular moment in time: 'Cinema has been a tangle of paradoxes on the threshold between the material and the immaterial for over a century' (in Cullinan, 2012: 61). The potential reasons for these contradictory phenomena could be considered 'as a way of managing the force of this future shock [. . .] the idea of cinema persists in the term 'digital cinema,' as a way of easing the transition to a different world, now both here' (Rodowick, 2007: 176–7).

The Future of Digital Film Studies – Approaches and Methods

By bringing together Production Studies, Film Studies and Digital Humanities in this research, I have sought to unify the 'parting of the ways between materiality and representation, between film as a constellation of specific technologies and cinema as a set of institutionally inscribed practices' (Uricchio, 2014: 274) In doing so, I have been able to make sense of some of the issues of an industry in transition within the wider context of 'a field giving way to interdisciplinary imperatives as the boundaries demarcating film studies erode by the force of powerful waves of new and emerging media and visual technologies' (Betz, 2008: 341).

Moreover, this work was only made possible through a model of industry collaboration and embedded research, which will become an increasingly valid and validating approach within industry studies; many see its future potentialities (Holt, 2013), and its specific methodological challenges (Vonderau, 2014). Vonderau deploys a similar case-study method in order to study a particular facet of film production – in his case propmakers in Hollywood – through which to illuminate a much wider situational context (Vonderau, 2016).

I have proposed an analytical framework within which to understand these and future film texts, through the unification and cross-analyses of this tripartite of Text, Production Aesthetics and Representational Texts.

Although comparative analyses were not included in this book, I have suggested that one such useful way of doing this is through the data visualisation tool which takes production data and outputs it into a visualised production cycle (see figure 3.2, page 76). This could be a useful tool in the future for mapping and understanding the different labour cycles of film production.

As far as possible, I have attempted to capture, preserve, present and interpret the intermedial lineaments that were characteristic of this period, and have presented these for further contextual, comparative studies and historical analyses.

Conclusion

Despite the new cinematic innovations described at the start of this Chapter, we are yet to reach a post-digital state – the chimera of pure digital/data productions unfettered by their celluloid antecedents are yet to manifest. Nor have we yet experienced a process of disintermediation – when the intermediary processes and roles are no longer required to bridge the gaps between celluloid and digital. Nor have we witnessed the attendant 'false revolution' of digital cinema (Belton, 2002). As Lev Manovich has noted: 'The makers of software used in media production usually do not set out to create a revolution. On the contrary, software is created to fit into already existing production procedures, job roles, and familiar tasks' (2013: 323–4):

> In the case of colour, digital advancements have not created a rupture or **radical** change. Rather, the institutional pressures associated with Hollywood filmmaking, in particular the need to test and integrate new technologies, have encouraged a familiar aesthetic trajectory from demonstration to restraint. Apparently **revolutionary** approaches to the technology are most likely only a passing phase in the adoption of digital grading. (Higgins 2003: 74–5)

Instead we see the very gradual diminution of these celluloid referents and analogue analogies and remain in the inexorable, slow, inchoate progression towards a pure-digital future in which we continue to '. . . understand media convergence as a process instead of a static termination' (Thorburn and Jenkins, 2004: 3).

There is fear and reluctance across the academic and industry domains. Here we see Philippe Gauthier lamenting the inevitable impacts upon the field of study: 'What will become of film studies when (2014: 229) every stage in the production and dissemination of a film has been gradually 'dematerialized' (i.e. 'digitalized')? What will become of film studies when 'film' disappears?' (2014: 230). The following remark typifies the affective response of film industry professionals to the demise of celluloid film production and processing:

It's a sad time we are in. It's a very changeable time, but unfortunately film will become very niche and everybody's going to be shooting on an Alexa which is weird. The digital world is now what we have to embrace. A bit of the romance is gone Sarah. (Robbie Ryan, 26 October 2012)[2]

There is a seemingly persistent and obsessive hybridisation in semantics which are littered with portmanteau terms that merge these domains together: 'synthespians,'[3] the 'digitographic' (Hadjioannou 2012) and the 'digilogue' (Sorman-Nilsson, 2013). In this relentless meshing together of the analogue and digital we see that it is not just the film industry which is seduced by the lure of the analogue – it is also an enduring commercial strategy.

A lot has changed since 2012, when looking up the filmographies of each of the book's interviewees on IMDb, I was sad to observe that Ejvind Bording[4], Colour Timer, lists his last film as being *Ginger & Rosa*. It was the last film to be processed before the closure of the ShortCut Film Laboratory in Copenhagen. I was fortunate to have a tour around the facility which at the time was a combination of laboratory spaces and digital suites. But as the Facility Manager lamented of the speed of its demise: 'Right now, it's only the seven people. [. . .] A year ago, there were forty-five.'

Some of the other seasoned professionals look to have retired, *Ginger & Rosa*'s Script Supervisor and long-standing collaborator of Potter, Penny Eyles lists her last film was *Philomena* (2013). Speaking in 2012 when camera tests were conducted on both film and digital cine cameras, Robbie Ryan mourned the cessation of FujiFilm which announced its closure in 2012 and shut down its film production in 2013.

It has now taken another dive because Fuji film has closed its doors. They're not going to make any more film stock so my new mantra is if Fuji is dead, film is dead.[5]

It is Stephen Prince's contention that 'film is no longer a necessary condition for cinema' (2004: 30). But what is clear is that what has been lost in the materiality, as this book shows, has been symbolically and skeuomorphically preserved in all aspects of the process. The predominant 'legacy aesthetics' of this moment are communicated through a series of digital motifs. Whereas Mary Ann Doane has claimed that: 'What is lost in the move to the digital is the imprint of time, the visible degradation of the image [. . .] The historicity of a medium is traced in the physical condition of its objects' (2007: 144). I would argue to the contrary, as I discussed in Chapter 4, digital film does carry with it the imprint of time but through a far more complex and sophisticated sign-system.

The most fundamental phase of the film-to-data transition, the material and metaphoric digital 'switch over' has passed. What we are left with as a result of the 'digital film' interpolation is a series of residual, visual aftershocks; how long they will resonate, we do not know. Until the benign appendages – these skeuomorphs – of celluloid and film are eradicated, the Film/Data hybridisation will remain the heuristic mechanism through which to understand contemporary film production and film-industry aesthetics.

It is possible that this period of time – 2012 – will come to be viewed as characterised by a certain sublime, a 'look' that has been shaped by the production processes and creative/logistical decisions that have been made? After (and if) we have moved beyond the transitional phase into the pure digital, a retrospective historiography would be necessary to ascertain this, looking across the entirety of the 2012 digital film canon, characterised by the perpetually temporary conjuncture. So, for the time being at least, the notion of 'digital film' persists and is the most useful term to capture the enduring film-to-digital transitional moment.

Ginger & Rosa is a touchstone of this moment, in some ways it is a valedictory text, a transitionary ode to film, imbued both textually (in the story) and texturally (in the medium) with sadness and nostalgia. A unique group of people were brought together in this collective endeavour of collaborative autership in a moment on the cusp of a profound transition. Their imprints, their reactions, their impulses, and the traces of their labour are forever inscribed on the film.

Notes

1. As defined in Chapter 1 – I use the term craft-based to imply a film that uses traditional, physical and practical techniques wherever possible, in its creation of scenery, props, effects, etc. Craft-based films are always location-based where the use of digital VFX is kept to an absolute minimum. Craft-based films are normally those which pertain to realist drama conventions.
2. In an interview with the author 26 October 2012.
3. The synthespian – a portmanteau term combining the words synthetic and thespian to refer to a computer-generated version of a film actor.
4. As listed on 24 February, 2017.
5. In an interview with the author, 26 October 2012.

Practitioner Filmography

Listed below are the credit listings showing selected films of each of the interviewees included in the book (both leading up to, and after their work on *Ginger & Rosa*), and in the roles which they fulfilled in *Ginger & Rosa* (many have held different roles on other productions). For full, comprehensive filmographies for each individual, all have profiles on imdb.com

The full credit listing of *Ginger & Rosa* follows below.

Listed in alphabetical order:

Michael Aaglund: Assistant Editor
The Dark Matter of Love (2012) Directed by Sarah McCarthy
The End of the Line short (2009) Directed by Li Marhaban

Francesco Alberico: Key Hair
Snow White and the Huntsman (2012) Directed by Rupert Sanders
The Three Musketeers (2011) Directed by Paul W. S. Anderson
Harry Potter and the Deathly Hallows: Part 2 (2011) Directed by David Yates
Harry Potter and the Deathly Hallows: Part 1 (2010) Directed by David Yates
Green Zone (2010) Directed by Paul Greengrass
Cassandra's Dream (2007) Directed by Woody Allen

Mia Bang Stenberg: Digital Production Manager
The Party (2017) Directed by Sally Potter
Easy Skanking (2006) Directed by Hella Joof
Triple Dare (2006) Directed by Christina Rosendahl
True Spirit (2005) Directed by Martin Strange-Hansen

Ejvind Bording: Colour Timer
The Reunion (2011) Directed by Niels Nørløv Hansen
Minor Mishaps (2002) Directed by Annette K. Olesen

Peter Bose: Miso Film
Jensen & Jensen (2011) Directed by Craig Frank
Those Who Kill TV Series (2011–)
The Candidate (2008) Directed by Kasper Barfoed
Fallen Angels (2008) Directed by Morten Tyldum
Wallander TV Series (2005–6)

Carlos Conti: Art Director
On the Road (2012) Directed by Walter Salles
The Kite Runner (2007) Directed by Marc Forster
Yes (2004) Directed by Sally Potter
The Motorcycle Diaries (2004) Directed by Sally Potter
The Man Who Cried (2000) Directed by Sally Potter

Stella Corradi: Director's Assistant
Macbeth (2015) Directed by Justin Kurzel
A Late Quartet (2012) Directed by Yaron Zilberman

Lucy Donowho: Standby Costume
Bel Ami (2012) Directed by Declan Donnellan and Nick Ormerod
Sherlock Holmes: A Game of Shadows (2011) Directed by Guy Ritchie
Another Year (2010) Directed by Mike Leigh
The Wolfman (2010) Directed by Joe Johnston

Penny Eyles: Script Supervisor
Tamara Drewe (2010) Directed by Stephen Frears
The Queen (2006) Directed by Stephen Frears
Nanny McPhee (2005) Directed by Kirk Jones
Mrs Henderson Presents (2005) Directed by Stephen Frears
Yes (2004) Directed by Sally Potter
Dirty Pretty Things (2002) Directed by Stephen Frears
Gosford Park (2001) Directed by Robert Altman
The Man Who Cried (2000) Directed by Sally Potter
The Tango Lesson (1997) Directed by Sally Potter
Orlando (1992) Directed by Sally Potter
Monty Python and the Holy Grail (1975) Directed by Terry Gilliam and
    Terry Jones
Kes (1969) Directed by Ken Loach

Lizzie Francke: Senior Production Executive: BFI Film Fund
Berberian Sound Studio (2012) Directed by Peter Strickland
Broken (2012) Directed by Rufus Norris
The Deep Blue Sea (2011) Directed by Terence Davies
Shame (2011) Directed by Steve McQueen
We Need to Talk About Kevin (2011) Directed by Lynne Ramsay
Kill List (2011) Directed by Ben Wheatley
Tyrannosaur (2011) Directed by Paddy Considine

Antonia Gibbs: Production Buyer
About Time (2013) Directed by Richard Curtis
We'll Take Manhattan TV Movie (2012) Directed by John McKay
The Great Ghost Rescue (2011) Directed by Yann Samuell
It's a Wonderful Afterlife (2010) Directed by Gurinder Chadha

Alistair Hopkins: Post-production Supervisor
The Best Exotic Marigold Hotel (2011) Directed by John Madden
The Awakening (2011) Directed by Nick Murphy
Tamara Drewe (2010) Directed by Stephen Frears
The Damned United (2009) Directed by Tom Hooper
In Bruges (2008) Directed by Martin McDonagh
The Queen (2006) Directed by Stephen Frears

Michael Holm: Compositor
Nymphomaniac: Vol. I (2013) Directed by Lars von Trier
Only God Forgives (2013) Directed by Nicolas Winding Refn
The Girl with the Dragon Tattoo (2009) Directed by Niels Arden Oplev
The Killing Episode 3.10 (2012) Directed by Fabian Wullenweber

Anne Jensen: Re-recording Mixer
Love Is All You Need (2012) Directed by Susanne Bier
Melancholia (2011) Directed by Lars von Trier
The Girl Who Kicked the Hornet's Nest (2009) Directed by Daniel Alfredson
The Girl Who Played With Fire (2009) Directed by Daniel Alfredson
Dogville (2003) Directed by Lars von Trier

Irene Lamb: Casting Director
The Imaginarium of Doctor Parnassus (2009) Directed by Terry Gilliam
Rage (2009) Directed by Sally Potter
The Brothers Grimm (2005) Directed by Terry Gilliam
Wimbledon (2004) Directed by Richard Loncraine
The Man Who Cried (2000) Directed by Sally Potter
Star Wars (1980 and 1977) Directed by George Lucas

Sean Leonard: 2nd Assistant Camera
The Fifth Estate (2013) Directed by Bill Condon
Byzantium (2012) Directed by Neil Jordan
Neverland (2011–) TV mini series
Albert Nobbs (2011) Directed by Rodrigo García

Heidi Levitt CSA: Casting Director
The Artist (2011) Directed by Michel Hazanavicius
The Wicker Man (2006) Directed by Neil LaBute
Rage (2009) Directed by Sally Potter
Nixon (1995) Directed by Oliver Stone
Natural Born Killers (1994) Directed by Oliver Stone
JFK (1991) Directed by Oliver Stone

Andy Litvin: Producer
The Holding (2011) Directed by Susan Jacobson
Albatross (2011) Directed by Niall MacCormick

Chatroom (2010) Directed by Hideo Nakata
1 Day (2009) Directed by Penny Woolcock
Hunger (2008) Directed by Steve McQueen

Martin Madsen: Visual Effect Supervisor
The Girl Who Kicked the Hornet's Nest (2009) Directed by Daniel Alfredson
The Girl Who Played with Fire (2009) Directed by Daniel Alfredson
The Girl with the Dragon Tattoo (2009) Directed by Niels Arden Oplev

Andy Mannion: 2nd Assistant Director
The Sweeney (2012) Directed by Nick Love
The King's Speech (2010) Directed by Tom Hooper
Sherlock Holmes (2009) Directed by Guy Ritchie
The Dark Knight (2008) Directed by Christopher Nolan
28 Weeks Later (2007) Directed by Juan Carlos Fresnadillo

Andrea Matheson: Art Director
Cuban Fury (2014) Directed by James Griffiths
Pride (2014) Directed by Matthew Warchus
Alan Partridge (2013) Directed by Declan Lowney

Charles McDonald: Unit Publicist
Pina (2011) Directed by Wim Wenders
Brighton Rock (2010) Directed by Rowan Joffe
Over Your Cities Grass Will Grow (2010) Directed by Sophie Fiennes
Four Lions (2010) Directed by Christopher Morris
Nowhere Boy (2009) Directed by Sam Taylor-Johnson
Looking For Eric (2009) Directed by Ken Loach

Tara McDonald: Hair and Make-up Designer
Tinker Tailor Soldier Spy (2011) Directed by Tomas Alfredson
Submarine (2010) Directed by Richard Ayoade
It's a Free World . . . (2007) Directed by Ken Loach
My Summer of Love (2004) Directed by Pawel Pawlikowski

Jean-Paul Mugel: Production Sound Mixer
Cosmopolis (2012) Directed by David Cronenberg
Rage (2009) Directed by Sally Potter
The Happening (2008) Directed by M. Night Shysmalan
The Diving Bell and the Butterfly (2007) Directed by Julian Schnabel
A Good Year (2006) Directed by Ridley Scott
Paris, Jet'aime (2006) various directors
Hidden (Caché) (2005) Directed by Michael Haneke
Yes (2004) Directed by Sally Potter
The Man Who Cried (2000) Directed by Sally Potter
The Tango Lesson (1997) Directed by Sally Potter

James O'Dee: Stunt Coordinator
The Hobbit: An Unexpected Journey (2012) Directed by Peter Jackson
Skyfall (2012) Directed by Sam Mendes
Snow White and the Huntsman (2012) Directed by Rupert Sanders
X-Men: First Class (2011) Directed by Matthew Vaughn

Joe Oppenheimer: Executive Producer
Shadow Dancer (2012) Directed by James Marsh
The Awakening (2011) Directed by Nick Murphy
The Edge of Love (2008) Directed by John Maybury

Sally Potter: Writer & Director
Rage (2009)
Yes (2004)
The Man Who Cried (2000)
The Tango Lesson (1997)
Orlando (1992)

Graham Povey: Special Effects Supervisor
Prometheus (2012) Directed by Ridley Scott
War Horse (2011) Directed by Steven Spielberg
Prince of Persia: The Sands of Time (2010) Directed by Mike Newell
Black Hawk Down (2001) Directed by Ridley Scott
Gladiator (2000) Directed by Ridley Scott
Saving Private Ryan (1998) Directed by Steven Spielberg

Anders Refn: Editor
The Party (2017) Directed by Sally Potter
Antichrist (2009) Directed by Lars von Trier
Dancer in the Dark (2000) Directed by Lars von Trier
Breaking the Waves (1996) Directed by Lars von Trier

Robbie Ryan: Cinematographer
The Angels' Share (2012) Directed by Ken Loach
Wuthering Heights (2011) Directed by Andrea Arnold
Fish Tank (2009) Directed by Andrea Arnold
Brick Lane (2007) Directed by Sarah Gavron
Red Road (2006) Directed by Andrea Arnold
Isolation (2005) Directed by Billy O'Brien

Christopher Sheppard: Producer
Rage (2009) Directed by Sally Potter
Yes (2004) Directed by Sally Potter
The Man Who Cried (2000) Directed by Sally Potter
The Tango Lesson (1997) Directed by Sally Potter
Orlando (1992) Directed by Sally Potter

Eddie Simonsen: Supervising Sound Editor
Only God Forgives (2013) Directed by Nicolas Winding Refn
Dogville (2003) Directed by Lars von Trier

Jane Soans: Production Manager
Shadow Dancer (2012) Directed by James Marsh
Sherlock Holmes (2009) Directed by Guy Ritchie
Me and Orson Welles (2008) Directed by Richard Linklater
Alex Rider: Operation Stormbreaker (2006) Directed by Geoffrey Sax
Closer (2004) Directed by Mike Nichols

Thomas Therchilsen: Digital Colour Grading
The Hunt (2012) Directed by Thomas Vinterberg
Hold Me Tight (2010) Directed by Kaspar Munk
Villa Paranoia (2004) Directed by Erik Clausen
Day and Night (2004) Directed by Simon Staho

Beatrice Von Schwerin: Post-production Coordinator
All These Voices (2015) Directed by David Henry Gerson
Those Who Will Kill (Television) (2011)

Holly Waddinton: Costume Designer
Lincoln (2012) Directed by Steven Spielberg
War Horse (2011) Directed by Steven Spielberg
Clash of the Titans (2010) Directed by Louis Leterrier
Atonement (2007) Directed by Joe Wright

Wakana Yoshihara: Hair and Make-up Supervisor
Snow White and the Huntsman (2012) Directed by Rupert Sanders
Salmon Fishing in the Yemen (2011) Directed by Lasse Hallström
Tinker Tailor Soldier Spy (2011) Directed by Tomas Alfredson
Harry Potter and the Deathly Hallows: Part 2 (2011) Directed by David Yates

Ginger & Rosa Full Credit List

Opening title sequence, presented as single static slates:

1. BFI and BBC Films present
2. An Adventure Pictures Production
3. In association with
4. The Match Factory
5. Media House
6. Ingenious
7. MisoFilm
8. DFI
9. A film by SALLY POTTER
10. GINGER & ROSA

End credits, presented as single static slates:

11. Written and directed by SALLY POTTER
12. ELLE FANNING
13. ALESSANDRO NIVOLA
14. CHRISTINA HENDRICKS
15. TIMOTHY SPALL
16. OLIVER PLATT
17. JODHI MAY
18. and ANNETTE BENING
19. Introducing ALICE ENGLERT
20. Produced by CHRISTOPHER SHEPPARD
21. Producer ANDREW LITVIN
22. Co-producers PETER BOSE, JONAS, ALLEN, LENE BAUSAGER, MICHAEL WEBER
23. Executive Producers RENO ANTONIADES, AARON L. GILBERT, GOETZ GROSSMAN
24. Executive Producers HEIDI LEVITT, JOE OPPENHEIMER, PAULA ALVAREZ VACCARO
25. Director of Photography ROBBIE RYAN BSC
26. Editor ANDERS REFN
27. Production Designer CARLOS CONTI
28. Costume Designer HOLLY WADDINGTON
29. Hair and Make-up Designer TARA MCDONALD
30. Production Sound Mixer JEAN-PAUL MUGEL
31. Casting Directors IRENE LAMB, HEIDI LEVITT CSA

Rolling credits

CAST (in order of appearance)

Natalie	CHRISTINA HENDRICKS
Anoushka	JODHI MAY
Roland	ALESSANDRO NIVOLA
Rosa's father	LUKE CLOUD
Young Ginger	POPPY BLOOR
Young Rosa	MAGDALENE MOUNTFORD
Ginger	ELLE FANNING
Radio announcer	RAY LONNEN
Rosa	ALICE ENGLERT
Beatniks	BROCK EVERITT-ELWICK
	MAX SCULLY
Teddy boys in car	MARCUS SHAKESHEFF
	CHARLIE SMITH
Boy on beach	RUPERT RIXON
Mark	TIMOTHY SPALL
Tony	ANDREW HAWLEY
YCND boy	BEN WIMSETT
Bella	ANNETTE BENNING
Children playing	AINE GARVEY
	MADISON DELUCA-PERRY
	AMELIE DELUCA-PERRY
Boy in café	RORY JAMES
Roger	OLIVER MILBURN
Dinner guest	RICHARD STRANGE
Police doctor	STEPHEN BOXER

Then:

Production Executive	MICHAEL MANZI
First Assistant Director	MATTHEW HANSON
Associate Producer	KURBAN KASSAM
Line Producer	MARSHALL LEVITEN
Script Supervisor	PENNY EYLES
Location Manager	JANE SOANS
Production Accountant	FREYA PINSENT
Story Consultant	WALTER DONOHUE
Production Coordinator	AMELIA PRICE
Assistant Production Coordinator	RACHEL MARTIN
Director's Assistant	STELLA CORRADI
Production Assistant	LIAM THORNTON
Assistant Accountant	CHARLES PINSENT
2nd Assistant Directors	ANDY MANNION
	CHRISTIAN RIGG
3rd Assistant Director	DARREN PRICE
Floor Runners	VALENTINA BORFECCHIA

	SHIVA TALWAR
	MATT BENSLEY
	DANIEL BLISS
	KATIE SEYMOUR
1st Assistant Camera	ANDREW O'RELLY
2nd Assistant Camera	SEAN LEONARD
	RACHEL CLARK
Camera Assistant	NIALL BARRY
Key Grip	SIMON MUIR
Camera Trainee	JAMES PAUL THOMAS
Boom Operator	JONATHAN ACBARD
Sound Assistants	KYLE PICKFORD
	ALEX BRYCE
Art Director	ANDREA MATHESON
Set Director	LIZ GRIFFITHS
Production Buyer	ANTONIA GIBBS
Standby Art Director	OLIVER VAN DER VIJVER
Graphics	EMILY NORRIS
Illustrator	MAUD GIRCOURT
Art Department Assistant	TOM KNIGHT
Trainee Art Department Assistant	YASMIN ALVAREZ
Property Master	CRAIG PRICE
Dressing Props	NEIL GRIFFITHS
	RODDY DOLAN
Standby Props	MARK SINDALL
Prop Driver	JUSTIN ACKROYD
Construction Services	ROB ANDERSON
Special Effects Supervisor	GRAHAM POVEY
Costume Supervisor	HANNAH WALTER
Assistant Costume Designer	BARTHOLOMEW CARISS
Standby Costume	LUCY DONOWHO
Costume Assistant	EMMA HARDING
Key Hair	FRANCESCO ALBERICO
Hair and Make-up Supervisor	WAKANA YOSHIHARA
Hair and Make-up Artist	SOPHIE ROBERTS
Gaffer	ANDY COLE
Best Boy	PAUL CRONIN
Electricians	CHRIS TANN
	ADRIAN MACKAY
Rigger	TONI KELLY
Assistant Location Manager	GEORGETTE TURNER
Unit Manager	BEN BAILEY

Location Assistant	SARAH KATE LEWIS
Location Scouts	NICK OLIVER
	TOBIN HUGHES
Dialect Coaches	SANDRA FRIEZE
	CHARMIAN GRADWELL
Stunt Coordinator	JAMES O'DEE
Stunt Performers	GARY HOPTROUGH
	MARTIN WILDE
	TONY VAN SILVA
	ARRAN TOPHAM
	GARY ARTHURS
	ZARENE DALLAS
	DEREK LEA
	SARAH FRANZL
	CHRISTIAN KNIGHT
	BELINDA MCGINLEY
	RAY NICHOLAS
On-set Tutor	LAURA GARY
Chaperone	JESSICA CAPP
Music Tutors	KAREN STREET
	DER-SHIN HWANG
Unit Drivers	HASSAN BLAL
	ANDY BARTON
	MARK CHERRY
Minibus Driver	MICKY WATTS
Post-Production Supervisor	ALISTAIR HOPKINS
Assistant Editor	MICHAEL AAGLUND
Music Supervisor	AMY ASHWORTH
Music Consultant	ALAN LEWENS
Archive Consultant	JANE RUNDLE
Casting Associates	LAUREN FERNANDES
	LISA ESSARY
Title Design	MARTIN MADSEN
	STEPHEN MASTERS

DIGITAL INTERMEDIATE AND VISUAL EFFECTS BY NORDISK
FILM SHORTCUT

Post-Production Coordinator	MORTEN SYLVEST ARNOLDUS
Digital Production Manager	MIA BANG STENBERG
Digital Intermediate	PER SIDOR
Online Technician	RASMUS TOFT
Visual Effect Supervisor	MARTIN MADSEN
Compositors	MICHAEL HOLM
	DANN DAMGAARD SANDGREEN
	LASSE STRØM

Digital Colour Grading	THOMAS THERCHILSEN
Graphics	LASSE STRØM
	MORTEN SKYTTE
DCP Mastering	THOMAS CASPERSEN
Mastering	JENS LILLEDAL SØRENSEN
Colour Timer	EJVIND BORDING
Laboratory Production Manager	THOMAS SCHLEIN

SOUND DESIGN BY MAINSTREAM

Supervising Sound Editor	EDDIE SIMONSEN
Re-recording Mixer	ANNE JENSEN
Sound Assistant	LARS RAMUSSEN
Foley Artist	ANDREA KING
Additional Dialogue Editor	SIMON CHASE
Unit Publicists	CHARLES MCDONALD
	MATTHEW SANDERS
Stills Photographer	NICOLA DOVE
'Making-of' Director	JOSEPH MATTHEWS
EPK Production	PEEK AND BOO

ADVENTURE PICTURES

Legal Services	LAW OFFICE DIANE GELON
Accountants	RAWSE VARLEY AND CO
	PHILIP VARLEY
	NIGEL BARNETT
Production Assistants	JIMMY BARNETT
	MEAGAN MAUDSLEY
	DAVID MADISON

BFI FILM FUND

Head of Film Fund	TANYA SEGHATCHIAN
Senior Production Executive	LIZZIE FRANCKE
Head of Production	FIONA MORHAM
Head of Business Affairs	WILL EVANS
Head of Production Finance	IAN KIRK

BBC FILMS

Production Executive	MICHAEL WOOD
Head of Business Affairs	ZOE BROWN
Legal and Business Affairs Manager	SIMON GILIS
Development Editor	BETH PATTINSON

MEDIA HOUSE CAPITAL

Co-Executive Producers	PATRICK MURRAY
	MARGOT HAND

MISO FILM

Assistant Producer	CAROLINE BLANCO
Post-Production Coordinator	BEATRICE VON SCHWERIN

Co-producers	BETTIS PRODUCTIONS LTD
	CURTIS PRODUCTIONS LTD
Legal services	LEE & THOMPSON LLP
	LEE STONE
	ANWEN GRIFFITHS
	ANGELA SCURRAH
Completion Guarantee	EUROPEAN FILM BONDS A/S
AND DFG	DEUTSCHE
	FILMVERSICHERUNGS
	GENEINSCHAFT
Production Executive	SHEILA FRASER MILNE
Legal Services	REED SMITH LLP
	RICHARD PHILIPPS
	LAURA CROWLEY
Insurance Services	GALLAGHER ENTERTAINMENT
	KEVIN O'SHEA
Laboratory Services	NORDISK FILM SHORTCUT
Auditors	SHIPLEYS LLP
	STEPHEN JOBERNS
Clearances	DEBBIE BANBURY MORLEY
Camera Equipment	PANAVISION
	ROB GARVIE
Lighting Equipment	ARRI LIGHTING
	LAURA THOMPSON
Tracking Vehicles	BICKERS ACTION
Costume Hire	ANGELS COSTUMIERS
	CARLO MANZI
	ACADEMY COSTUMES
	MOVIETONE
Picture Vehicles	TLO FILM SERVICES
Accommodation Services	LIL AND KATE LONDON LTD
	MEDIA COM 24–7
Travel Services	ET TRAVEL
Set Groundworks	GPT GROUNDWORK SERVICES
Editing Equipment	HYPERACTIVE
Health and Safety Advisers	JHA SAFETY
	MICK HURRELL
Paramedics	TEAM SERVICES
Unit Catering	ACE CATERING
	RUSSELL BOSWELL
Unit Security	THE MOVIE LOT
Walkie-talkies	AUDIOLINK
Location Facilities	ON-SET FACILITIES

Filmography

Addams Family, The, directed by Barry Sonnenfeld, USA: Orion Pictures, 1991.

A Field in England, directed by Ben Wheatley, UK: Film4, 2013.

A Little Touch of Harry, directed by Mary Gwatkin, UK: Mindseye Films, 1989.

American Beauty, directed by Sam Mendes, USA: DreamWorks, 1999.

Anatomy of a Film, directed by Sarah Atkinson and Clare Holden, UK: Artificial Eye, 2012.

Angels Share, The, directed by Ken Loach, UK: Sixteen Films, 2012.

Annie, directed by John Huston, USA: Columbia Pictures, 1982.

A Nightmare on Elm Street, directed by Wes Craven, USA: New Line Cinema, 1984.

Anna and the King, directed by Andy Tennant, USA: Fox 2000 Pictures, 1999.

Apocalypse Now, directed by Francis Ford Coppola, USA: Zoetrope Studios, 1979.

Artist, The, directed by Michel Hazanavicius, USA: Studio 37, 2011.

Backdraft, directed by Ron Howard, USA: Imagine Films Entertainment, 1991.

Back in Time, directed by Jason Aron, USA: Malka Media Group, 2015.

Back to the Future, directed by Robert Zemeckis, USA: Universal Pictures, 1985.

Batman Begins, directed by Christopher Nolan, USA: Warner Bros., 2005.

Behind the Screen, directed by Charlie Chaplin, USA: Lone Star Corporation, 1916.

Ben-Hur, directed by William Wyler, USA: Metro-Goldwyn-Mayer (MGM), 1959.

Berberian Sound Studio, directed by Peter Strickland, UK: Warp X, 2012.

Blow Out, directed by Brian De Palma, USA: Cinema 77, 1981.

Bolt, directed by Byron Howard and Chris Williams, USA: Walt Disney Animation Studios, 2008.

Birdman, directed by Alejandro G. Iñárritu, USA: New Regency Pictures, 2014.

Breakfast Club, The, directed by John Hughes, USA: Universal Pictures, 1985.

Breaking the Waves, directed by Lars von Trier, Denmark: Argus Film Produktie, 1996.

Broken, directed by Rufus Norris, UK: BBC Films, 2012.

Burden of Dreams, directed by Les Blank, Netherlands: Flower Films, 1982.

Buttercup Bill, directed by Remy Bennett and Émilie Richard-Froozan, UK: Blonde to Black Pictures, 2014.

Byzantium Director: Neil Jordan, UK: Demarest Films, 2012.

Chris Kenneally: The Making of 'Side by Side' Documentary, directed by Alexandros Maragos, Greece: Momentum Visuals, 2014.

Cinematographer Style, directed by Jon Fauer, USA: T-shop Production, 2006.

Citizen Kane, directed by Orson Welles, USA: RKO Radio Pictures, 1941.

Cleopatra, directed by Joseph L. Mankiewicz and Rouben Mamoulian, USA: Twentieth Century Fox Film Corporation, 1963.

Day for Night, directed by François Truffaut, USA: Les Films du Carrosse, 1973.

Dreamy Dud: He Resolves Not to Smoke, directed by Wallace A. Carlson, The Essanay Film Manufacturing Company, 1915.

Dumbo, directed by Samuel Armstrong, USA: Walt Disney Productions, 1941.

Earthquake, directed by Mark Robson, USA: Universal Pictures, 1974.

8 ½, directed by Federico Fellini, USA: Cineriz, 1963.

Elephant Man, The, directed by David Lynch, USA: Brooksfilms, 1980.

English Patient, The directed by Anthony Minghella, USA: Miramax, 1996.

Erin Brockovich directed *by* Steven Soderbergh, USA: Universal Pictures, 2000.

Everyday, directed by Michael Winterbottom, UK: Revolution Films, 2012.

Eyes Wide Shut, directed by Stanley Kubrick, USA: Warner Bros., 1999.

Fifty Shades of Grey, directed by Sam Taylor-Johnson, USA: Focus Features, 2015.

FILM, Installation, by Tacita Dean 2012, UK: Tate, Unilever, 2012.

Forever Ealing, directed by Andrew Snell, UK: Channel 4 Television Corporation, 2002.

Forbidden Zone, Theatre production, directed by Katie Mitchell, UK: 59 Productions, 2014.

For Your Consideration, directed by Christopher Guest, USA: Shangri-La Entertainment, 2006.

From Borehamwood to Hollywood: The Rise and Fall and Rise of Elstree, directed by Howard Berry, UK: TheCurators! Productions, 2014.

Full Metal Jacket, directed by Stanley Kubrick, UK: Natant, 1987.

Game of Thrones, television series, created by David Benioff and D.B. Weiss, USA: Home Box Office (HBO), 2011–.

Ginger & Rosa, directed by Sally Potter. UK: Adventure Pictures, 2013.

Goodbye, Dragon Inn, directed by Tsai Ming-liang, UK: Homegreen Films, 2003.

Goodfellas, directed by Martin Scorsese, USA: Warner Bros, 1990.

Gravity, directed by Alfonso Cuarón, USA: Warner Bros., 2013.

Gravity, Installation, designed by 59 Productions and Framestore UK, 2014.

Greed, directed by Erich von Stroheim, USA: Metro-Goldwyn Pictures Corporation, 1925.

Hearts of Darkness, A Filmmaker's Apocalypse, directed by Fax Bahr, George Hickenlooper and Eleanor Coppola, USA: American Zoetrope & Cineplex-Odeon Films, 1991.

Hellraiser, directed by Clive Barker, UK: Cinemarque Entertainment BV, 1987.

Hellzapoppin', directed by H.C. Potter, USA: Mayfair Productions Inc., 1941.

Henry V, directed by Kenneth Branagh, UK: Renaissance Films, 1989.

Holy Motors, directed by Leos Carax, France: Pierre Grise Productions, 2012.

How Animated Cartoons Are Made, directed by Wallace Carlson, USA: J. R. Bray Studios, 1919.

How the Fleischer Studios, Miami, Florida, made 'Aladdin and His Wonderful Lamp,' directed by Dave Fleischer, USA: Fleischer Studios, 1939.

How Walt Disney Cartoons are Made, director unknown. USA: Walt Disney, 1937

Hugo, directed by Martin Scorsese, USA: Paramount Pictures, 2011.

Hulk, directed by Ang Lee, USA: Universal Pictures, 2003.

Hustler, The, directed by Robert Rossen, USA: Rossen Films, 1961.

I, Anna, directed by Barnaby Southcombe, UK: Embargo Films, 2012.

Inception, directed by Christopher Nolan, USA: Warner Bros., 2010.

Inception, Installation, designed by 59 Productions and Double Negative UK, 2014.

Intolerance, directed by D.W. Griffith, USA: Triangle Film Corporation, 1916.

Jaws, directed by Steven Spielberg, USA: Zanuck/Brown Productions, 1975.

Jerry Maguire, directed by Cameron Crowe, USA: TriStar Pictures, 1996.

Kill Bill: Vol. 1, directed by Quentin Tarantino, USA: Miramax, 2003.

Kill Bill: Vol. 2, directed by Quentin Tarantino, USA: Miramax, 2004.

La La Land, directed by Damien Chazelle, USA: Black Label Media, 2016.

Le Mépris (Contempt), directed by Jean-Luc Godard, USA: Les Films Concordia, 1963.

Lawrence of Arabia, directed by David Lean, UK: Horizon Pictures (II), 1962.

Lifeboat, directed by Alfred Hitchcock, USA: Twentieth Century Fox Film Corporation, 1944.

Life of Pi, directed by Ang Lee, USA: Fox 2000 Pictures, 2012.

Living in Oblivion, directed by Tom DiCillo USA: JDI Productions, 1995.

London's Hollywood, UK: LAB Broadcast and Fire Mountain Productions/ITV1, 2006.

Lost in La Mancha, directed by Keith Fulton and Louis Pepe, UK: Quixote Films, 2002.

Lost in London Live, directed by Woody Harrleson, UK: Waypoint Entertainment, 2017.

Making of Ginger & Rosa, directed by Joseph Matthews, UK: Adventure Pictures, 2012.

Making 'The Shining', directed by Vivian Kubrick, USA: Eagle Film SS, 1980.

Maps to the Stars, directed by David Cronenberg, USA: Prospero Pictures, 2014.

Matrix, The, directed by Lana Wachowski and Lilly Wachowski, USA: Warner Bros., 1999.

Miss Peregrine's Home for Peculiar Children, directed by Tim Burton. USA: Twentieth Century Fox Film Corporation, 2016.

Mutiny on the Bounty, directed by Frank Lloyd, USA: Metro-Goldwyn-Mayer (MGM), 1935.

New Nightmare, directed by Wes Craven, USA: New Line Cinema, 1994.

Oh Brother Where Art Thou?, directed by Joel and Ethan Coen, 2000, USA: Touchstone Pictures, 2000.

Orlando, directed by Sally Potter, UK: Adventure Pictures, 1992.

Oz The Great and Powerful, directed by Sam Raimi, USA: Walt Disney Pictures, 2013.

Papadopoulos & Sons, directed by Marcus Markou, UK: Double M Films, 2013.

The Peanuts Movie, directed by Steve Martino USA: Twentieth Century Fox Animation, 2015.

Peeping Tom, directed by Michael Powell, USA: Michael Powell (Theatre), 1960.

Philomena, directed by Stephen Frears, UK: The Weinstein Company, 2013.

Pi, directed by Darren Aronofsky, USA: Harvest Filmworks, 1998.

Pleasantville, directed by Gary Ross, USA: New Line Cinema, 1998.

Prometheus, directed by Ridley Scott, USA: Twentieth Century Fox Film Corporation, 2012.

Pulp Fiction, directed by Quentin Tarantino, USA: Miramax, 1994.

Rage, directed by Sally Potter, UK: Adventure Pictures, 2009.

Raging Bull, directed by Martin Scorsese, USA: Chartoff-Winkler Productions, 1980.

Reluctant Dragon, The, directed by Alfred L. Werker, USA: Walt Disney Studios, 1941.

Reservoir Dogs, directed by Quentin Tarantino, USA: Live Entertainment, 1992.

Room 237, directed by Rodney Ascher, USA: Highland Park Classics, 2012.

Rope, directed by Alfred Hitchcock, USA: Warner Bros., 1948.

Run Lola Run, directed by Tom Tykwer, Germany: X-Filme Creative Pool, 1999.

Russian Ark, directed by Aleksandr Sokurov, Russia: The State Hermitage Museum, 2002.

Shepperton Babylon, directed by Ben McPherson, UK: BBC, 2005.

Shining, The, directed by Stanley Kubrick, USA: Warner Bros., 1980.

Sightseers, directed by Ben Wheatley, UK: StudioCanal, 2012.

Side by Side, directed by Chris Kenneally, USA: Company Films, 2012.

Singin' in the Rain, directed by Stanley Donen and Gene Kelly, USA: Metro-Goldwyn-Mayer (MGM), 1952.

Sixth Sense, directed by M. Night Shyamalan, USA: Hollywood Pictures, 1999.

Snow White and the Seven Dwarves, supervising director David Hand, USA: Walt Disney Productions, 1937.

Stagecoach, directed by John Ford, USA: Walter Wanger Productions, 1939.

Stanley Kubrick's Boxes, directed by Jon Ronson, UK: World of Wonder Productions, 2008.

State and Main, directed by David Mamet, France: Filmtown Entertainment, 2000.

Suicide squad, directed by David Ayer, USA: Atlas Entertainment, 2016.

Tango Lesson, directed by Sally Potter, UK: Adventure Pictures, 1997.

The Cutting Edge: Magic of Editing, directed by Wendy Apple, USA: A.C.E, 2004.

The Madness of King George, directed by Nicholas Hytner, UK: The Samuel Goldwyn Company, 1994.

The Player, directed by Robert Altman, USA: Avenue Pictures, 1992.

Timecode, directed by Mike Figgis, USA: Screen Gems, 2000.

Transformers: Age of Extinction, directed by Michael Bay, USA: Paramount Pictures, 2014.

Transformers: The Premake, directed by Kevin B. Lee, USA: Kevin B. Lee, 2014.

20th Century Fox Studio Tour, directed by Jimmy Fidler, USA: Twentieth Century Fox Film Corporation, 1936.

The Party, directed by Sally Potter, UK: Adventure Pictures, 2017.

The Twilight Saga: Breaking Dawn – Part 1, directed by Bill Condon, USA: Summit Entertainment, 2011.

24-hour Party People, directed by Michael Winterbottom, UK: Revolution Films, 2002.

Vampire Diaries, The, TV Series, *Midnight Rider* episode (2012), directed by Randall Miller, USA: Alloy Entertainment, 2009–.

Who Needs Sleep? directed by Haskell Wexler, USA: The Institute for Cinema Studies, 2006.

Wizard of Oz, The, directed by Victor Fleming, George Cukor Metro-Goldwyn-Mayer (MGM), 1939.

Victoria, directed by Sebastian Schipper, Germany: MonkeyBoy, 2015.

Wolf of Wall Street, The, directed by Martin Scorsese, USA: Red Granite Pictures, 2013.

Yes, directed by Sally Potter, UK: Adventure Pictures, 2000.

You Make the Movies campaign video, UK: Industry Trust for IP Awareness, 2009.

Bibliography

Academy of Motion Picture Arts and Sciences (2007). *The Digital Dilemma: Strategic Issues in Archiving and Accessing Digital Motion Picture Materials*, Hollywood: Academy of Motion Picture Arts and Sciences.

Academy of Motion Picture Arts and Sciences (2012), *The Digital Dilemma 2: Perspectives from Independent Filmmakers, Documentarians and Nonprofit Audiovisual Archives*, Hollywood: Academy of Motion Picture Arts and Sciences.

Acland, C. R. and Hoyt, E. (2016). *The Arclight Guidebook to Media History and the Digital Humanities*, retrieved from http://projectarclight.org/book.

Adorno, T. W. and Horkheimer, M. (1997), *Dialectic of Enlightenment* (J. Cumming, trans.), New York: Verso.

Alberge, D. (15 August 2015), 'Sadie Frost turns academic to highlight lack of film production roles for women', *The Guardian*, retrieved from http://www.theguardian.com/lifeandstyle/2015/aug/15/sadie-frost-turns-academic-women-film-production-buttercup-bill?CMP=share_btn_tw

Allen, J. T. (1980), 'The Industrial Context of Film Technology: Standardisation and Patents', in T. De Lauretis and S. Heath (eds), *The Cinematic Apparatus* (pp. 26–36), New York: St. Martin's Press.

Allon, Y., Cullen, D. and Patterson, H. (eds) (2001), *Contemporary British and Irish Film Directors*, London: Wallflower.

Andrew, D. (2000), 'The unauthorized auteur today, in R. Stam and T. Miller (eds), *Film and Theory: An Anthology* (pp. 20–9), Oxford: Blackwell.

Andrew, D. (2016), 'Time for Epic Cinema in an Age of Speed', *Cinema Journal*, 55(2), 135–46.

Archer, N. (2016), 'Speeds of Sound: On Fast Talking in Slow Movies', *Cinema Journal*, 55(2), 130–5.

Arri (2011), ALEXA Anamorphic De-squeeze White Paper.

Arthur, M. B. and Rousseau, D. M. (eds) (1996), *The Boundaryless Career*, Oxford: Oxford University Press.

Arthur, P. (2004), '(In)Dispensable Cinema: Confessions of a "making-of" addict', *Film Comment*, 40(4), 38–42.

Arthur, P. (2008, 25.10.08), 'Digital Fabric, Narrative Threads', from http://www.paularthur.com/2008/10/25/digital-fabric-narrative-threads/

Ashton, D. (2015), 'Making Media Workers: Contesting Film and Television Industry Career Pathways', *Television & New Media*, 16(3), 275–94.

Atkinson, S. (2011), 'Stereoscopic-3D storytelling – Rethinking the conventions, grammar and aesthetics of a new medium', *Journal of Media Practice*, 12(2), 139–56.

Atkinson, S. (2012a), 'Sparking ideas, making connections: Digital Film Archives and collaborative scholarship', *Frames Cinema Journal*, 1(1).

Atkinson, S. (2012b), 'Film and Audiovisual Media OERs: The case of SP-ARK', The Sally Potter Film Archive A HEA/JISC Open Educational Resources Case Study.

Atkinson, S. (2014), *Beyond the Screen: Emerging Cinema & Engaging Audiences*, New York: Bloomsbury.

Atkinson, S. (2015a), 'Interactive "making-of" machines: The performance and materiality of the processes, spaces and labor of VFX production', *Spectator: The University of Southern California Journal of Film and Television Criticism*, 35(2), 36–46.

Atkinson, S. (2015b), 'Gravity: towards a stereoscopic poetics of deep space', in M. Spöhrer (ed.), *The Aesthetic and Narrative Dimensions of 3D Films: New Perspectives on Stereoscopy*, Wiesbaden: Springer.

Atkinson, S. (2016), 'Digitally Preserving Potter: The Dailiness and Feminization of Labor within Digital Filmmaking and Archiving', *Feminist Media Histories*, 2(1), 29–44.

Atkinson, S. (2016), *Prevention is Better Than More: From Criminalization to Commercialization of Mass-Pirating-Publics*, paper presented at the SCMS 2016, Atlanta, Georgia.

Atkinson, S. (2016), *simulacinema*, paper presented at the TFTV Research Seminar Series, Department of Theatre, Film and Television, University of York.

Atkinson, S. (2017), *simulacinema: Production as reception in contemporary spaces of film consumption*, paper presented at the Situation Space, How Spatial Images Define the User's Disposition, International conference, Humboldt University, Berlin.

Atkinson, S. and Whatley, S. (2015), 'Digital archives and open archival practices', *Convergence: The International Journal of Research into New Media Technologies*, 21(1), 3–7.

Baillieu, B. and Goodchild, J. (2002), *The British Film Business*, Chichester: John Wiley and Sons.

Baker, W. E. and Faulkner, R. R. (1991), 'Role as Resource in the Hollywood Film Industry', *American Journal of Sociology*, 97(2), 279–309.

Balcerzak, S. and Sperb, J. (eds) (2009), *Cinephilia in the Age of Digital Reproduction: Film, Pleasure and Digital Culture Vol. 1*, London: Wallflower.

Balcerzak, S. and Sperb, J. (eds) (2012), *Cinephilia in the Age of Digital Reproduction: Film, Pleasure and Digital Culture Vol. 2*, London: Wallflower.

Balcon, M. (1969), *Michael Balcon presents . . . A Lifetime of Films*, London: Hutchinson.

Ball, V. and Bell, M. (2013), 'Working Women, Women's Work: Production, History, Gender: Introduction', *Journal of British Cinema and Television*, 10(3), 547–62.

Banks, M. (2009), 'Gender Below-the-Line: Defining Feminist Production Studies', in V. Mayer, M. Banks and J. T. Caldwell (eds), *Production Studies: Cultural Studies of Media Industries* (pp. 87–98), New York: Routledge.

Banks, M., Conor, B. and Mayer, V. (eds) (2016), *Production Studies, The Sequel!*, New York: Routledge.

Barlow, A. (2005), *The DVD Revolution: Movies, Culture & Technology*, Westport: Praeger.

Barnwell, J. (2004), *Production Design: Architects of the Screen*, London and New York: Wallflower.

Barr, C. (1998), *Ealing Studios* (3rd edn), Berkeley: University of California Press.

Barrow, S. (2011), 'The British film industry: creativity and constraint', *British Politics Review*, 6(1).

Baudry, J.-L. and Williams, A. (1974–5), 'Ideological Effects of the Basic Cinematographic Apparatus, *Film Quarterly*, 28(2), 39–47.

Bazin, A. (1957), 'De la politique des auteurs', *Cahiers du cinéma*, 70, 2–11.

Bechky, B. A. (2006), 'Gaffers, Gofers and Grips: Role-Based Coordination in Temporary Organizations', *Organization Science*, 17(1), 3–21.

Beckman, K. (2016), 'The Tortoise, the Hare and the Constitutive Outsiders: Reframing Fast and Slow Cinemas', *Cinema Journal*, 55(2), 125–30.

Bell, M. and Williams, M. (eds) (2010), *British Women's Cinema*, London: Routledge.

Bellantoni, P. (2005), *If it's Purple, Someone's Gonna Die: The Power of Colour in Visual Storytelling*, Oxford: Focal Press.

Belton, J. (2002), 'Digital Cinema: A False Revolution', *October*, 100 (Obsolescence), 98–114.

Benjamin, W. (2007), *Illuminations* (H. Zohn, trans.), New York: Shocken Books.

Bennett, B. (2015), 'The cinema of Michael Bay: an aesthetic of excess', *Senses of Cinema*, 75.

Bennett, J. and Brown, T. (2008), *Film and television after DVD*, London: Routledge.

Berg, M. and Seeber, B. (2016), *Slow Professor: Challenging the Culture of Speed in the Academy*, Toronto: University of Toronto Press.

Bernstein, S. (2004), *Film Production*, Oxford: Focal Press.

Berry, D. M. (ed.) (2012), *Understanding Digital Humanities*, Basingstoke: Palgrave Macmillan.

Berry, D. M., van Dartel, M., Dieter, M., Kasprzak, M., Muller, N., O'Reilly, R. and de Vicente, J. L. (2012), *New aesthetic, new anxieties*, Rotterdam.

Betz, M. (2008), 'Little Books', in L. Grieveson and H. Wasson (eds), *Inventing Film Studies*, Durham, NC and London: Duke University Press.

Betz, M. (2010), 'In Focus: Cinephilia', *Cinema Journal*, 49(2), 130–2.

BFI (2011), 'BFI Collection Policy', 16 November 2011, in BFI (ed.), London: BFI.

BFI (2012), *BFI Statistical Yearbook 2012*, London: BFI.

BFI (2012), *CID STYLISTICS MANUAL*, London: BFI.

Bilton, C. (2007), 'Managing creative work through release and control', in C. Bilton (ed.), *Management and creativity* (pp. 66–90), Oxford Blackwell Publishing.

Blair, H. (2001), 'You're Only as Good as Your Last Job: the Labour Process and Labour Market in the British Film Industry', *Work, Employment and Society*, 15(1), 149–69.

Blair, H. (2003), 'Winning and Losing in Flexible Labour Markets: the Formation and Operation of Networks of Interdependence in the UK Film Industry', *Sociology*, 37(4), 677–94, doi: 10.1177/00380385030374003

Bloore, P. (2009), 'Re-defining the Independent Film Value Chain', in U. F. Council (ed.), London: UK Film Council.

Boaden, H. (2016), 'BBC Radio Director Helen Boaden resigns, criticising state of journalism', *The Independent*, retrieved from http://www.independent.co.uk/news/media/tv-radio/bbc-radio-director-helen-boaden-to-announce-resignation-at-prix-italia-preview-in-lampedusa-a7337181.html

Bolter, J. D. and Grusin, R. (2001), *Remediation: Understanding New Media*, Cambridge, MA: MIT Press.

Bonini, T. and Gandini, A. (2016), 'Invisible Workers in an Invisible Medium: An Ethnographic Approach to Italian Public and Private Freelance Radio Producers', in M. Banks, B. Conor and V. Mayer (eds), *Production Studies, The Sequel!* (pp. 138–49), New York: Routledge.

Bordwell, D. (2012), *Pandora's Digital Box: Films, Files, and the Future of Movies*, Madison: The Irvington Way Institute Press.

Bordwell, D., Staiger, J. and Thompson, K. (1985), *The Classical Hollywood Cinema: Film Style and Mode of Production to 1960*, London: Routledge.

Bordwell, D. and Thompson, K. (2011), *Minding Movies: Observations on the art, craft, and business of filmmaking*, Chicago: The University of Chicago Press.

Bordwell, D. and Thompson, K. (2013), *Film Art: An Introduction* (10th edn), Madison: University of Wisconsin Press.

Boughey, D. (1921), *The Film Industry*, London: Sir Isaac Pitman and Sons.

Brereton, P. (2012), *Smart Cinema, DVD Add-Ons and New Audience Pleasures*, Basingstoke: Palgrave Macmillan.

Brereton, P. (2015), Smart New Audiences: A Pilot Study (DVD Bonus Features – A New Form of Cineaste Experience!), *Quarterly Review of Film and Video*, 32, 367–83.

Brisbin, D. (2009, December 2009–January 2010), 'Instant Fan-Made Media', *Perspective*, 56–7.

Brown, B. (2015), *The Filmmakers Guide to Digital Imaging*, Oxford: Focal Press.

Brown, W. (2013), *Supercinema Film-Philosophy for the Digital Age*, New York: Berghahn.

Brownlow, K. (1968), *The Parade's Gone By*, London: Secker and Warburg.

Brunel, A. (1933), *Filmcraft: The art of picture production*, London: George Newnes.

Bruno, G. (2008) 'Yes, it's about Time: A Virtual Letter to Sally Potter from Giuliana Bruno.' *Journal of visual culture*, 7.1, 27–40.

Brunsdon, C. (2008), 'In Focus: The British Film Institute: In the Dark: The BFI Archive', *Cinema Journal*, 47(4), 152–5.

Bulletin, T. K. (2013, 05/02/2013), 'UK film production spending declines; Skyfall tops 2012 box office', *The Knowledge Bulletin*.

Buscombe, E. (1985), 'Notes on Columbia Pictures Corporation 1926–1941', in B. Nichols (ed.), *Movies and Methods: Volume 2* (pp. 92–108), Berkeley: University of California Press.

Butler, I. (1971), *The Making of Feature Films*, Harmondsworth: Penguin.

Caldwell, J. T. (2008a), *Production Culture: Industrial Reflexivity and Critical Practice in Film and Television*, Durham, NC: Duke University Press.

Caldwell, J. T. (2008b), 'Prefiguring DVD Bonus Tracks: Making-ofs and Behind-the-Scenes as Historic Television Programming Strategies Prototypes', in J. Bennett and T. Brown (eds), *Film and television after DVD* (pp. 149–71), London: Routledge.

Caldwell, J. T. (2009a), 'Screen studies and industrial "theorizing" ', *Screen*, 50(1), 167–79.

Caldwell, J. T. (2009b), 'Cultures of Production: Studying Industry's Deep Texts, Reflexive Rituals, and Managed Self-Disclosures', in J. Holt and A. Perren (eds), *Media Industries: History, Theory, and Method* (pp. 199–212), Chichester: Wiley-Blackwell.

Caldwell, J. T. (2013), 'Para-Industry: Researching Hollywood's Blackwaters', *Cinema Journal*, 52(3), 157–65.

Caldwell, J. T. (2014), 'Para-Industry, Shadow Academy', *Cultural Studies*, 28(4), 720–40. doi: 10.1080/09502386.2014.888922

Callahan, V. (ed.) (2010), *Reclaiming the Archive: Feminism and Film History*, Detroit: Wayne State University Press.

Campagnoni, D. P. (2006), 'The preservation, care and exploitation of documentation related to the cinema: an unresolved issue', *Film History: An International Journal*, 18(3), 306–18.

Carman, E. (2016), *Independent Stardom: Freelance Women in the Hollywood Studio System*, Austin: University of Texas Press.

Carringer, R. L. (1985), *The Making of Citizen Kane*, London: John Murray.

Carringer, R. L. (2001), Collaboration and Concepts of Authorship, *PMLA*, 116(2), 370–9.

Case, D. (2005), *Film Technology in post production*, Oxford: Focal Press.

Castle, A. (2008), *The Stanley Kubrick Archives*, Köln: Taschen.

Chanan, M. (1976), *Labour Power in the British Film Industry*, London: BFI.

Chanan, M. (1980), 'Labour power and aesthetic labour in film and television in Britain', *Media, Culture & Society*, 2.2 117–37.

Chang, J. (2011), *FilmCraft: Editing*, Lewes: Ilex.

Chávez Heras, D. (2011), 'The Malleable Computer: Software and the Study of the Moving Image', *Frames Cinema Journal*, 1(1).

Christian, A. J. (2011), 'Joe Swanberg, Intimacy, and the Digital Aesthetic', *Cinema Journal*, 50(4), 117–35.

Christopherson, S. and Storper, M. (1989), 'The Effects of Flexible Specialization on Industrial Politics and the Labor Market: The Motion Picture Industry', *Industrial and Labor Relations Review*, 42(3), 331–47.

Chun, W. H. K. (2011), *Programmed visions: Software and memory*, Cambridge, MA: MIT Press.

Clevé, B. (2005), *Film Production Management* (3rd edn), Abingdon: Focal Press.

Coates, P. (2010), *Cinema and Colour: The Saturated Image*, London: Palgrave Macmillan BFI.

Cobley, P. and Haeffner, N. (2011), 'Narrative Supplements: DVD and the Idea of the "Text"', in R. E. Page and B. Thomas (eds), *New Narratives: Stories and Storytelling in the Digital Age*, Lincoln: University of Nebraska Press.

Cohendet, P. and Simon, L. (2007), 'Playing across the playground: paradoxes of knowledge creation in the videogame firm', *Journal of Organizational Behavior*, 28(5), 587–605.

Comolli, J.-L. (1980), 'Machines of the Visible', in T. De Lauretis and S. Heath (eds), *The Cinematic Apparatus* (pp. 121–42), New York: St. Martin's Press.

Conant, M. (1960), *Antitrust in the Motion Picture Industry, Economic and Legal Analysis*, Cambridge: Cambridge University Press.

Conor, B. (2014), *Screenwriting:creative labor and professional practice*, London: Routledge.

Cook, B.C. (1916), 'The Film Surgeon' in *Picture Play Magazine*, May 1916, IV, 3, 220–4.

Cook, P. (1996), *Fashioning the Nation: Costume and Identity in British Cinema*, London: BFI.

Cook, P. and Dodd, P. (eds) (1993), *Women and Film: A Sight and Sound Reader*, London: Scarlett Press.

Cook, T. (1993), 'The Concept of Archival Fonds and the Post-Custodial Era: Theory, Problems and Solutions', *Archivaria* (35), 24–37.

Corrigan, T. (1991), *A Cinema Without Walls: Movies and Culture After Vietnam*, New Brunswick, NJ: Rutgers University Press.

Corrigan, T. (2016), Still Speed: Cinematic Acceleration, Value and Execution. *Cinema Journal*, 55(2),

Corrigan, T. and White, P. (2012), *The Film Experience: An Introduction*, Boston: Bedford/St. Martin's Press.

Cowan, P. (2012a), Underexposed: The Neglected Art of the Cinematographer, *Journal Media Practice*, 13(1), 75–96.

Cowan, P. (2012b), 'Authorship and the Director of Photography: A Case Study of Gregg Toland and Citizen Kane', *Networking Knowledge*, 5(1), 231–45.

Crisp, V. (2015), *Film distribution in the digital age: pirates and professionals*, Basingstoke: Palgrave Macmillan.

Crittenden, R. (2006), *Fine Cuts: The Art of European Film Editing*, Oxford: Focal Press.

Cucco, M. (2010), 'The borders of the domestic market and their importance for the economy of the film industry: The Swiss case study', *European Journal of Communication*, 25(2), 153–67. doi: 10.1177/0267323110363648

Cullinan, N. (ed.) (2012), *Tacita Dean: Film*, London: Tate Publishing.

Curtin, M. and Sanson, K. (eds) (2016), *Precarious Creativity: Global Media Local Labor*, Oakland: University of California Press.

Curtin, M. and Vanderhoef, J. (2014), A Vanishing Piece of the Pi: The Globalization of Visual Effects Labor, *Television & New Media*, 1–21.

Daly, K. M. (2009), New Mode of Cinema: How Digital Technologies are Changing Aesthetics and Style, *Kinephanos*, 1(1).

Davidson, A. (5 May 2015), 'What Hollywood Can Teach Us About the Future of Work', *The New York Times Magazine*.

Davy, C. (ed.) (1938), *Footnotes to the film*, London: Lovat Dickson.

de Esteban, M.-J. (2013), 'Film, Data, Action! the BFI Collections Are Now Just a Click Away', *Journal of Film Preservation*.

de Kuyper, E. (1994), 'Anyone for an aesthetic of film history?' *Film History*, 6, 100–9.

De Lauretis, T. and Heath, S. (eds) (1980), *The Cinematic Apparatus*, New York: St. Martin's Press.

Decherney, P. (2012), *Hollywood's Copyright Wars: From Edison to the Internet*, New York: Columbia University Press.

DeFillippi, R. J. and Arthur, M. B. (1998), 'Paradox in project-based enterprise: The case of film making', *California Management Review*, 40(2), 125–39.

Denton, B. (20–1 January 1925), 'Thru Death Valley with von Stroheim: How the Director of Greed and His Workers Braved Death for the Sake of Realism', *Motion Picture Magazine*, 92.

Derrida, J. and Prenowitz, E. (1995), 'Archive Fever: A Freudian Impression', *Diacritics*, 25(2), 17.

Desjardins, M. (2016), 'Performance, Labor and Stardom in the Era of the Synthespian in Banks', in M. Banks, B. Conor and V. Mayer (eds), *Production Studies, The Sequel!* (pp. 11–22), New York: Routledge.

Deuze, M. (2006), 'Collaboration, participation and the media', *New Media & Society*, 8(4), 691–8, doi: 10.1177/1461444806065665

Deuze, M. (2007), *Media Work*, Cambridge: Polity.

Deuze, M. (2009), 'Convergence Culture and Media Work, in J. Holt and A. Perren (eds), *Media Industries: History, Theory, and Method* (pp. 144–56), Chichester: Wiley-Blackwell.

Dick, B. F. (2010), *Anatomy of Film* (6th edn), Boston: Bedford/St. Martin's Press.

Directors Guild of America (2004), 'Possessory Credit Timeline', retrieved 7 January 2016, from http://www.dga.org/Craft/DGAQ/All-Articles/0402-Feb-2004/Possessory-Credit-Timeline.aspx

Doane, M. A. (1980), 'Ideology and Practice of Sound Editing and Mixing', in T. De Lauretis and S. Heath (eds), *The Cinematic Apparatus* (pp. 47–56), New York: St. Martin's Press.

Doane, M. A. (2002), *The Emergence of Cinematic Time: Modernity, Contingency, the Archive*, Cambridge, MA: Harvard University Press.

Doane, M. A. (2007), 'The Indexical and the Concept of Medium Specificity', *A Journal of Feminist Cultural Studies*, 18(1).

Du Gay, P. (ed.) (1997), *Production of Culture: Cultures of Production*, London: Sage.

Duchovnay, G. (ed.) (2004), *Film Voices: Interviews from Post Script*, Albany: State University of New York Press.

Ebbers, J. J. and Wijnberg, N. M. (2009), 'Latent organizations in the film industry: Contracts, rewards and resources', *Human Relations*, 62(7), 987–1009.

Eberts, J. and Ilott, T. (1990), *My Indecision is Final: The Rise and Fall of Goldcrest Films*, London: Faber and Faber.

Ede, L. N. (2010), *British Film Design*, London: I. B. Tauris.

Egan, K. (2015), 'Precious footage of the auteur at work: framing, accessing, using, and cultifying Vivian Kubrick's Making the Shining', *New Review of Film and Television Studies*, 13(1), 63–82.

Elsaesser, T. (1998a), 'Digital Cinema – Delivery Event, Time', in T. Elsaesser and K. Hoffmann (eds), *Cinema Futures: Cain, Abel or Cable? – The Screen Arts in the Digital Age* (pp. 201–22), Amsterdam: Amsterdam University Press.

Elsaesser, T. (1998b), 'Fantasy Island: Dream Logic as Production Logic', in T. Elsaesser and K. Hoffman (eds), *Cinema Futures: Cain, Abel or Cable? The Screen Arts in the Digital Age* (pp. 143–58), Amsterdam: Amsterdam University Press.

Elsaesser, T. (2014a), 'Digital Cinema: Convergence or Contradiction?', in C. Vernallis, A. Herzog and J. Richardson (eds), *The Oxford Handbook of Sound and Image in Digital Media* (pp. 13–44), New York: Oxford University Press.

Elsaesser, T. (2014b), 'Pushing the contradictions of the digital: "virtual reality" and "interactive narrative" as oxymorons between narrative and gaming', *New Review of Film and Television Studies*, 12(3), 295–311.

Enticknap, L. (2005), *Moving Image Technology: From zoetrope to digital*, London: Wallflower.

Ettedgui, P. (ed.) (1999), *Production Design & Art Direction*, Switzerland: Screencraft.

Fairservice, D. (2001), *Film Editing: History, Theory and Practice*, Manchester: Manchester University Press.

Feinberg, S. (2013, 12/11/2013), 'Top Directors Reveal How Female Film Editors Shaped Their Movies', *The Hollywood Reporter*.

Ferguson, K. L. (2015), Volumetric Cinema. *[in] Transition*, 2(1).

Figgis, M. (2007), *Digital Film-Making*, London: Faber and Faber.

Fischer, L. (2004), '"Dancing through the Minefield": Passion, Pedagogy, Politics, and Production in "The Tango Lesson"', *Cinema Journal*, 43(3), 42–58.

Fitzgerald, J. (2010), *Studying British Cinema: 1999–2009*, Leighton Buzzard: Auteur.

Flanagan, M. (2004), 'The Hulk, an Ang Lee Film: Notes on the Blockbuster Auteur', *New Review of Film and Television Studies*, 1, 19–35.

Flaxton, T. (2011), 'HD Aesthetics', *Convergence: The International Journal of Research into New Media Technologies*, 17(2), 113–23.

Follows, S. (2014a), 'What percentage of a UK film crew is female?' Retrieved from https://stephenfollows.com/percentage-uk-film-crew-female/

Follows, S. (2014b), 'Gender within film crews', *Stephen Follows Film Data and Education* (Vol. 22).

Follows, S. (2014c), 'Gender within UK film crews', *Stephen Follows Film Data and Education*.

Follows, S. (2014d), 'Gender in Film Industry', *Stephen Follows Film Data and Education* (p. 49).

Follows, S. (2015a), 'How many people work on independent films in the UK?', retrieved from http://stephenfollows.com/how-many-people-work-on-independent-films-in-the-uk/

Follows, S. (2015b), 'The full costs and income of a £1million indie film', retrieved from http://stephenfollows.com/the-full-costs-and-income-of-a-1million-indie-film

Fortmueller, K. (2015), 'Performing Labor in the Media Industries: Editor's Introduction', *Spectator: The University of Southern California Journal of Film and Television Criticism*, 35(2), 5–9.

Fossati, G. (2011), *From Grain to Pixel: The Archival Life of Film in Transition* (2nd edn), Amsterdam: Amsterdam University Press.

Foucault, M. (2002), *The Archaeology of Knowledge*, London: Routledge.

Fowler, C. (2009), *Contemporary Film Directors*, Urbana: University of Illinois Press.

Frick, C. (2009), 'Manufacturing Heritage: The Moving Image Archive and Media Industry Studies' in J. Holt and A. Perren (eds), *Media Industries: History, Theory, and Method* (pp. 34–44), Chichester: Wiley-Blackwell.

Frick, C. (2011), *Saving Cinema: The Politics of Preservation*, Oxford: Oxford University Press.

Gans, H. J. (1963), 'The Creator–Audience Relationship in the Mass Media: An Analysis of Movie Making', in B. Rosenberg and D. Manning White (eds), *Mass Culture: The popular arts in America* (pp. 315–24), New York: The Free Press of Glencoe.

Ganz, A. and Khatib, L. (2006), 'Digital cinema: The transformation of film practice and aesthetics', *New Cinemas: Journal of Contemporary Film*, 4(1), 21–36.

Gaudreault, A. and Marion, P. (2015), *The End of Cinema? A Medium in Crisis in the Digital Age* (T. Barnard, trans.), New York: Columbia University Press.

Gaut, B. (1997), 'Film Authorship and Collaboration', in R. Allen and M. M. Smith (eds), *Film Theory and Philosophy* (pp. 149–72), Oxford: Clarendon Press.

Gauthier, P. (2014), 'What will film studies be? Film caught between the television revolution and the digital revolution', *New Review of Film and Television Studies*, 12(3), 229–33.

Geertz, C. (1973), *The Interpretation of Cultures*, New York: Basic Books.

Genette, G. (1987), *Paratexts: Thresholds of Interpretation*, Cambridge: Cambridge University Press.

Geuens, J.-P. (2007), 'The Space of Production', *Quarterly Review of Film and Video*, 24(5), 411–20.

Geuens, P. (1996), 'Through the Looking Glasses: From the Camera Obscura to Video Assist', *Film Quarterly*, 49(3), 16–26.

Ghosal, T. (2015), 'Unprojections, or, Worlds Under Erasure in Contemporary Hollywood Cinema', *Media-N: Journal of the New Media Caucus*, 11(1).

Gill, R. (2014), 'Unspeakable inequalities: Post feminism, entrepreneurial subjectivity, and the repudiation of sexism among cultural workers', *Social Politics: International Studies in Gender, State & Society*, 21(4), 509–28.

Gitelman, L. (2006), *Always Already New: Media, History, and the Data of Culture*, Cambridge, MA: MIT Press.

Godard, J.-L. (1956), 'Montage, mon beau souci', in Jean-Luc-Godard par Jean-Luc Godard, *Cahiers du cinéma*, 1986, 94: Paris.

Goldsmith, B. and O'Regan, T. (2005), *The Film Studio: Film Production in the Global Economy*, Lanham: Rowman and Littlefield.

Gomery, D. (1985), 'Writing the History of the American Film Industry: Warner Brothers and Sound', in B. Nichols (ed.), *Movies and Methods: Volume 2* (pp. 109–61), Berkeley: University of California Press.

Goodridge, M. (2012), *FilmCraft: Directing*, Lewes: Ilex.

Govil, N. (2013), 'Recognizing "Industry"', *Cinema Journal*, 52(3), 172–6.

Grant, C. (2000), 'www.auteur.com?', *Screen*, 41(1), 101–8.

Grant, C. (2008), 'Auteur Machines? Auteurism and the DVD', in J. Bennett and T. Brown (eds), *Film and television after DVD*, London: Routledge.

Grant, C. (2012), 'Film and Moving Image Studies: Re-Born Digital?', *Frames Cinema Journal*, 1(1).

Gray, J. (2010), *Show Sold Separately: Promos, Spoilers and Other Media Paratexts*, New York: New York University Press.

Gray, L. S. and Seeber, R. L. (eds) (1996), *Under the Stars: Essays on Labor Relations in Arts and Entertainment*, Ithaca: Cornell University Press.

Greenwald, S. R. and Landry, P. (2009), *This Business of Film: A practical guide to achieving success in the film industry*, New York: Lone Eagle.

Grierson, J. (1966), 'The First Principles of Documentary' in *Grierson on Documentary* in Hardy, F. (ed.), London: Faber and Faber, 145–56.

Grieveson, L. (2012), 'The Work of Film in the Age of Fordist Mechanization', *Cinema Journal*, 51(3), 25–51.

Grieveson, L. (2013), 'What is the Value of a Technological History of Cinema?', *Alphaville: Journal of Film and Screen Media*, 6.

Griffiths, K. (2003), 'The Manipulated Image', *Convergence: The International Journal of Research into New Media Technologies*, 9(4), 12–26.

Grodal, T., Larsen, B. and Laursen, I. T. (eds) (2004), *Visual Authorship: Creativity and Intentionality in Media*, Copenhagen: Museum Tusculanum Press.

Grugulis, I. and Stoyanova, D. (2009), 'I don't know where you learn them: skills in film and TV', in A. McKinlay and C. Smith (eds), *Working in the Creative Industries* (pp. 135–55), New York: Palgrave Macmillan.

Grugulis, I. and Stoyanova, D. (2011), 'The missing middle: communities of practice in a freelance labour market', *Work, employment and society*, 25(2), 342–51.

Grugulis, I. and Stoyanova, D. (2012), 'Social Capital and Networks in Film and TV: Jobs for the Boys?', *Organization Studies*, *33*(10), 1311–331, doi: 10.1177/0170840612453525

Grusin, R. (2007), DVDs, Video Games and the Cinema of Interactions, in J. Lyons and J. Plunkett (eds), *Multimedia Histories: From the Magic Lantern to the Internet*, Exeter: University of Exeter Press.

Gubbins, M. (2011), 'Lost Demographics: Industry analyst Michael Gubbins examines the facts behind the UK Film Council's final study of diversity in film', *MovieScope Magazine*. http://www.moviescopemag.com/24-fps/industryinsider/lost-demographics/

Gunning, T. (2004), 'Re-Newing Old Technologies: Astonishment, Second Nature, and the Uncanny in Technology from the Previous Turn-of-the-Century', in D. Thorburn and H. Jenkins (eds), *Rethinking Media Change – The Aesthetics of Transition* (pp. 39–60), Cambridge, MA: MIT Press.

Gurevitch, L. (2016), 'Cinema Designed: Visual Effects Software and the Emergence of the Engineered Spectacle', in S. Denson and J. Leyda (eds), *Post-Cinema: Theorizing 21st-Century Film*, Falmer: REFRAME Books.

Hadjioannou, M. (2012), *From Light to Byte: Toward an Ethics of Digital Cinema*, Minneapolis, MN: University of Minnesota Press.

Hagener, M., Hediger, V. and Strohmaier, A. (eds) (2016), *The State of Post-Cinema Tracing the Moving Image in the Age of Digital Dissemination*, Basingstoke: Palgrave.

Hallam, J. and Roberts, L. (2011), 'Mapping, memory and the city: Archives, databases and film historiography', *European Journal of Cultural Studies*, *14*(3), 355–372. doi: 10.1177/1367549411399939.

Halligan, F. (2012), *Film Craft: Production Design*, Lewes: Ilex.

Hampton, B. B. (1931), *A History of the Movies*, New York: Covici-Friede.

Hand, M. (2008), *Making Digital Cultures: Access, Interactivity, and Authenticity*. Farnham: Ashgate.

Harbord, J. (2002), *Film Cultures*, London: Sage.

Harper, S. (2000), *Women in British Cinema: Mad, Bad and Dangerous to Know*, New York: Continuum.

Hatch, K. (2013), 'Cutting Women: Margaret Booth and Hollywood's Pioneering Female Film Editors', in J. Gaines, R. Vatsal and M. Dall'Asta (eds), Women Film Pioneers Project, in C. f. D. R. a. Scholarship (Series Edn.), New York: Columbia University Libraries. Retrieved from <https://wfpp.cdrs.columbia.edu/essay/cutting-women/>.

Havens, T. and Lotz, A. D. (2012), *Understanding Media Industries*, New York: Oxford University Press.

Havens, T., Lotz, A. D. and Tinic, S. (2009), 'Critical Media Industry Studies: A Research Approach', *Communication, Culture & Critique*, 2, 234–53.

Hayles, N. K. (2007), 'Narrative and Database: Natural Symbionts', *PMLA*, 122(5), 1603–8.

Heath, S. (1980), 'The Cinematic Apparatus: Technology as Historical and Cultural Form', in De Lauretis, T. and Heath, S. (eds) (1980), *The Cinematic Apparatus*, pp. 1–13, New York: St. Martin's Press.

Hediger, V. and Vonderau, P. (2009), *Films that Work : Industrial Film and the Productivity of Media*, Amsterdam: Amsterdam University Press.

Hesmondhalgh, D. (2010), 'Media industry studies, media production studies', in J. Curran (ed.), *Media and Society* (pp. 145–63), London: Bloomsbury.

Hesmondhalgh, D. (2013), *The Cultural Industries* (3rd edn), London: Sage.

Hesmondhalgh, D. and Baker, S. (2008), 'Creative Work and Emotional Labour in the Television Industry', *Theory, Culture & Society*, 25(7–8), 97–118.

Hesmondhalgh, D. and Baker, S. (2015), 'Sex, Gender and Work Segregation in the Cultural Industries', in B. Conor, R. Gill and S. Taylor (eds), *Gender and Creative Labour, Sociological Review Monographs*, Hoboken: Wiley-Blackwell.

Higgins, S. (2003), 'A New Color Consciousness: Color in the Digital Age', *Convergence: The International Journal of Research into New Media Technologies*, 9(4), 60–76.

Hill, E. (2014), 'Recasting the Casting Director: Managed Change, Gendered Labor, in D. Johnson, D. Kompare and A. Santo (eds), *Making Media Work: Cultures of Management in the Entertainment Industries*, New York: New York University Press.

Hill, E. (2016), *Never Done: A History of Women's Work in Media Production*, New Brunswick, NJ: Rutgers University Press.

Hilmes, M. (2009), 'Nailing Mercury: The Problem of Media Industry Historiography', in J. Holt and A. Perren (eds), *Media Industries: History, Theory, and Method* (pp. 21–33), Chichester: Wiley-Blackwell.

Hilmes, M. (2013), 'On a Screen Near You: The New Soundwork Industry', *Cinema Journal*, 52(3), 177–82.

Hine, C. (2015), *Ethnography for the internet: Embedded, embodied and everyday*, New York: Bloomsbury.

Holt, J. (2013), 'Two-Way Mirrors: Looking at the Future of Academic-Industry Engagement', *Cinema Journal*, 52(3), 183.

Holt, J. and Perren, A. (eds) (2009), *Media Industries: History, Theory, and Method*, Chichester: Wiley-Blackwell.

Honthaner, E. L. (2001), *The Complete Film Production Handbook* (3rd edn), Burlington: Focal Press.

Horak, J.-C. (2007), 'The Gap Between 1 and 0 Digital Video and the Omissions of Film History, *Spectator*, 27(1), 29–41.

Horne, H. L. (2010), *The Relationship among Career Anchors, Negative Career Thoughts, Vocational Identity, and Hope in Freelance Production Crew for Film and Television* (Doctor of Philosophy), Florida State University, Florida (3775).

Hoskins, C., McFadyen, S., Finn, A. and Jackel, A. (1995), 'Film and Television Co-Production: Evidence from Canadian-European Experience', *European Journal of Communication*, 10(2), 221–43, doi: 10.1177/0267323195010002004.

Hoxter, J. and Horton, A. (2014), *Screenwriting*, London: I. B. Tauris.

Huettig, M. D. (1944), *Economic Control of the Motion Picture Industry: A Study in Industrial Organization*, Philadelphia: University of Pennsylvania Press.

Huff, J. (2012), 'Beyond the Surface: 15 Years of Desktop Aesthetics', *Rhizome*.

Huhtamo, E. and Parikka, J. (eds) (2011), *Media archaeology: Approaches, applications, and implications*, Berkeley: University of California Press.

Institution, B. S. (2010), 'Film identification. Enhancing interoperability of metadata', Element sets and structures BS EN 15907:2010: British Standards Institution.

Isaacs, B. (2013), *The Orientation of Future Cinema: Technology, Aesthetics, Spectacle*, New York: Bloomsbury Academic.

James, N. (2010), 'Syndromes of a new century', *Sight & Sound*.

Jenkins, H. (2006a), *Convergence Culture: Where Old and New Media Collide*, New York: New York University Press.

Jenkins, H. (2006b), 'Prohibitionists and Collaborationists: Two Approaches to Participatory Culture', retrieved from http://henryjenkins.org/2006/07/prohibitionists_and_collaborat.html

Jenkins, H., Ford, S. and Green, J. (2013), *Spreadable Media: Creating Value and Meaning in a Networked Culture*, New York: New York University Press.

Jeong, S.-h. and Szaniawski, J. (eds) (2016), *The Global Auteur: The Politics of Authorship in 21st Century Cinema*, New York: Bloomsbury.

Jin, D. Y. (2012), 'Transforming the global film industries: Horizontal integration and vertical concentration amid neoliberal globalization', *International Communication Gazette*, 74(5), 405–22, doi: 10.1177/1748048512445149

Jobes, G. (1966), *Motion Picture Empire*, Hamden, CT: Archon Books.

Johns, J. (2010), 'Manchester's Film and Television Industry: Project Ecologies and Network Hierarchies', *Urban Studies*, 47(5), 1059–77, doi: 10.1177/0042098009353628

Johnson, D. (2014), 'Authorship Up for Grabs: Decentralized Labor, Licensing, and the Management of Collaborative Creativity', in D. Mann (ed.), *Wired TV: Laboring Over an Interactive Future* (pp. 32–52), New Brunswick, NJ: Rutgers University Press.

Johnson, D., Kompare, D. and Santo, A. (eds) (2014), *Making Media Work: Cultures of Management in the Entertainment Industries*, New York: New York University Press.

Jones, C. (1996), 'Careers in Project Networks: The Case of the Film Industry', in M. B. Arthur and D. M. Rousseau (eds), *The Boundaryless Career: A New Employment Principle for a New Organizational Era* (pp. 58–75), Oxford: Oxford University Press.

Jones, C. and DeFillippi, R. J. (1996), 'Back to the future in film: Combining industry and self-knowledge to meet the career challenges of the 21st century', *Academy of Management Executive*, 10(4), 89–103.

Kann, M. (1938), 'Hollywood and Britain – three thousand miles apart', in C. Davy (ed.), *Footnotes to the film* (pp. 185–202), London: Lovat Dickson Ltd.

Kapsis, R. (1986), 'Hollywood Filmmaking and Audience Image', in S. Ball-Rokeach and M. G. Cantor (eds), *Media, Audience, and Social Structure* (pp. 161–73), London: Sage.

Katz, J. (1991), 'Archiveology', *Cinematograph*, 4, 96–7.

Kawin, B. (1987), *How Movies Work*, Oakland: University of California Press.

Kendall, T. (2016), 'Staying on, or Getting off (the Bus): Approaching Speed in Cinema and Media Studies, *Cinema Journal*, 55(2), 112–18.

Kipnis, L. (2000), 'Film and Changing Technologies', in J. Hill and P. Church Gibson (eds), *World Cinema: Critical Approaches* (pp. 211–20), Oxford: Oxford University Press.

Klinger, B. (2001), 'The Contemporary Cinephile: Film Collecting in the Post-Video Era', in M. Stokes and R. Maltby (eds), *Hollywood Spectatorship: Changing Perceptions of Cinema Audiences* (pp. 132–51), London: British Film Institute.

Klinger, B. (2008), 'The DVD Cinephile: Viewing Heritages and Home Film Cultures', in J. Bennett and T. Brown (eds), *Film and Television After DVD* (pp. 19–44), New York: Routledge.

Knight, J. (2007), 'DVD, Video and Reaching Audiences: Experiments in Moving-Image Distribution', *Convergence: The International Journal of Research into New Media Technologies*, 13(1), 19–41, doi: 10.1177/1354856507072858.

Knight, J. (2012), *How visible will our history be?*, paper presented at Cultural Attitudes Towards Technology and Communication 2012, Murdoch University, Australia.

Knowles, K. (2016), 'Slow, Methodical and Mulled Over: Analogue-Film Practice in the Age of the Digital', *Cinema Journal*, 55(2), 146–51.

Koepnick, L. (2014), *On Slowness: Toward an Aesthetic of the Contemporary*, New York: Columbia University Press.

Kogen, L. (2005), 'The Spanish Film Industry: New Technologies, New Opportunities', *Convergence: The International Journal of Research into New Media Technologies*, 11(1), 68–86, doi: 10.1177/135485650501100106.

Koltun, L. (1999), 'The promise and threat of digital options in an archival age', *Archivaria*, 1(47).

Kozloff, S. (1988), *Invisible Storytellers: Voice-over narration in American fiction film*, Berkeley: University of California Press.

Kuehn, K. (2013), 'Hope Labor: The Role of Employment Prospects in Online Social Production', *The Political Economy of Communication*, 1(1), 9–25.

Kuhn, V., Alan Craig, Kevin Franklin, Simeone, M., Arora, R. and Dave Bock, L. M. (2012), *Large Scale Video Analytics: On-demand, iterative inquiry for moving image research*, paper presented at E-Science (e-Science), 2012 IEEE 8th International Conference.

Langham, J. (1996), *Lights, Camera, Action: Working in Film, Television and Video*, London: British Film Institute.

Larsen, L. R. and Nissen, D. (eds) (2006), *100 years of Nordisk Film*, Copenhagen: Danish Film Institute.

Lauzen, M. M. (2012), 'The celluloid ceiling: behind-the-scenes film employment of women in the top 250 films of 2012', San Diego: Center for the Study of Women in Film and Television.

Lauzen, M. M. (2014), 'The Celluloid Ceiling: Behind-the-Scenes Employment of Women on the Top 250 Films of 2013', San Diego: Center for the Study of Women in Television and Film, San Diego State University, San Diego.

Lauzen, M. M. (2015), 'The Celluloid Ceiling: Behind-the-Scenes Employment of Women on the Top 250 Films of 2014', San Diego: Center for the Study of Women in Television and Film, San Diego State University.

Lazzarato, M. (1996), 'Immaterial labour', *Radical thought in Italy: A potential politics*, 133–47.

Lee, B. (2015, August 11, 2015), 'Meryl Streep's Writers Lab reveals first group of female screenwriters', *The Guardian*, retrieved from http://www.the-guardian.com/film/2015/aug/11/meryl-streep-female-writer-program-reveals-participants

Lee, L. (2013), 'Between Frames: Japanese Cinema at the Digital Turn', *Alphaville: Journal of Film and Screen Media*, 5.

Lees, D. and Berkowitz, S. (1981), *The Movie Business*, New York: Vintage Books.

Lehmann, J., Atkinson, S. and Evans, R. (2015), *Applying Semantic Technology to Film Production*, paper presented at The Semantic Web: ESWC 2015 Satellite Events, Portorož, Slovenia.

Leung, W. F., Gill, R. and Randle, K. (2015), 'Getting in, getting on, getting out? Women as career scramblers in the UK film and television industries', *The Sociological Review*, 63(1), 50–65.

Levine, E. (2001), 'Toward a paradigm for media production research: Behind the scenes at general hospital', *Critical Studies in Media Communication*, 18(1), 66–82.

Lewis, H. T. (1933), *The Motion Picture Industry*, New York: D. Van Nostrand Company, Inc.

Lindeperg, S. (2013), 'Film Production as a Palimpsest', in P. Szczepanik and P. Vonderau (eds), *Behind the Screen: Inside European Production Cultures* (pp. 73–87), New York: Palgrave Macmillan.

Lissitzky, E., K. (1965), 'und Pangeometrie', in U. Conrads (ed.), *Rußland: Architektur für eine Weltrevolution* (pp. 122–9), Berlin: Ullstein.

Lobato, R. (2009), 'The politics of digital distribution: exclusionary structures in online cinema', *Studies in Australasian Cinema*, 3(2), 167–78.

Lobato, R. (2012), *Shadow Economies of Cinema: Mapping Informal Film Distribution*, Basingstoke: Palgrave Macmillan.

Lohmann, F. von. (2007), 'Fair Use, Film, and the Advantages of Internet Distribution', *Cinema Journal*, 46(2), 128–33.

Lovell, A. and Sergi, G. (2005), *Making Films in Contemporary Hollywood*, London: Hodder Education.

Lumet, S. (1995), *Making Movies*, New York: Bloomsbury.

Lunenfeld, P. (1999), *The digital dialectic: New essays on new media*, Cambridge, MA: MIT Press.

MacNab, G. (1993), *J. Arthur Rank and the British Film Industry*, London: Routledge.

Mahurter, S. (2007), *The Stanley Kubrick Archive at University of the Arts London*, paper presented at the EVA, London, http://www.eva-conferences.com/sites/eva-conferences.com/files/public/active/0/12-Mahurter.pdf

Mangolte, B. (2003), 'Afterward: A Matter of Time. Analog Versus Digital, the Perennial Question of Shifting Technology and Its Implications for an Experimental Filmmaker's Odyssey'. In R. Allen and M. Turvey (eds), *Camera*

Obscura, Camera Lucida (pp. 261–74), Amsterdam: Amsterdam University Press.

Manovich, L. (2010), 'Digital Cinema and the History of a Moving Image', in M. Furstenau (ed.), *The Film Theory Reader: Debates and Arguments* (pp. 245–55), London: Routledge.

Manovich, L. (2011), *The Language of New Media*, Cambridge, MA: MIT Press.

Manovich, L. (2013), *Software Takes Command*, New York: Bloomsbury.

Marks, L. U. (2002), *Touch: Sensuous Theory and Multisensory Media*, University of Minnesota Press.

Mathieu, C. (2013), 'The "Cultural" of Production and Career', in P. Szczepanik and P. Vonderau (eds), *Behind the Screen: Inside European Production Cultures* (pp. 45–60), New York: Palgrave Macmillan.

Mathieu, C. and Strandvad, S. M. (2008), 'Is this what we should be comparing when comparing film production regimes? A systematic typological scheme and application', *Creative Industries Journal*, 1(2), 171–92.

Mayer, S. (2008), 'Expanding the frame: Sally Potter's digital histories and archival futures', *Screen*, 49(2), 194–202, doi: 10.1093/screen/hjn028.

Mayer, S. (2009), *The Cinema of Sally Potter: A Politics of Love*, London: Wallflower.

Mayer, V. (2011), *Below the Line: Producers and Production Studies in the New Television Economy*, Durham, NC: Duke University Press.

Mayer, V. (2016), 'The Production of Extras in a Precarious Creative Economy', in M. Curtin and K. Sanson (eds), *Precarious Creativity: Global Media Local Labor*, Oakland: University of California Press.

Mayer, V., Banks, M. J. and Caldwell, J. T. (eds) (2009), *Production Studies: Cultural Studies of Media Industries*, New York: Routledge.

Mayne, J. (1990), *The Woman at the Keyhole: Feminism and Women's Cinema*, Bloomington: Indiana University Press.

McClean, S. T. (2008), *Digital Storytelling: The Narrative Power of Visual Effects in Film*, Cambridge, MA: MIT Press.

McDonald, P. (2013), 'IN FOCUS: Media Industries Studies – Introduction', *Cinema Journal*, 52(3), 145–9.

McDonald, P. and Wasko, J. (eds) (2008), *The Contemporary Hollywood Film Industry*, Oxford: Blackwell.

McKim, K. (2006), 'Sally Potter', *Senses of Cinema*, 40.

McKinlay, A. and Smith, C. (eds) (2009), *Creative Labour. Working in the Creative Industries*, New York: Palgrave Macmillan.

McNeil, E. (1911), 'Outline of how to write a photoplay', *The Moving Picture World*, 9(1).

McPherson, T. (2009), 'In Focus: Digital Scholarship and Pedagogy', *Cinema Journal*, 48(2), 119–60.

McPherson, T. (2012), 'US Operating Systems at Mid-Century: The Intertwining of Race and UNIX', in L. Nakamura and P. Chow-White (eds), *Race after the Internet* (pp. 21–37), New York: Routledge.

McVeigh-Schultz, J. (2011), 'Movie Tagger Alpha: Critical Tagging in Emerging Methods of Media Scholarship', *Frames Cinema Journal*, 1(1).

Medhurst, A. (1991), 'In Search of a Rogue', *Sight and Sound*, 1(1).

Metz, C. (1974), *Film Language*, New York: Oxford University Press.

Millard, K. (2010), 'After the typewriter: the screenplay in a digital era', *Journal of Screenwriting*, 1(1), 11–25.

Miller, T. (2011), 'The New International Division of Cultural Labour', in M. Deuze (ed.), *Managing Media Work*, Los Angeles: Sage.

Miller, T., Govil, N., McMurrin, J., Maxwell, R. and Wang, T. (2005), *Global Hollywood 2*, London: BFI Publishing.

Misek, R. (2010), 'The 'look' and how to keep it: cinematography, postproduction and digital colour', *Screen*, 51(4), 404–9, doi: 10.1093/screen/hjq045

Moseley, R. and Wheatley, H. (2008), 'Is Archiving a Feminist Issue? Historical Research and the Past', *Cinema Journal*, 47(3), 152.

Mroz, M. (2012), *Temporality and Film Analysis*, Edinburgh: Edinburgh University Press.

Mukherjee, D., Gupta, G., Bhasin, R. and Kumar, P. (2013), 'And Action! Making Money in the Post-production Services Industry', in A. T. Kearney, http://www.atkearney.com/communications-media-technology/ideas-

Mulvey, L. (2006), *Death 24x a Second: Stillness and the Moving Image*, London: Reaktion Books.

Murphy, R. (ed.) (2010), *The British Cinema Book* (3rd edn), Basingstoke: Palgrave Macmillan.

Murray, J. (2012), *Inventing the Medium: Principles of Interaction Design as a Cultural Practice*, Cambridge, MA: MIT Press.

Neumann, P. and Appelgren, C. (2007), *The Fine Art of Co-Producing* (2nd edn), Copenhagen: Neumann Publishing.

Ng, J. (2010), 'The Myth of Total Cinephilia', *Cinema Journal*, 49(2), 146–51.

Nichols, B. (1975), 'Style, Grammar, and the Movies', *Film Quarterly*, 28(3), 33–49.

Nichols, B. (2002), *Introduction to Documentary*, : Bloomington: Indiana University Press.

North, D. (2008), *Performing Illusions: Cinema, Special Effects and the Virtual Actor*, London: Wallflower.

Orgeron, K. (2007), 'La Camera-Crayola: Authorship Comes of Age in the Cinema of Wes Anderson', *Cinema Journal*, 46(2), 40–65.

Osthoff, S. (2009), *Performing the Archive: The Transformation of the Archive in Contemporary Art from Repository of Documents to Art Medium*, New York: Atropos Press.

Oxford Economics (2012), *The Economic Impact of the UK Film Industry*, Oxford: Oxford Economics.

Pandian, A. (2011), 'Reel time: ethnography and the historical ontology of the cinematic image', *Screen*, 52(2), 193–214.

Paul, A. and Kleingartner, A. (1996), 'The Transformation of Industrial Relations in the Motion Picture and Television Industries: The Talent Sector', in L. Gray and R. Seeber (eds), *Under the Stars: Essays on Labor Relations in Arts and Entertainment* (p. 161), Ithaca: ILR Press.

Peacock, S. (2010), *Colour*, Manchester: Manchester University Press.

Pearlman, K. (2009), *Cutting Rhythms: Shaping the film edit*, Burlington: Focal Press.

Perkins, R. and Stollery, M. (2004), *British Film Editors: the heart of the movie*, London: BFI.

Perkins, V. F. (1972), *Film as Film: understanding and judging movies*. Harmondsworth: Penguin.

Perren, A. (2013), 'Rethinking Distribution for the Future of Media Industry Studies', *Cinema Journal*, 52(3), 165–71.

Perrons, Diane (1999), 'Flexible working patterns and equal opportunities in the European Union', *European Journal of Women's Studies*, 6(4), 391–418.

Perry, G. (1981), *Forever Ealing: A Celebration of the Great British Film Studio*, London: Pavilion.

Petrie, D. (1996a), *The British Cinematographer*, London: BFI.

Petrie, D. (ed.). (1996b). *Inside Stories: Diaries of British Film-makers at Work*. London: BFI.

Petrie, D. and Stoneman, R. (2014), *Educating Film-Makers: Past, Present and Future*, Bristol: Intellect.

Philisphen, H. (2009), 'Constraints in Film Making Processes Offer an Exercise to the Imagination: A Pleading Based on Experiences in Denmark', *Seminar.net – International Journal of Media, Technology and Lifelong Learning*, 5(1), 12.

Pietrzyk, K. (2012), 'Preserving digital narratives in an age of present-mindedness', *Convergence: The International Journal of Research into New Media Technologies*, 18(2), 127–33, doi: 10.1177/1354856511433689.

Pollock, G. (2007), *Encounters in the Virtual Feminist Museum: Time, space and the archive*, London: Routledge.

Posner, M. (2016), 'How Is a Digital Project Like a Film?', in C. R. Acland and E. Hoyt (eds), *The Arclight Guidebook to Media History and the Digital Humanities* (pp. 184–94), Falmer: REFRAME/Project Arclight.

Potter, S. (2014), *Naked Cinema: Working with Actors*, New York: Faber and Faber.

Powdermaker, H. (1951), *Hollywood: The Dream Factory – An Anthropologist Looks at the Movie-Makers*, Boston: Little, Brown and Company.

Powdermaker, H. (1963), 'Hollywood and the USA', in B. Rosenberg and D. Manning White (eds), *Mass Culture: The popular arts in America* (pp. 278–93), New York: The Free Press of Glencoe.

Pratt, A. (2000), 'New media the new economy and new spaces', *Geoforum*, 31(4), 425–36.

Prescott, A. (ed.) (2015), *Big Data in the Arts and Humanities: Some Arts and Humanities Research Council Projects*, Glasgow: University of Glasgow.

Price, S. and Pallant, C. (2015), *Storyboarding, A Critical History*, Basingstoke: Palgrave.

Prince, S. (2004), 'The Emergence of Filmic Artifacts: Cinema and Cinematography in the Digital Era', *Film Quarterly*, 57(3), 24–33.

Purse, L. (2013), *Digital Imaging in Popular Cinema*, Edinburgh: Edinburgh University Press.

Randle, K. and Culkin, N. (2009), 'Getting In and Getting On in Hollywood: Freelance Careers in an uncertain industry', in A. McKinlay and C. Smith (eds), *Creative Labour. Working in the Creative Industries* (pp. 93–115), New York: Palgrave Macmillan.

Randle, K., Forson, C. and Calveley, M. (2015), 'Towards a Bourdieusian analysis of the social composition of the UK film and television workforce', *Work, employment and society*, 29(4), 590–606.

Reiss, J. (2010), *Think Outside the Box Office: The ultimate guide to film distribution and marketing for the digital era*, New York: Hybrid Cinema LLC.

Reynolds, S. (1998), 'The face on the cutting-room floor: women editors in the French cinema of the 1930s', *Labour History Review*, 63(1), 66–82.

Reynolds, S. (2012, Dec 19 2012), '"Les Misérables": Behind the scenes on the Pinewood set', *Movies News* Retrieved 24/02/2013, 2013, from http://www.digitalspy.co.uk/movies/news/a446136/les-miserables-behind-the-scenes-on-the-pinewood-set.html

Rich, A. (1979), *Lies, Secrets and Silence*, New York: Norton.

Rodowick, D. N. (2007), *The Virtual Life of Film*, Cambridge, MA: Harvard University Press.

Rombes, N. (2009), *Cinema in the Digital Age*, London: Wallflower.

Rose, F. (2011), *The Art of Immersion: How the digital generation is remaking Hollywood, Madison Avenue, and the way we tell stories*, New York: W. W. Norton and Company.

Rosenbaum, J. (2010), *Goodbye Cinema, Hello Cinephilia: Film Culture in Transition*, Chicago: The University of Chicago Press.

Ross, M. (2015), *3D Cinema: Optical Illusions and Tactile Experiences*, Basingstoke: Palgrave Macmillan.

Ross, P. (1944) 'Continuity', in 'Women Talking: A Symposium on the Part Played by Women Technicians in Film Production', *Royal Photographic Society pamphlet*, 14–19 and 16.

Rosten, L. (1941), *Hollywood: The Movie Colony, the Movie Makers*, New York: Harcourt, Brace and Company.

Rowlands, L. and Handy, J. (2012), 'An addictive environment: New Zealand film production workers' subjective experiences of project-based labour. *Human Relations*, 65(5), 657–80, doi: 10.1177/0018726711431494.

Salt, B. (1985), 'Statistical Style Analysis of Motion Pictures', in B. Nichols (ed.), *Movies and Methods, Vol 2*. Berkeley: University of California Press.

Salt, B. (2009), *Film Style and Technology: History and Analysis*, London: Starword.

Sandhu, S. (9 March 2012), '"Slow cinema" fights back against Bourne's supremacy', *The Guardian*.

Sarris, A. (2007), 'Notes on the "Auteur" Theory in 1962', *Kwartalnik Filmowy* (59), 6–17.

Sayad, C. (2013), *Performing Authorship: Self-inscription and Corporeality in the Cinema*, London: I. B. Tauris.

Schaap, R. (2011), 'No Country for Old Women: Gendering Cinema in Conglomerte Hollywood', in H. Radner and R. Stringer (eds), *Feminism at the*

Movies: Understanding Gender in Contemporary Popular Cinema, New York: Routledge.

Schatz, T. (2009a), 'New Hollywood New Millenium', in W. Buckland (ed.), *Film Theory and Contemporary Hollywood Movies*, New York: Routledge.

Schatz, T. (2009b), 'Film Industry Studies and Hollywood History', in J. Holt and A. Perren (eds), *Media Industries: History, Theory, and Method* (pp. 45–56), Chichester: Wiley-Blackwell.

Schatz, T. (2014), 'Film Studies, Cultural Studies, and Media Industries Studies', *Media Industries Journal*, 1(1), 39–43.

Schoonover, K. (2012), 'Wastrels of Time: Slow Cinema's Laboring Body, the Political Spectator, and the Queer', *Framework: The Journal of Cinema and Media*, 53(1), 65–78.

Schrey, D. (2014), 'Analogue Nostalgia and the Aesthetics of Digital Remediation', *Media and Nostalgia: Yearning for the past, present and future, Kathatrina Niemeyer* (pp. 27–38), Basingstoke: Palgrave Macmillan.

Scott, A. J. (2000), 'Multimedia and digital visual effects workers in Southern California', in A. J. Scott (ed.), *The Cultural Economy of Cities* (pp. 155–69), London: Sage.

Sellors, P. (2007), 'Collective Authorship in Film', *The Journal of Aesthetics and Art Criticism*, 65(3), 263–71.

Shaw, J. and Weibel, P. (eds) (2003), *Future Cinema: The Cinematic Imaginary after Film*, Cambridge, MA: MIT Press.

Sim, G. (2012), 'When and Where is the Digital Revolution in Cinematography?', *Projections: the journal for movies and mind*, 1, 79–100.

Singer, M. (1998), *A Cut Above: 50 Film Directors talk about their craft*, Los Angeles: Lone Eagle.

Skillset, C. (2012), 'Employment census of the creative media industries', London: Skillset.

Small, Edward S. and Eugene Levinson, 'Toward a Theory of Animation', *The Velvet Light Trap* 24 (Fall 1989): 67–74.

Smith, C. (2012), 'A Future For British Film. It begins with the audience . . . A UK film policy review', London: Department for Culture, Media and Sport.

Smith, S. L., Choueiti, M., Scofield, E. and Pieper, K. (2013), 'Gender inequality in 500 popular films: Examining on-screen portrayals and behind-the-scenes employment patterns in motion pictures released between 2007–2012', Los Angeles: University of Southern California Annenberg School for Communication and Journalism.

Smith, S. L., Pieper, K. and Choueiti, M. (2013), 'Exploring the Barriers and Opportunities for Independent Women Filmmakers', Los Angeles: Sundance Institute.

Snickars, P. and Vonderau, P. (eds) (2009), *The You Tube Reader*, Stockholm: The National Library of Sweden.

Sorensen, I. E. (2012), 'Crowdsourcing and outsourcing: the impact of online funding and distribution on the documentary film industry in the UK', *Media, Culture & Society*, 34(6), 726–743, doi: 10.1177/0163443712449499.

Sorman-Nilsson, A. (2013), *Digilogue: How to Win the Digital Minds and Analogue Hearts of Tomorrow's Customer*, Chichester: Wiley-Blackwell.

Spadoni, R. (2007), *Uncanny Bodies: The Coming of Sound Film and the Origins of the Horror Genre*, Berkeley: University of California Press.

Sperb, J. (2016), *Flickers of Film: Nostalgia in the Time of Digital Cinema*, New Brunswick, NJ: Rutgers University Press.

Sperlich, R. (2011), 'The mixed blessing of autonomy in digital cultural production: A study on filmmaking, press photography and architecture in Austria', *European Journal of Communication*, 26(2), 133–46, doi: 10.1177/0267323111401611.

Spicer, A. and McKenna, A. T. (2013), *The Man Who Got Carter: Michael Klinger, Independent Production and the British Film Industry, 1960–1980*, London: I. B. Tauris.

Spielmann, Y. (1999), 'Expanding film into digital media', *Screen*, 40(2), 131–45.

Spottiswoode, R. (1950), *A Grammar of the Film*, Berkeley: University of California Press.

Stahl, M. (2009), 'Privilege and Distinction in Production Worlds: Copyright, Collective Bargaining, and Working Conditions in Media Making', in V. Mayer, M. J. Banks and J. T. Caldwell (eds), *Production Studies: Cultural Studies of Media Industries*, New York: New York.

Staiger, J. (1977), 'Dividing labour for production control', unpublished seminar paper, University of Wisconsin-Madison.

Staiger, J. (1981), *The Hollywood Mode of Production: The construction of divided labor in the film industry*, Madison: University of Wisconsin.

Staiger, J. (1985), 'The Politics of Film Canons', *Cinema Journal*, 24(3), 4–23.

Standards, B. (2012), 'Guidelines for implementors of EN 15744 and EN 15907': Standard Number: PD CEN/TS 16371:2012: BSI Standards Limited.

Starkey, K., Barnatt, C. and Tempest, S. (2000), 'Beyond networks and hierarchies: Latent organizations in the UK television industry', *Organization Science*, 11(3), 299–305.

Steele, D. (2013), 'Succès de plume? Female Screenwriters and Directors of UK Films, 2010–2012', London: BFI Research and Statistics Unit.

Stewart, G. (2007), *Framed Time: Toward a postfilmic cinema*, Chicago: The University of Chicago Press.

Stollery, M. (2009), 'Technicians of the unknown cinema: British critical discourse and the analysis of collaboration in film production', *Film History*, 21, 373–93.

Strandvad, S. M. (2012), 'Attached by the Product: A Socio-Material Direction in the Sociology of Art', *Cultural Sociology*, 6(2), 163–76.

Strandvad, S. M. (2013), 'Analyzing Production from a Socio-material Perspective', in P. Szczepanik and P. Vonderau (eds), *Behind the Screen: Inside European Production Cultures* (pp. 27–43), New York: Palgrave Macmillan.

Sweet, M. (2005), *Shepperton Babylon: The Lost Worlds of British Cinema*, London: Faber and Faber.

Szczepanik, P. (2014), 'Globalization through the Eyes of Runners: Student Interns as Ethnographers on Runaway Productions in Prague', *Media Industries Journal*, 1(1), 56–61.

Szczepanik, P. and Vonderau, P. (eds) (2013), *Behind the Screen: Inside European Production Cultures*, New York: Palgrave Macmillan.

Tasker, Y. (2010), 'Vision and Visibility: Women Filmmakers, Contemporary Authorship, and Feminist Film Studies', in V. Callahan (ed.), *Reclaiming the Archive: Feminism and Film History*, Detroit: Wayne State University Press.

Taylor, T. and Hsu, M. (2003), *Digital Cinema: The Hollywood Insider's Guide to the Evolution of Storytelling*, Studio City: Michael Wiese.

Theophanidis, P. and Thibault, G. (2016), 'Media Hysteresis: Persistence Through Change', *Alphaville: Journal of Film and Screen Media*, 12, 8–23.

Thompson, R. (2002), *Grammar of the Shot*, Oxford: Focal Press.

Thompson, R. and Bowen, C. J. (2009), *Grammar of the Edit* (2nd edn), Burlington: Elsevier.

Thorburn, D. and Jenkins, H. (eds) (2004), *Rethinking Media Change – The Aesthetics of Transition*, Cambridge, MA: MIT Press.

Threadgall, D. (1994), *Shepperton Studios: An Independent View*, London: BFI.

Tiago de, L. and Nuno Barradas, J. (eds) (2015), *Slow Cinema*, Edinburgh: Edinburgh University Press.

Toles, G. (2010), 'Rescuing Fragments: A New Task for Cinephilia', *Cinema Journal*, 49(2), 159–66.

Toulmin, V., Popple, S. and Russell, P. (eds) (2004), *The Lost World of Mitchell and Kenyon: Edwardian Britain on Film*, London: BFI.

Truffaut, F. (1954), 'Une certaine tendance du cinéma français', *Cahiers du cinéma*, 31, 15–29.

Tryon, C. (2009), *Reinventing Cinema: Movies in the age of media convergence*, New Brunswick, NJ: Rutgers University Press.

Tryon, C. (2013), *On-demand Culture: Digital delivery and the future of movies*, New Brunswick, NJ: Rutgers University Press.

Tudor, D. (2008), 'The Eye of the Frog: Questions of Space in Films Using Digital Processes', *Cinema Journal*, 48(1), 90–110.

Tudor, D. (2010), 'Light Bouncing: Digital Processes Illuminate the Cultural Past', *Jump Cut: A Review of Contemporary Media*, 52.

Turnock, J. (2013), 'Removing the Pane of Glass: The Hobbit, 3D High Frame Rate Filmmaking, and the Rhetoric of Digital Convergence', *Film Criticism*, 3(1), 37–8.

Turow, J. (2014), 'The Case for Studying In-Store Media', *Media Industries Journal*, 1(1), 62–8.

Tyberj, C. (2004), 'The Makers of Movies: Authors, Subjects, Personalities, Agents?', in T. Grodal, B. Larsen and I. T. Laursen (eds), *Visual Authorship: Creativity and Intentionality in Media* (pp. 37–65), Copenhagen: Museum Tusculanum Press.

Tzioumakis, Y. (2006), 'Marketing David Mamet: Institutionally Assigned Film Authorship in Contemporary American Cinema', *Velvet Light Trap*, 57, 60–75.

Uricchio, W. (2014), 'Film, cinema, television . . . media?' *New Review of Film and Television Studies*, 12(3), 266–79.

Ursell, G. (2006), 'Working in the media', in D. Hesmondhalgh (ed.), *Media Production*, Maidenhead: Open University Press.

Usai, P. C. (2001), *The Death of Cinema: History, Cultural Memory, and the Digital Dark Age*, London: British Film Institute.

Utterson, A. (2011), *From IBM to MGM: Cinema at the dawn of the digital age*, London: BFI.

Vanderhoef, J. and Curtin, M. (2016), 'The Crunch Heard 'Round The World: The Global Era of Digital Game Labor', in M. Banks, B. Conor and V. Mayer (eds), *Production Studies, The Sequel!* (pp. 196–264), New York: Routledge.

Vaughan, D. (1983), *Portrait of an Invisible Man: The working life of Stewart McAllister, Film Editor*, London: BFI.

Velios, A. (2011), 'Creative Archiving: a case study from the John Latham Archive', *Journal of the Society of Archivists*, 32(2), 255–71.

Venkatasawmy, R. (2013), *The Digitization of Cinematic Visual Effects*, Lanham: Lexington Books.

Verevis, C. (2005), 'Mike Figgis: Time Code and the Screen', in N. Rombes (ed.), *New Punk Cinema*, Edinburgh: Edinburgh University Press.

Verhoeven, D. (2016), 'Visualising Data in Digital Cinema Studies: More than Just Going through the Motions?', *Alphaville: Journal of Film and Screen Media*, 11, 92–104.

Vonderau, P. (2013), 'Borderlands, Contact Zones, and Boundary Games: A Conversation with John T. Caldwell', in P. Szczepanik and P. Vonderau (eds), *Behind the Screen: Inside European production cultures* (pp. 13–25), New York: Palgrave Macmillan.

Vonderau, P. (2014), 'Industry Proximity',. *Media Industries Journal, 1*(1), 69–74.

Vonderau, P. (2016), 'How Global is Hollywood? Division of Labor from a Prop-Making Perspective', in M. Banks, B. Conor and V. Mayer (eds), *Production Studies, The Sequel!* (pp. 23–36), New York: Routledge.

Walker, A. (1974), *Hollywood England: The British Film Industry in the Sixties*. London: Michael Joseph.

Wasko, J. and Meehan, E. R. (2013), 'In Focus: Media Industries Studies: Critical Crossroads or Parallel Routes? Political Economy and New Approaches to Studying Media Industries and Cultural Products', *Cinema Journal*, 52.3 (Spring 2013), 150–7.

Wasser, F. (2009), *Veni, vidi, video: The Hollywood empire and the VCR*, Austin: University of Texas Press.

Waugh, P. (1984), *Metafiction: The Theory and Practice of Self-conscious Fiction*, London: Routledge.

Weller, M. (2011), *The Digital Scholar: How technology is transforming scholarly practice*, London: Bloomsbury Academic.

Wernimont, J. (2013), 'Whence Feminism? Assessing Feminist Interventions in Digital Literary Archives', *Digital Humanities Quarterly*, 7(1).

Whissel, K. (2010), 'The Digital Multitude', *Cinema Journal*, 49(4), 90–110.

Williams, M. (2013), 'The Continuity Girl: Ice in the Middle of Fire', *Journal of British Cinema and Television*, 10(3), 603–17.

Wood, A. (2007), 'Pixel Visions: Digital Intermediates and Micromanipulations of the Image', *Film Criticism*, 32(1), 72–94.

Wood, A. (2013), 'Intangible spaces: Three-dimensional technology in Hugo and IMAX in The Dark Knight', *Convergence: The International Journal of Research into New Media Technologies*, 1–13.

Wood, A. (2014), *Software, Animation and the Moving Image: What's in the Box?*, Basingstoke: Palgrave Macmillan.

Wood, R. E. (2001), 'Toward an Ontology of Film: A Phenomenological Approach', *Film-Philosophy*, 5(24).

Wright, J. (2009), *Making the Cut: Female Editors and Representation in the Film and Media Industry*, paper presented at the Thinking Gender, LA.

Wyatt, J. (1994), *High concept: Movies and marketing in Hollywood*, Austin: University of Texas Press.

Young, F. and Petzold, P. (1972), *Work of the Motion Picture Cameraman*, New York: Focal Press.

Zeppelzauer, M., Mitrović, D. and Breiteneder, C. (2012), 'Archive Film Material – A Novel Challenge for Automated Film Analysis' | Frames Cinema Journal, *Frames Cinema Journal*, 1(1).

Zito, S. (1977), 'George Lucas Goes Far Out', *American Film*, 2, 8–13.

Žižek, S. (1997), *The plague of fantasies*, London: Verso.

Zuckerman, E. W. (2004), 'Do Firms and Markets Look Different? Repeat collaboration in the feature film industry, 1935–1995', unpublished manuscript.

Index

EU representative:
Easy Access System Europe
Mustamäe tee 50, 10621 Tallinn, Estonia
Gpsr.requests@easproject.com

www.ingramcontent.com/pod-product-compliance
Lightning Source LLC
Chambersburg PA
CBHW071411050326

40689CB00010B/1825